Tonya,

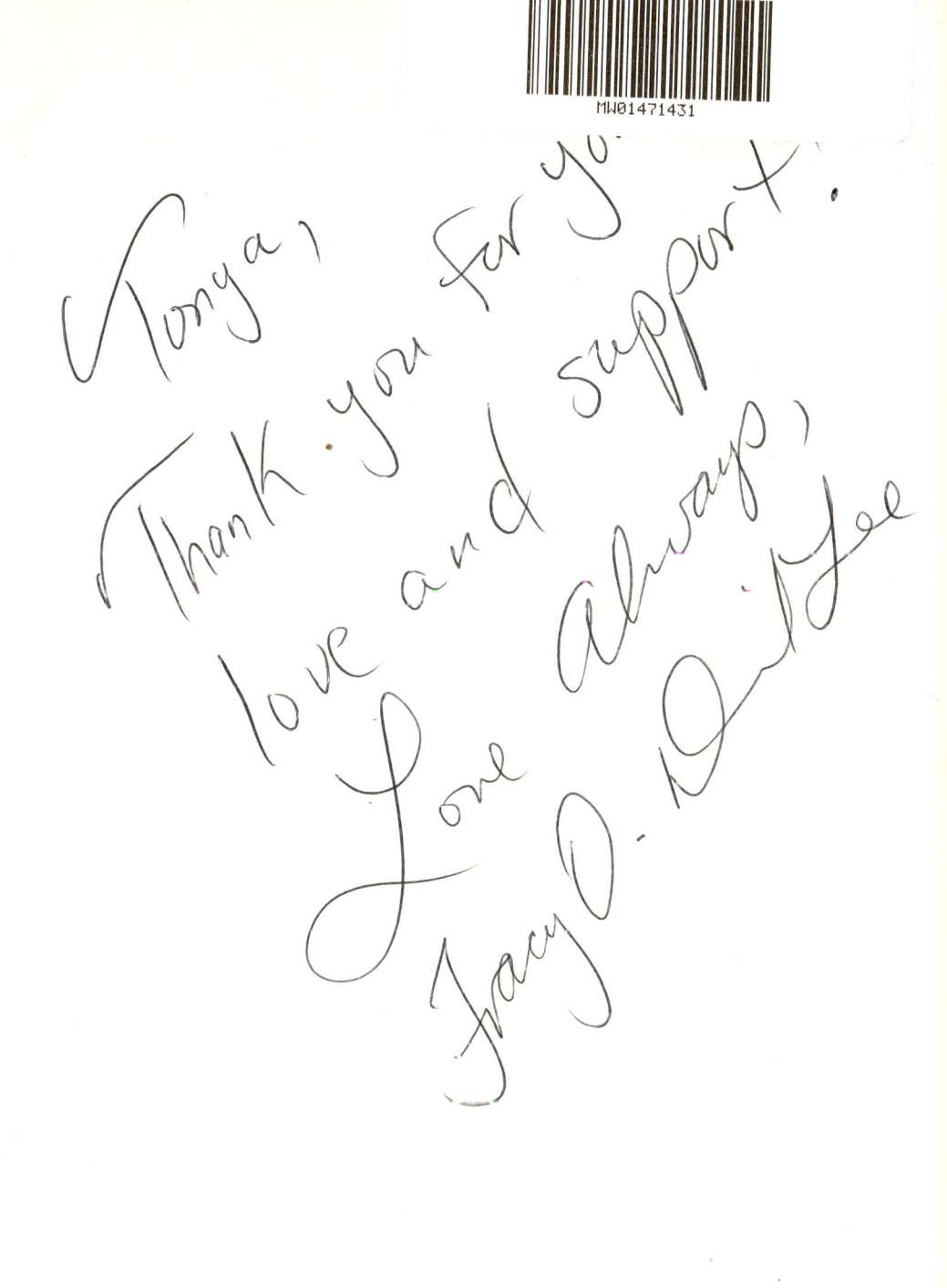

Thank you for your love and support.

Love always,
Tracy D. ...

God's Girl

Also by
Tracy O'Neal-Daniel

Somber Trials but Supernatural Triumphs!
Good Morning Saints!
God Made You Special

Acclaim for God's Girl

Dear Daughter Tracy,

We think you have a bestseller on your hands! We recommend this book not only to single women going through a major struggle with loss in their lives but to *all women*. This book is like a blueprint to recovery; it gives steps and direction that only come from a life that has been lived. We've often heard that confession is good for the soul; however, it takes a person who totally trusts God to be as real and as naked before Him as you have been in this book.

This book will be a Godsend to any of its readers because they will readily feel the sincerity of the author's heart from which she writes. Thank you, Daughter, for putting into words how many of us feel but are not able to communicate. This is a testament of the workings of God in your life, so keep it up. As your youth pastors, we have always been proud of you ever since you were a young girl, but now you are making us even prouder!

Pastors Nathaniel and Valencia Newsome
Spirit Filled Life Full Gospel Church—Fort Pierce, Florida

Greetings to Every Reader of This Book!

I am Pastor George R. Keys of Omaha, Nebraska, and I can say with an assurance that Sister Tracy is indeed God's girl. From the first day we met her back in 1992, she always displayed the true character of God as one of his daughters, and we found her dedication as a wife, mother, friend, and dedicated member of the body of Christ to be second to none.

When she and her husband were stationed in Omaha, Nebraska, miles away from their family while facing some very tumultuous trials, my family and I became their family and stuck with them during their difficult and confusing circumstances. I was with God's girl when she, through our help, reflected on the mystery of her God/Father's providence.

As Tracy has done, we all must discover that none of us is the leading character in the story of our own life. God is. Therefore, we are not being led to see Him in our stories but our stories in His. Being a daughter of the most high, Tracy realizes that God is the bigger context and plot in which all of our stories are found and He is always reliable but never predictable. As you read this book, know that your Father has a plan for you as well and He is behind everything that has happened and is happening in your life.

We love our spiritual daughter Tracy, for she has lived a crucified life in Christ, a life of self-denial. She has walked day after day dying to herself, her own desires and wishes, faithfully living her life for Jesus Christ and His kingdom. Before you read this book, I speak a prophetic word in and over your life: *God will do a new thing in your life at the conclusion of this book.*

Pastor George R. Keys and First Lady Daty Keys
New Testament Church of God in Christ—Bellevue, Nebraska

God's Girl

Living My Life for His Glory

Tracy O'Neal Daniel Lee

WestBow Press
A DIVISION OF THOMAS NELSON
& ZONDERVAN

Copyright © 2017 Tracy O'Neal Daniel Lee.

All rights reserved. No part of this book may be used or reproduced by any means, graphic, electronic, or mechanical, including photocopying, recording, taping or by any information storage retrieval system without the written permission of the author except in the case of brief quotations embodied in critical articles and reviews.

This book is a recount of events in the life of Tracy O'Neal Daniel Lee according to the author's recollection and perspective. While all the stories are true, certain names and identifying details have been altered to protect the privacy of those involved.

Scripture quotes marked (KJV) are taken from the King James Version of the Bible.

Scripture quotes marked (NKJV) are taken from the New King James Version®. Copyright © 1982 by Thomas Nelson. Used by permission. All rights reserved.

Scripture quotations marked (NIV) are taken from the Holy Bible, New International Version®, NIV®. Copyright © 1973, 1978, 1984, 2011 by Biblica, Inc.™ Used by permission of Zondervan. All rights reserved worldwide.

Scripture quotations marked (TLB) are taken from The Living Bible copyright © 1971. Used by permission of Tyndale House Publishers, Inc., Carol Stream, Illinois 60188. All rights reserved.

Scripture quotations are taken from the Holy Bible, New Living Translation, copyright ©1996, 2004, 2007, 2013, 2015 by Tyndale House Foundation. Used by permission of Tyndale House Publishers, Inc., Carol Stream, Illinois 60188. All rights reserved.

Front and back cover photography by Juanita Hogan
Makeup by Jasmine R. Daniel
Hair by Tavares Gilbert

WestBow Press books may be ordered through booksellers or by contacting:

WestBow Press
A Division of Thomas Nelson & Zondervan
1663 Liberty Drive
Bloomington, IN 47403
www.westbowpress.com
1 (866) 928-1240

Because of the dynamic nature of the Internet, any web addresses or links contained in this book may have changed since publication and may no longer be valid. The views expressed in this work are solely those of the author and do not necessarily reflect the views of the publisher, and the publisher hereby disclaims any responsibility for them.

Any people depicted in stock imagery provided by Thinkstock are models, and such images are being used for illustrative purposes only. Certain stock imagery © Thinkstock.

ISBN: 978-1-5127-9922-4 (sc)
ISBN: 978-1-5127-9921-7 (hc)
ISBN: 978-1-5127-9923-1 (e)

Library of Congress Control Number: 2017913337

Print information available on the last page.

WestBow Press rev. date: 9/6/2017

To my eight daughters, my two sons, my two daughter-in-laws, my soon-to-be son in-law, and my grandson. I felt an urgency to write this memoir as a testament to you and others of what God can do with the life of a willing vessel.

I also dedicate this memoir to young women and girls everywhere, who may at some point in their lives be faced with tough troubles and trials, as I've had to face in my own life.

When I thought God was being unfair to me by allowing so many trials to come my way, in hindsight I realize He was simply allowing life to groom me for my calling. Those trials are what He used to break me, to mold me, to shape me, and to make me a godly example and mouthpiece for Him.

Listen, God is not a respecter of persons. Just as He has blessed and anointed my life because of my willingness and obedience to do His will, even in the face of tough obstacles, He can and will do the same for you. A willing vessel with a heart turned perfectly toward Him is all He requires to begin the process of transforming you into His girl or His son.

Contents

Foreword by Dr. Willie B. O'Neal xi
Introduction: My Story xv

1. Child of a Preacher Man 1
2. Growing up Not Very Brady 13
3. God's Girl in the Making 20
4. Mr. Right 26
5. Waiting for My Fairy Tale to Begin 34
6. My God, Why Have You Forsaken Me? 40
7. It Is Well with My Soul 51
8. Starting All over Again 62
9. Another Faith Test 73
10. Trials on Every Hand 77
11. Nothing's Too Hard for God 88
12. The Goal to Do God's Will 101
13. Busy Working for the Lord 114
14. Staying Alive 117
15. What's Going On? 128
16. Something's Coming 135
17. Blindsided 141
18. The Good Wife and Mom 161
19. Too Tired to Cry 183
20. My Apocalypse 213
21. God, Why? 235
22. Mistakes of a Broken Heart 246
23. The Climb 272

24. From Mourning to Dancing 284
25. God's Girl 323

Acknowledgments 341
About the Author 349

Foreword

It seems like it was just yesterday that my beautiful, bald baby girl was born. I was a young nineteen-year-old in a new marriage, and her mother and I had just lost a baby boy the year before her birth. We were so happy when she arrived safe and healthy.

Tracy was such a good natured baby. I felt even then a special attachment to her. Her mother, Teresa, gave me the freedom to take her to Sunday school with me every Sunday morning while I served as the superintendent. I enjoyed spending that time with my baby girl, but I didn't realize until now that the incorruptible seed of the Word of God was being sown into her spirit. A seed that has produced the anointed woman of God she has become today.

When my marriage crumbled and I found myself being swept away into a fairy-tale world to try to escape my depressing reality, it was the love, affection, and expectation of my little girl that kept me grounded enough to confront life just as it was. I remember so vividly how every Friday evening she and my son William would look forward to their weekend visits with me. They would pack their clothes in a brown paper sack and sit by the window anticipating my arrival. If I wasn't there at the time that I promised, Tracy would call my mother and ask, "Grannie, have you seen my daddy?" and my mother wouldn't stop searching until she had located me for Tracy. Not wanting to let my little girl down is what pushed me to keep pressing through my tumultuous life. To this day, I still remind her that she was born for me.

After I remarried and became the pastor of Mount Canaan, Tracy, along with the rest of my children, was instantly confronted with the sometimes-grim scrutiny that comes along with being "the pastor's children." Not only that, but because I was in the very throes of a personal spiritual transition that included making some major ministry changes, our home life began to be governed by a strict, new set of rules. And though it was tough on my children, Tracy never complained. She simply complied with every request. So it was no surprise that God allowed her to be the first of my seven children to be filled with the Holy Ghost.

I will never forget the night that I laid hands on her. It was during a Saturday night in the early 1980s when my wife, Patricia, and I were returning from a night of ministering salvation to others at the church. The anointing of God was still upon me so heavily that when we stepped onto our porch and knocked at the front door, I told God that I was going to lay hands on whoever was on the other side of that door. And who happened to be on the other side of the door but my twelve-year-old daughter, Tracy. After leading her through the prayer of salvation, I laid my hands on her, and God immediately took control. She was crying and speaking in tongues so clearly that my eyes just welled up with tears. It was such a supernatural experience because she was not familiar with the Holy Ghost or speaking tongues. But, through faith, she received them both.

Throughout her childhood and now in her adult life, I have watched Tracy grow up spending her life working for the Lord. She was always a faithful and obedient young lady who never gave her parents any real problems. I have always recognized that the hand of God is upon her, as He has endowed her with many gifts and talents that she has constantly used for the glory of God. Ever since she was a young child, she possessed a unique ability to tell captivating stories through writing. And although she has used her gift for Mount Canaan in many ways, the most memorable has been the creative ways she has shared Patricia's and my life stories with the congregation during our annual birthday celebrations. And today, after years of sharing our stories, God is giving her the stage to share her own.

As her father and then as her pastor, I have walked with my daughter through many of the trials and tribulations you will read about in this book. And I have encouraged her time and time again with these words, "Nothing happens to us unless it first passes through the hands of God." Just knowing that God examined each situation before allowing them to come her way has always given her and me both so much peace.

Tracy has been an exemplary daughter, an exemplary wife, and an exemplary mother because of the way she has handled life. I can honestly say that her trials have grown her up spiritually and have increased her in wisdom, knowledge, and faith. By sharing her story with the world, she is yelling back down the road to those who might be experiencing some of the same trials she's faced, saying, "If God can fix it for me, He can surely fix it for you too!"

I have no doubt that you will be blessed by the words Tracy has written in this book. She is not preaching a sermon, nor attempting to write you a prescription for life. But rather, she is allowing her life story to witness for her through the sincere words on these pages. Her mother and stepfather, Teresa Murray and Dewey Murray, her third mother, Marilyn Daniel, her in-laws, John and Martha Calloway, her stepmother, Patricia O'Neal, and I, as well as her siblings are all extremely proud of her and this great body of work she has produced through the power of the Holy Ghost. And now, without further ado, allow me to present to some and introduce to others an extraordinary woman of God with an extraordinary story for you, Mrs. Tracy O'Neal Daniel Lee … God's girl.

Dr. Willie B. O'Neal, Senior Pastor
Mount Canaan Full Gospel Church
Birmingham, AL

Introduction

My Story

Everyone on this earth has a story. And everyone's story is a combination of life's events, both good and bad, which ultimately results in who and where he or she is today. Many people choose to share their stories publicly, and then there are those who feel their stories are better kept private. But it's funny how I never had the opportunity to make either of those choices concerning my story, as God made the choice for me when He turned me into a preacher's kid at a very young age. As we all know, there is nothing private in the life of a preacher and his family. Once a man declares that he has been called by God to preach, his and his family's lives are suddenly fair game for scrutiny. Needless to say, my family's life has been on display ever since my dad said *yes* to God just before I turned five years old.

Growing up in the church, I've often heard testimonies (personal stories) from the older saints about the many wonderful things God has done for them. Their testimonies ranged from vivid recollections of their past sinful lives and the miraculous way God delivered them to stories of how God healed them from a terrible sickness or disease. They would also testify of how God allowed them to escape a horrifying near-death experience, or how He showed up on time with supernatural finances to meet specific needs.

Because I've always loved a good story, testimony time never failed to fascinate me. But it also had an adverse effect, as it left me with feelings of inadequacy. I harbored these feelings because I assumed I'd never have a spectacular testimony like the ones I grew up hearing, as I was just a young girl who got saved very young, long before I was old enough to even think about committing some of the sins these people had committed and were being delivered from. There was nothing too impressive about my life that would captivate the attention of a congregation and make them want to shout and rejoice with me. But little did I know all of that would soon change.

Fast-forward to 1993, during the first of many devastating episodes in my life. In the midst of my heartbreaking dilemma, God commissioned me to "Write." That one simple word is what I heard in my spirit as I picked up an ink pen from the floor of a hospital in Omaha, Nebraska. At that time, I was twenty-four years old, and my story was still fresh in the making.

It wasn't too surprising that God would say this to me, as writing was a gift He'd given me as a young child and one that He is yet developing even today. Ever since I discovered pen and paper as a toddler, I always loved writing. I used my gift often while growing up in the church, writing poetry, songs, and even holiday dramas. But at this particular moment in time, while standing in that Midwest hospital, 935 miles away from my southern roots, God took a second to reveal to me a tiny portion of His massive plan for my life. He was in the process of developing my testimony and transforming me into a mouthpiece for Him. Mine would be a story that slowly unfolded throughout the years and involved several agonizing events. It was a story that God wanted me to write about and share with the world.

I toyed with several titles for my story before settling with its present title. As the words "God's Girl" crossed my mind, my spirit leaped in confirmation as I felt those words described me and the story of my life perfectly because my ultimate goal in life has always been to please Him. I am in no way saying that I've lived a perfect life; quite the contrary. I am saying that for much of my imperfect life, my heart, mind, and soul have remained focused on one agenda, trying to please God in all that I do and say. And although it was never very easy, something within me always knew that living for Him would be worth the effort. But I soon found out that my idea of *worth it* was not what God had in mind.

Believe it or not, I spent much of my life mentally chasing a fairy tale. I assumed that if I did my best to live for God, I would eventually be rewarded with the happily-ever-after life for which I'd always longed.

In this *happy life*, I expected troubles to be few, relationships to be great, health to be excellent, money to be plenteous, and marriage to last forever and ever. I know that sounds crazy, but it's true; this was my mentality.

I desperately looked forward to this fairy-tale type of life, especially after I married at age twenty-two and moved from Birmingham, Alabama, to Omaha, Nebraska. I really believed that my life was about to become far better than the one I was leaving behind, as I not only grew up as a preacher's kid, but I grew up in a highly frustrating and very public split-family situation from which I was quite anxious to run away. Little did I know I was in for a rude awakening as my brand-new life, in a brand-new city and state, with my brand-new husband came with even more trials than I had experienced in my previous life. It wasn't at all the perfect little fairy tale that I had dreamed of.

In 2003, I finally self-published the book that God commissioned me to write, and I titled it *Somber Trials but Supernatural Triumphs*. In it, I simply shared many of the devastating episodes my husband and I endured during our marriage and how God blessed us to triumph supernaturally over them all.

I assumed after writing the book that life would turn happily ever after for us, but that was far from the truth as life only tossed more troubles in our direction. Yet I stood steadfast in my belief that when the dust finally settled, all would be well, and we would continue our journey toward our trouble-free happy place.

I literally spent twenty-one years of marriage waiting patiently for our happily ever after to manifest. That is, until I was forced to endure the most heartbreaking trial of my life, a trial that made me face the reality that there is no such thing as happily ever after, at least not in the form that I expected. In an instant, my faith, hope, dreams, and silly fairy-tale desires all faded to black, and so did my desire to continue living for God.

I was hurt and disappointed in Him, and I seriously considered aborting any other plans He had for my life because obviously His plans were no longer working. I decided it was time to do things my way, as there was no point in trying to live for Him when heartbreak always seemed to be my reward. As far as I was concerned, I'd made all the lemonade I could from the many lemons life was constantly handing me. I was tired of making lemonade! It just didn't taste good anymore!

But though I tried to give up on God, He never once thought about giving up on me. In fact, during my days of confusion and semi-rebellion, He did nothing but love on me. And, in subtle ways, He kept me assured of His presence. He never left me, nor did He forsake me, just as He promised in His Word. Then one day, when I least expected it, He showed up for me like a superhero by plunging down, scooping me up, and rescuing me from my own self-destruction. I'm still reeling in amazement!

Recently God revealed to me that with each trial I faced in my life, I was actually evolving into a new person. And today, because of those trials, I have become a wise, humble, faithful, and extraordinary woman of God with an extraordinary family, living an extraordinary life. The very storms that I felt were hindering me from reaching the happily-ever-after goal I had set for my life were actually blowing me toward an amazing destiny that God had prepared just for me. A destiny that included a new level of happiness and, more importantly, peace!

Friend, God encouraged me to pour out my heart to you within the pages that follow, in hopes that you will identify with me at some point during my story and, in turn, receive your healing as I have mine. I especially pray that through my story you will ultimately see in yourself the extraordinary person that God is transforming you into via your trials. So come on inside, put on your seat belt, and get ready to join me on this passionate journey as I reflect on my past, reexamine my present, and eagerly look ahead to my bright and exciting future as God's girl, boldly living my life for His glory.

Let's go!

1

Child of a Preacher Man

> Train up a child in the way he should go: and when he is old, he will not depart from it.
> —Proverbs 22:6 (KJV)

There I was standing in the church foyer on May 30, 2015, arm in arm with my dad and adorned in a lovely ivory wedding gown and veil. Daddy was about to give me away in marriage for the second time in my life.

I never thought I'd be in such a place in life. Remarried that is. I had spent the twenty-one years of my first marriage being so careful to do life just right in order to avoid making the same marital mistakes my parents and grandparents and so many others before me had made. I wanted to be the one in my family to break the generational curse of divorce. I wanted my first marriage to be my only marriage. I wanted it to be perfect and to last forever. But a storm arose in 2012, which brought our wedding vows, "for better, for worse, for richer, for poorer, in sickness and in health, to love and to cherish, till death do us part" full circle, thereby forcing my forever to end much too soon.

So, as I stated, there I was, about to walk down the aisle once again, in an effort to give marriage a second chance and very excited about embarking on this brand-new chapter of life. But before I continue to divulge that story, it's important that I travel back in time and share with you the events of my life that led up to this moment and ultimately transformed me into the woman I am today, a woman honored to be considered God's girl.

I call myself God's girl because I've spent my entire life living and working for Him and watching Him do miraculous things in my life as a result. Honestly, my entire forty-eight years here on this earth have been filled with church and God, God and church. Growing up as a preacher's kid, I had no idea what life was like apart from church. For me, going to church was just as natural as going to the restroom. My family attended church so much that even while home in bed sound asleep, I would still be at church in my dreams. And though it may sound like it, I'm actually not complaining, as I loved God and church very much during my childhood, and I still love both today. In fact, in my heart, I hold many fond memories of the lessons, songs, Bible verses, friends, and mentors I acquired while growing up in the ministry.

To be honest, my earliest church memory is not so fond, as it left me with a scar on my right knee that remains today. I must have been somewhere around three or four years old. I can remember walking along one of the side aisles near a floor register. I don't know how or why, but I tripped and fell, and my knee landed on that register. After that, I only remember blood, pain, tears, and somebody picking me up.

This painful incident happened at Friendship Baptist Church, located in the small community of Brighton, Alabama, where my parents were born and raised. Brighton, which is about fourteen miles outside of Birmingham, is not only where my parents both grew up but also where they met, got married, and started their family.

My mom and dad, who actually got married as teenagers while attending Brighton High School, had one significant thing in common; they both possessed sensitive hearts toward God. And though their parents didn't attend church regularly, they made sure their children attended faithfully.

My mom, Teresa Davis, born to Ms. Elaine Newell and the late Mr. Willie Davis, was the oldest of her mother's ten children. My mom was always a prayer warrior, long before she knew what the term actually meant. As a very young girl, she could always be caught praying during any free moment. And even if there wasn't a free moment, she'd create one and go before the Lord in prayer. Whether it was in a stall of a public restroom or in a congested closet at home, it didn't matter. All that mattered to her was her obedience to God's Word, which encourages us to pray without ceasing. Her heart for God resulted in God's amazing favor on her life, especially in the area of business. While taking home economics in high school, my mom discovered her passion and her gift for sewing. Becoming Mrs. Mildred Dickerson's favorite student, my mom excelled so well in the class that she became an entrepreneur while still in grade school, making clothing for her teachers, family members, friends, and of course herself.

My dad, Willie Bruce O'Neal, born to Ms. Eddie Mae Henderson and the late Mr. Preston O'Neal, was affectionately known as "Luke" in the community of Brighton. He was the oldest of his mother's three children. Because he had such a fear of death and hell, my dad eagerly gave his life to Christ at the young age of twelve and spent much of his childhood working in the church. At age fifteen, he was given the position of junior Sunday school superintendent of Friendship Baptist Church, a position he held until age nineteen, after which he was promoted to Sunday school superintendent. He had been placed in these positions because church leaders recognized his oratorical gift. At such a young age, his gift of speaking and drawing crowds was making room for him.

Because they had conceived a child out of wedlock, my parents decided to do what they thought was right and marry, although they were still in high school. Their son, whom they named Willie Bruce after my dad, was born two months after they married. However, the baby died immediately after birth. While enduring this painful loss, my parents graduated high school together that May, and then they began trying for another child to heal the wound in their hearts. Conceiving another child didn't take long, as they conceived me the very same year, and on March 19, 1969, almost an exact year from the birth date of their deceased son, I entered their world. Their grieving hearts were happy once again, and I, being their rainbow baby, received all the love and admiration that they carried in their hearts for their deceased son and for me. Thirteen months later, they were surprised with another son, whom they named William Bruce.

Immediately after William's birth, my mom encouraged my dad, who was working for the United States Steel Company, to purchase for them a newly constructed three-bedroom, one-bath split-level home in the flourishing city of Hueytown, Alabama. The ability to purchase a home of this caliber at such a young age was a major feat for young African Americans during this time, which is why he and my mom were so proud when God blessed them in such a miraculous way. My dad often tells the story of an older Caucasian coworker who gave him a ride home from work one day. When they pulled up in front of Daddy's new house, the coworker asked, "Is this your parents' home?" And Daddy proudly responded, "No, this is *my* house," to which the coworker looked terribly puzzled.

After filling his new house with brand-new everything from Sears & Roebuck, my young dad soon discovered that material things are not what make a house a home nor what holds a marriage together, as his marriage began turning rocky very rapidly. And to make matters worse, Sears & Roebuck's repo men showed up one day and took everything away.

Personally, I feel the breakdown of my parents' marriage was inevitable due to their marrying so young; in addition, they had no good examples of married couples in their families to follow, as my dad's father never married his mom, and my mom's father was divorced from her mom. Simply put, Willie Bruce O'Neal and Teresa Davis were two immature and misinformed children, playing house in a highly complicated adult world. Consequently, heavy issues arose, such as miscommunication, financial troubles, disrespect, mental abuse, physical abuse, and adultery, which ultimately destroyed their brief union.

After spending about a year and a half away from the church, separated from my mom and shacking up with a new woman named Patricia Bodley, Daddy spent much of his time wallowing in depression and indulging in sin, trying to, as he put it, *heal himself*. But I thank God that in his desperate mental state he had enough fight in him not to become the typical deadbeat dad. Though he may have wandered at times, he never faded away into the darkness of his depression, ultimately disappearing from my and my brother's lives. Rather than disappear, he fought hard to remain visible. In fact, my mom, who was also going through a great deal of depression as a woman scorned, never kept William and me from our dad. She continued to allow us to visit him, even at the home of the other woman. I truly admire her for that.

While my dad was so-called healing himself, doing many sinful things that were totally out of character for him, he was actually running from the calling God had placed on his life. But he finally surrendered to God while at work on a Sunday morning in January 1974.

On this particular day, with tears streaming down his face, he abruptly left his job at US Steel and drove directly to Friendship Baptist Church, never taking the time to freshen up or change out of his street clothes into something more church appropriate.

The urgency he felt in his spirit that morning was the result of several attempts God had made over a period of time to get his attention. The first attempt was in a dream God had given him months earlier as he slept in Patricia's bed. In the dream, he said he was standing in the midst of a city that was on fire. There were buildings burning and falling and many young people screaming and running for their lives. While watching all of this in horror, Daddy said he suddenly heard the voice of God say to him, "I told you to tell them. I told *you* to tell them!" And he replied, "Lord, if you just give me another chance, I'll tell them! I'll tell them!"

Daddy said he woke up in tears, determined to obey God's orders, but as days passed, life got in the way, and he never made good on his promise. As a result, God applied more pressure. On the first of January, 1974, Patricia, who was expecting a baby by my dad, went into labor with serious complications. The doctor tried to force my dad to make a decision, asking him whether to save the mother or the child. Not being able to make such a decision, Daddy says he pleaded with the doctor to save them both. Then he ran into a phone booth and called his mom and several other family members. After making those phone calls, he placed a very important phone call to God.

In that phone booth, Daddy promised God that if He would spare Patricia's life and the life of their unborn child, he would do whatever God wanted him to do. So God answered his prayer when, before the New Year's Day was done, Patricia gave birth by cesarean section to my half sister Franchesca, whom we affectionately call Fran. And on that Sunday morning, when God touched my dad's heart and led him from his job straight to the church, God was simply reminding him that it was time to make good on his promise.

Daddy ended up in a brief scuffle with an usher as he tried to enter the church sanctuary. The usher wouldn't allow him to enter because of his inappropriate attire, especially the big brown apple cap he wore on his head. However, because of my dad's constant persistence, the usher finally allowed him entrance while snatching the cap off his head and pressing it hard into his chest.

With a wild look in his eyes and holding his cap tightly to his chest, Daddy entered the sanctuary as everyone stared at him in bewilderment. His pastor, W. J. Sankey, then said to him, "Follow me to my office."

In the office, Daddy shared with Pastor Sankey his encounter with God, and Pastor Sankey was not at all surprised as he told him, "God told me you were coming." Then he asked him, "When do you want to preach your trial sermon?" Daddy was shocked, as he had not yet told his pastor that God had called him to preach, but his pastor was already asking him about a trial sermon. Pastor Sankey then took it upon himself to pick a date. He remembered that his pastoral anniversary was coming up in a few weeks, and he decided to schedule my dad to preach his trial sermon on that special day, which was a great honor.

Daddy and Pastor Sankey returned to the pulpit where Pastor Sankey allowed my dad to address the congregation. As he stood before the people, Daddy boldly declared that God had called him to preach. Suddenly, the entire church went up in praise, and it wasn't long before the news of his announcement spread throughout the community of Brighton like wildfire. In fact, many people still talk about it to this day.

Though that announcement shocked many people, and made some

feel as if Daddy had lost his mind, it wasn't very surprising to several of the church's older members who had the opportunity to watch him grow up. Like Pastor Sankey, they expected my dad to preach one day because they had witnessed the gift God had given him to captivate an audience during his years as a young Sunday school superintendent. No, they were not at all surprised about this announcement. Their purpose for celebrating on that fateful Sunday morning was because their prodigal son had found his way home.

My mom, who wasn't at church on this particular Sunday, was at home kneeling in the windowsill of my bedroom, which she often used as her prayer room. Over the years, she has often shared with me how during her prayers that day, she happened to be praying for my dad. My mom knew the life he was presently living was the total opposite of the person she knew him to be. The *Luke* she had grown up with was a God-fearing, churchgoing young man who cared very much how God and others viewed him. But this new Luke was very different and in the worse way.

Mama prayed, "Lord, if he never comes back to me, please bring him back to you," and she stayed there in the windowsill praying for a very long time. She said she had determined not to stop praying until God gave her a sign. After a while, she suddenly saw an image of Jesus before her, and it appeared as if He was kneeling and praying with her. That's when she finally stopped praying and went into the kitchen to finish cooking her Sunday dinner. A while later, her phone was ringing off the hook with call after call from friends, family, and church members telling her what my dad said at Friendship that day. Mama knew then that God had answered her prayer.

In February 1974, Daddy preached his trial sermon, and I've been told that there was literally standing room only in Friendship's sanctuary, as it seemed nearly everyone in the Brighton community was interested in hearing Luke preach. His sermon, which was titled "Repent Ye for the Kingdom of Heaven is at Hand," and subtitled "Running with a Message," proved that God's anointing was truly upon his life because there were many young people who accepted Christ into their hearts that day after hearing his message.

In obedience to his pastor, Daddy stopped shacking with Patricia and went back home to live with his mom. And after he and my mom divorced, he and Patricia married that April in a small ceremony in my grandmom's living room.

Patricia, whom I respectfully call Mama as well, but will call Mama Trish in this book as not to confuse you, entered their marriage with my half sister Franchesca Horatio O'Neal and her two other children from her previous marriage. My stepsister Triola Michelle Ellis, nicknamed "Tree," and my stepbrother Willie James Ellis, nicknamed "Chop," were older than William and me, and amazingly their ages fell in sequence with ours, as we were about seven, six, five, and four years of age when our parents married. Five years after they wed, my half brother Dedrick Dewayne O'Neal was born, and twenty-one months after his birth, a seventh child was added when they adopted Mama Trish's nephew, JaCarlos DeJuan O'Neal, bringing their total number of children to seven. And when my cousin Patrick Jonathan Fisher came down from New York to stay with us every summer, there were eight of us.

So, in my dad's household, I had seven siblings, which were two sisters, four brothers, and a cousin. And in my mom's household, as she had also remarried, I had two siblings, my brother William (whom I count in both households), and my half brother Philemon Williams. This resulted in my place in the family changing frequently, depending on which house I was in at the time. For instance, I was the oldest child in my mom's house, but in my dad's house, I was the third oldest.

Three years after Daddy preached his trial sermon, our family, who was like an African American version of the television sitcom *The Brady Bunch*, became the first family of Mount Canaan Missionary Baptist Church. Mt. Canaan's building was a tiny white A-frame structure that rested deep within the tree-covered hills of the Garden Highland community in Birmingham, Alabama. There were somewhere between seven to twelve faithful members upon our arrival, who were only having Sunday services twice a month. However, under my dad's leadership, the church grew and changed drastically. This special place is where my siblings and I all grew up in the Lord and where my dad and stepmom work in full-time ministry as pastor and co-pastor to this very day.

It wasn't long after being called to pastor Mt. Canaan Missionary Baptist Church that my dad grew tired of operating in traditional Baptist etiquette and preaching unfruitful messages that were not changing lives. His desire was to have a life-changing ministry, which he prayed for fervently, and God wasted no time answering his prayers. During this time, God sent people into his life to teach him about the Holy Spirit, and before long, he had received it. And my stepmom, who had received the Holy Spirit as a child due to being raised in a holiness church, rededicated her life to God and experienced a refilling of the Holy Spirit. Then Daddy struck a goldmine of spiritual knowledge when he was introduced to the seminar teachings of Minister William "Bill" Gothard Jr., founder of the nondenominational organization, Institute in Basic Life Principles.

Through Bill Gothard's ministry, my dad learned such things as God's structure of the family, His principles of finance, and other godly principles of life, which he soon began putting into practice in his home and in his church. Soon afterward, God anointed him to preach powerful messages of grace, repentance, and salvation that led to word of this anointed young preacher and his life-changing messages quickly spreading across Birmingham and its surrounding cities. As a result, Mt. Canaan grew so rapidly that there was standing room only every Sunday morning as men stood around the walls, allowing the women and children to sit during services.

Daddy's prayers for a more effective ministry had been answered, as his ministry was having a great impact on the lives of many young men, women, and children who were in search of answers for their miserable lives. There was no doubt that the young people who were finding their way to Mt. Canaan were those he saw in that impacting dream God gave him in 1973 when he saw a city burning and young people running for their lives.

Realizing that the direction of the church was changing with the introduction of the Holy Spirit and the teaching of godly principles, my dad was inspired to change the church from Baptist to nondenominational. He also changed the name to Mt. Canaan Full Gospel Church and added the motto, *a family church with a teaching ministry, reaching world for Christ.*

This is where it all started for me. My introduction to another level in God that is. I am honored to say that I was one of those whose life was tremendously impacted very early in my dad's ministry, as I happened to be the first of my siblings and our young friends at church to receive salvation and the Holy Spirit, when I was around twelve years old. To be honest, being so young, I had never heard of the Holy Spirit or of being saved; nevertheless, God gave me the most magnificent rendezvous with Him that I shall never forget.

It was a Saturday night, and William and I were spending the weekend at my dad's house as normal. As we played with our siblings in the back room of the house, there was a knock at the front door. My oldest sister, Triola, whom our parents always put in charge of us when they were away, suggested that I go answer the door.

At the door were my dad and stepmom, returning home from a night of ministering. The power of God was still heavy upon my dad, and he was anxious to lay hands on whoever was standing on the other side of that door. It just happened to be me.

Like a madman, he rushed into the house, grabbed me by the hand, and led me to one of the two rocking chairs in his bedroom. At that moment, I didn't understand what was happening. I thought I was in trouble or something. *What did I do?* I wondered. But now I realize that it was just *my night* as I had been chosen by God to receive the gift of salvation and His precious Holy Spirit. This gift from Him would change my life forever.

As Daddy sat down in the other rocking chair across from me, he questioned me in urgency as to whether I'd asked God to save me or if I'd ever asked Him for the Holy Spirit. I was nervous as I thought to myself,

Did I forget to do that? Then I thought, *Wait a minute. What in the world is that?*

While flipping through the pages of my mind, I quickly remembered the day that I was baptized. I must have been around eight or nine years old. *Is that what Daddy was talking about?* Well maybe not because he already knew I'd been baptized, so he wouldn't be questioning me about that. As I continued thinking, God interrupted my thoughts with the memory of a prayer that I had prayed several weeks earlier at bedtime. I shared with Daddy how I mentioned to God that I wanted more of Him. However, at the time of that prayer, I really didn't know what *more of Him* consisted of. I just knew that deep inside I felt a need for more. Unbeknownst to me, I was about to get just what I'd asked for and more.

After quoting Romans 10:9, which states, "If you confess with your mouth the Lord Jesus and believe in your heart that God has raised Him from the dead, you will be saved," my dad went on to explain salvation to me. He shared with me how Jesus had died on the cross for my sins and that all I needed to do was accept Him into my heart and He would forgive me of my sins with the promise of a home in heaven with Him when I die.

Then Daddy asked me if I wanted to receive this salvation. Of course, I said, "Yes." So he told me to raise my hands as he led me through a prayer of repentance. What happened next is what I consider a seat belt moment.

Daddy told me to say, "Thank You, Jesus," repeatedly, and I did, with my whole heart. Suddenly, my mouth began to say things that I didn't understand or have any control over. I was speaking in tongues! Pretty soon, I started to feel as light as a feather.

That entire experience was so emotional and overwhelming for me. I can hardly explain it any better than that. At one point, it felt as if I were having a brief out-of-body experience because I could feel myself float to the other side of the room, and from there I could actually see myself sitting in that rocking chair. My hands were raised, my mouth was going forth in tongues, and my face was full of tears. It was amazing!

That experience proved to me, beyond a shadow of doubt, that God *is* real. If I ever had any doubts about His existence, they all instantly vanished. Just think about it; at only twelve years of age, not knowing anything about salvation or the Holy Spirit, and having nothing to go on but faith in God and in my dad, I stepped out into the deep. And as I stepped, God instantly swooped me up and carried me into a place that only He could take me. Those sincere tears streaming down my face, that sudden ability to speak in a new tongue, and that awesome feeling of joy that flooded my soul; yes, I can honestly say that God is real!

The next day, which was a Sunday morning, my siblings and I were all silently wondering, *Now what?* We wondered if there was going to be some kind of instant and or noticeable change in me. *Will I look different? Will I act different?* I remember the uncomfortable feelings of being watched by my siblings all morning as we dressed for Sunday school. Finally, when William asked me a question to which I responded in a way he didn't particularly care for, he loudly exclaimed, "Naw, she ain't changed! She's still the same!"

What neither my brother nor the rest of us realized was, though the change in me was not yet visible, there was definitely some changing going on inside, as that supernatural event marked the beginning of my evolution. Through the process of time and experience, I was slowly but surely evolving into the woman of God I am today.

2

Growing up Not Very Brady

> Jesus replied, "You do not realize now what I am doing, but later you will understand."
> —John 13:7(NIV)

The Brady Bunch, a popular television sitcom back in the 1970s, was the story of a man named Mike Brady who, after raising his three sons alone, met and married a lady named Carol who had three daughters. After an eventful backyard wedding, these eight people went on to become a big, happy blended family. This family-friendly sitcom was one of my all-time favorite television shows growing up, but it was also partially to blame for my very naive fairy-tale mentality.

Because I happened to be growing up in a real-life blended family during the run and syndication of that television series, and I was not familiar with others my age that were living in such a family, I instantly accepted the Bradys as the prototype for all blended families.

Imagine the disappointment I faced when my own family failed to measure up to the standards of the blissful Bradys. I was left assuming that something was terribly wrong with us because the *Brady Bunch* producers never emphasized the broken family situations from which this new beautifully blended family had derived.

For instance, it was made clear in the beginning that Mike's previous wife was deceased, but where was Carol's former husband? Did the girls ever go visit their dad, and was Carol receiving child support payments from him? Did Carol's former husband have issues with Mike being in his daughters lives, or did Mike have any issues with him? And if there were issues, did the girls suffer mentally from the continued animosity between them? Also, did the boys truly feel loved by Carol? And did the girls truly feel loved by Mike?

It took some time, but I finally grasped that the Bradys were only an exaggerated TV version of a blended family, which in no way could compare to my broken/blended family, as mine was the raw, real-life version.

In my version, I grew up in two homes, and my childhood was spent going back and forth between my mom's house during the week and my dad's house on the weekends and during the summer months. With those two homes came a different set of rules for each, and as you can imagine, that was very tough to deal with at times. But because my parents separated and divorced when I was very young, it was the only lifestyle I ever knew. So God blessed me to survive it, though it was not painless.

It was not only tough going back and forth between the two homes, but having to deal with my parents' turbulent relationship was even tougher. As their oldest child, I often felt caught in the middle of their animosity, living much of my childhood in depression due to carrying the weight of their heavy grown-up issues in my young mind. I desperately wished for a way to fix their relationship so that we all could be happy and harmonious like the Bradys, but I didn't know how. These matters and more plagued my youth. Thus my constant longing for a happy fairy-tale life was born.

Some of our church members, who likened my dad's family to *The Brady Bunch*, would sometimes refer to us as *The O'Neal Bunch*. And many of them agreed that, as with the Bradys, our family blended so well that they had a hard time figuring out which child belonged to which parent. I must admit that was all God.

In fact, on several occasions, there were church people who said to me, "You look just like your mama." Those words would always confuse me because I'd think they were referring to my biological mom, to which I'd reply, "Oh, do you know my mama?" Then a look of confusion would come over their face as they silently wondered why I would ask such a silly question. Clearly, they knew her; she was the first lady of the church. After experiencing several of these awkward scenarios, to which I would give the same never-ending explanation of our family dynamics, "First Lady O'Neal is my stepmom, and Pastor O'Neal is my dad," I started to wonder if I had been doing something wrong in exposing that bit of information because of the look of shock they would give me. Also, as I tried to figure out why so many people were seeing my stepmom on my face, I came up with my own explanation. I've always heard people say that husbands and wives tend to look alike through time. If that is the case, then when people assumed they were seeing Mama Trish on my face, the person they were actually seeing was my dad, whom I look very much alike. So with that understanding, I've learned to just smile and say, "Thank you."

Unlike Mr. Brady, my dad didn't have a huge, extravagant home for his large family to grow up in, as he really couldn't afford one. However, around 1975, he and Mama Trish counted themselves blessed to find and remodel a tiny, decrepit, three-bedroom, one-bath home in the city of Brighton that they purchased for about $4,700. And they lived in that tiny house for twenty years until God blessed them with one much greater in 1996.

But every weekend and during the summer, that tiny old house was filled to capacity with my dad, my stepmom, my six siblings, our cousin Patrick, and me. And as you can imagine, at bedtime, the sleeping arrangements for us kids were all over the place—the floor, the den sofa, and even doubled up in twin beds.

Just as the Brady kids delved into all sorts of daily shenanigans, our being preacher's kids made my siblings and I no different. If anything, I'd say our shenanigans were way more fun. We made the most of our weekends and summer times together. From the front yard to the backyard, in the ditch, up the street, around the corner and several blocks away, we explored the neighborhood of Parker Springs in Brighton, Alabama, to the fullest and enjoyed every moment.

Having a cool brother like Chop, who was very gifted at creating exciting games for us to play, building the coolest forts and constructing the craziest go-carts, made summertime super memorable for us. While I was too scared to ever spend the night in his forts or ride on his go-carts, just watching him, my brother, William, and our cousin Patrick enjoy them was fun enough for me.

The spiritual modifications that were taking place within our church were also taking place in our home, as Daddy had turned into a saved, sanctified, Holy Spirit-filled preacher man who lived his life as if Jesus would be showing up at any minute. Therefore, for the sake of holiness, he put many restrictions upon his church members and his family, especially his wife, his daughters, and the women in our church. For example, he abruptly stopped us from wearing pants. We were only allowed to wear skirts and dresses. And our hems had to fall below the knee, not above. We wore skirts and dresses year-round and for every event, including picnics, skating, bowling, and baseball, at which point we would add socks and sneakers, which made for a very bizarre-looking outfit. The only thing remotely close to pants that we were allowed to wear was culottes, which were basically wide-legged pants that resembled skirts. And when it came to swimming, Daddy made sure he found my sisters and me one-piece swimming suits with short skirts attached.

Also, we couldn't wear any makeup whatsoever to enhance our beauty. So, as teens, when Triola and I discovered clear lip gloss, we thought we had struck gold as we shined our lips to the max! One Sunday morning while sitting in our Sunday school class, which Daddy was teaching, our lips were shinning so bright that Daddy could hardly concentrate on the lesson. He suddenly stopped teaching, reached into his suit pocket, pulled out a handkerchief, and handed it to us while firmly stating, "Wipe it off!" in front of all of our friends. How embarrassing. Daddy said he was trying to help us be modest and holy women, but sometimes we felt more like dull and unattractive creatures.

In high school, my sisters and I were not allowed to go to our proms. In fact, we never even pressed the issue when prom season rolled around, as we already knew how our dad felt about the subject. But our brothers, on the other hand, did press the issue, and without Daddy's blessing or help, they attended and thoroughly enjoyed their senior proms.

When it came to dating, my sisters and I were not allowed to entertain any young man that did not go through our dad first. This rule always made us uneasy, as Daddy wanted to drill the guy about everything from "Who are your parents?" to "Do you know Jesus?" As with all rules, this one was broken a number of times, but regardless, it was still his rule.

There's a particular memory that my siblings and I shall never forget, and that was the summer the TVs disappeared. One summer day, in the early 1980s, a few of my siblings were in the den watching television. At the same moment that Daddy happened to walk through the den, one of the characters on TV yelled a curse word. The D word to be exact. Without warning, Daddy yanked the plug and snatched up the TV. Then he went through the house, snatched up all the other TVs, and stored them all in a closet in his bedroom.

After hearing so much ungodly chatter coming into his house via the television and corrupting his kids, Daddy had finally had enough. But we assumed he had lost his mind or something. Even Mama Trish was dumbfounded at his actions, but as a good wife, she didn't kick against his authority; she just trusted the God in him.

A day or so after the televisions disappeared, Daddy went out and purchased construction paper and markers and gave me the task of transcribing scriptures onto the paper while he taped several to walls all around the house. But he not only placed scriptures on the walls, Daddy started giving us scriptures and even whole chapters to memorize, as it was his desire that we absorb God's Word rather than the bad words and ungodly lifestyles coming at us via television.

Daddy even gave Mama Trish a scripture to memorize during that time, which was Romans 8:28, "And we know that all things work together for good to them that love God, to them who are the called according to his purpose" (KJV). This appalled her because she felt as if he was treating her like one of the children. But despite her feelings, she obeyed him by faith, and it turns out Romans 8:28 is now her most favorite scripture to this day.

I remember one summer Daddy gave us the assignment to learn chapter 6 of Romans and an incentive for doing so. He promised dinner at our favorite restaurant to the one who could recite it from beginning to end. I happened to learn it first. After reciting it verbatim, I was awarded the opportunity to enjoy a meal at Bonanza, a local steak restaurant. Joining me were my dad and Brother Robert Dismukes, one of our faithful church members whom I affectionately refer to as Uncle D. Uncle D was so proud of me that he later presented me with my first Bible; it was a burgundy Open Bible, which was beautifully engraved with my name on the lower right-hand corner.

Our no-television, scripture-memorizing lifestyle lasted longer than we expected. In fact, half of my siblings and I had grown up and moved away before the televisions finally returned. Though our childhood was much different from that of our peers, which sometimes made us feel as if we were missing out on real life, my siblings and I all agree that we are grateful to have had that experience, as we are reaping the benefits of Daddy's abrupt decision today. Not only did we develop a greater bond between us as siblings, but also we absorbed a never-ending supply of the Word of God deep inside our souls that prepared us to handle the trials and tribulations that were awaiting us down the road.

However, I'm still grateful for my brother Chop, whom I'd venture to say was anointed to create fun for us during that season of our lives. We had so much fun playing his made-up games and laughing uncontrollably until we really didn't have time to miss watching television.

Daddy kept us very active in the church, as we were some of the first children to make up the church's youth department and youth choir. We were always attending youth meetings, choir rehearsal, Sunday school, Sunday service, revivals, and every other service the church offered.

My friends LaShonda Carlisle, LaTanya Tarver, Benfordnetti Morgan, and I enjoyed meeting up at church because there was just something about being there that literally energized us. The fellowship, the praise and worship, the dancing and shouting, and the Word of God were all things to which we looked forward. Having been separated all week, going to our individual schools, coming together at Mt. Canaan on the weekends was the highlight of our lives.

Our youth department, which we dubbed the YICs and the YACs, short for Youth in Christ and Young Adults in Christ, was where we met and fell in love with many of the mentors that supported us spiritually throughout our youth and young adulthood. Such people include our youth pastors Nathaniel and Valencia Newsome, whom we dubbed Daddy and Mama Newsome, and their youth coordinators like Sister Aleshia Poscy, Sister Cynthia Ward, Sister Freda Sutton, Sister Willa Dean Lundy, and many more. These people played active roles in our raising whether they realize it or not. They spent quality time with us, always had a listening ear, and never ceased to love, guide, and encourage us during our formative years, thereby helping to groom us into the successful men and women we are today.

Today I realize that church was the escape route God gave me to deal with the frustrations I faced in the drama between my parents. You see, although they were saved and very much in the church, they were still human, dealing with very sensitive issues. Issues that, for some reason, I tended to carry heavily on my shoulders. And as much as I desired and prayed for our lives to mirror the Bradys' happy lifestyle, God didn't allow it. However, He gave me something better, He gave me Himself, which helped me to cope with the life that I had been born into. But what I didn't know then and am well aware of now is that He was allowing me to experience and absorb lessons from my broken/blended family that I would need to take with me to another life that He had waiting for me down the road.

3

God's Girl in the Making

> And ye shall be holy unto me: for I the Lord am holy, and have severed you from other people, that ye should be mine.
> —Leviticus 20:26 (KJV)

A close bond is what my dad and I have always shared since my birth, making me a bona fide Daddy's girl. This in no way meant I loved my mother any less, because I loved her just as much, but there was a connection between my dad and me that just couldn't be explained.

I would venture to say that the bond between us started to fuse immediately after my birth, as I was their rainbow baby, a replacement for the child he and my mom had recently lost. Then the bond between us grew stronger as he hurried home after work each day, anxious to spend time with his baby girl. On Sunday mornings, we bonded as my mom gave him the freedom to carry me to Sunday school with him each week. He proudly entered the building with his baby girl in tow, gaining the attention of several excited little girls who begged to hold me. Our bond gained even more strength as he relished in my many milestones, such as the time he grabbed me up, ran through the alley to his mom's house, and stood me before her to show off my newest feat … walking!

Growing closer as I grew older, my dad became my confidant and best friend. No matter how many friends I had, Daddy was my closest. He understood me, and I understood him. Our special relationship is what helped me in my young adulthood, as I was able to see clearly which guys were good for me and which guys were simply up to no good. The love and respect he showered me with made it hard for me to settle with just any guy. That guy would have to come as close as possible to the standards my dad had already set.

However, during my preteen years, when I was not yet good at discerning a guy's motives, my dad's discernment kicked in, and his fervent prayers always protected me. When I think back on the times I gave in to a certain guy's sweet talk and ended up behind the church or in the church basement learning how to French-kiss without Daddy's knowledge, I'm truly grateful to God for my dad's fervent prayers that covered me like a blanket and protected me like a shield.

One such episode of my dad's fervent prayers was brought on by a shameful act I committed one day during my middle school years. While home alone after school, my brother William happened to peep out the window and caught a glimpse of my boyfriend and me French-kissing on the front porch. Though I felt very uneasy about what we were doing, I allowed his charm and persistence to reel me in, but I had no idea that William or anyone else in our neighborhood had witnessed our ignorant love scene.

A few days later, an older teenaged boy named Christopher, who lived down the street, told me what he had witnessed. Christopher assured me that he would not tell my mom if I promised not to let it happen again. Through this wise young man, God was protecting me because Christopher's words put enough fear in me to make me give him my utmost promise. But that wasn't the end of the situation as I had hoped.

For several weeks, William never spilled the beans until one night when I ratted on him for something he did earlier in the day. That's when he used his secret weapon.

To get Mama off his back, he told her all about my kissing incident. Suddenly she stopped tearing into him and swiftly pounced on me. Then she picked up the phone and called my dad. He was *her* secret weapon. She knew the relationship he and I possessed and that if anyone could put me in my place it would be him. Daddy was so upset that he declared he would be at our house the next day. And sure enough, he was there.

I just knew I was going to get a whipping. But Daddy surprised me. All he did was talk to me. Heart to heart. One on one. And during our talk,

I told him about the older boy down the street who saw what happened and what he had said to me.

Grateful to know that God had used that young man to speak into my life, Daddy sent me down the street to get Christopher. When he and I returned, Daddy thanked him and commended him for watching over me. Then he asked us to join hands, and he prayed.

Every day from that point on, my dad increased his private prayers for me. He specifically asked God to shield me and to make my boyfriend lose interest in me. He later shared how he prayed over me as I slept at his house one night because he was very serious about God removing that boy from my life.

And suddenly it happened. I remember it so clearly. I was sitting in the lunchroom at school one day when my boyfriend walked in unexpectedly. He came straight over to me and said, "Tracy, I don't think we need to see each other anymore." Because I had already begun to lose interest in him, I simply agreed. And just like that, our toxic relationship was over.

That abrupt ending was very weird to me, and I assumed my dad must have called this boy or his parents and possibly threatened him or something. But when I questioned Daddy about it, he replied, "Baby, I didn't call anybody. I just prayed." And that's when I learned just how true God's Word is … "The effectual fervent prayer of a righteous man availeth much" (James 5:16b KJV).

I'm sure that not having my dad living in the house with me is what caused me to readily accept the love this boy was offering, because his sweet and charming ways filled a void that was created by my dad's absence. But there was also another void, one that even my dad couldn't fill, and that was the space in my heart that could only be filled by God. It wasn't long after that kissing episode that I gave my life to the Lord, as I shared with you in chapter 1. On that Saturday night when I accepted Jesus into my heart, I became more than just Daddy's girl; I became God's girl, and I wanted nothing more than to please Him with my life.

Though I had my share of errors, for the most part I tried my best to please God and my parents and to make them proud. Therefore, I tried my best not to give them any problems when it came to obeying. Even if I didn't always agree with them, I didn't voice my grievances very often. I simply obeyed. Never wanting to cause disappointment and grief, I tried to live by their wisdom and examples.

I guess many would say I lived my life in safe mode, never venturing out to learn life for myself through trial and error. My thinking was, and still is, *Why suffer undo hardship when someone has already done the work for you?* If my parents and others who have already traveled the road of life and made their mistakes along the way decided to yell back down the road to me in an effort to point out which bumps and potholes I needed to avoid, I'd be a fool to yell, "Stop telling me! Let me find them by myself!" Therefore, if living life in safe mode gets me to success much quicker in life, then safe mode it is!

As teens, my friends at church and I, who had accepted Jesus Christ and the Holy Spirit, were serious as a heart attack about our faith as we tried to live our best lives for God. We were not your average teenagers, as we lived our lives "sold out" for Him. And having the awesome support system of our youth ministry leaders made living for God not as hard as it could have been.

I remember on Fridays overhearing some of my classmates at school discuss their plans for the weekend as they were planning to attend parties or nightclubs. But I would just sit there and daydream about going to Friday night praise service at church. And when they would return to school on Monday discussing the good time they had over the weekend, partying and drinking and such, I would quietly reminisce on the great time I had at church all weekend praising the Lord with my friends. Of course, this did not make me a very popular student. But thank God, popularity was never an issue with me; all I wanted to do was serve God.

Though I loved God with all my heart, it was never easy going against the grain. Wearing dresses to school every day and being different from my peers made me stick out like a sore thumb, and no one likes to be singled out among his or her peers in a negative light. I felt those dresses were screaming loudly, clearly, and very negatively, "This girl is strange!" And if the dresses didn't scream loud enough, there were a few kids who did, as those who didn't know me very well referred to me as "that sanctified girl." It didn't feel very good to be laughed at.

I drudged on through high school, spending my days looking forward to the weekends to be with my church family. It was so hard to stay focused in my classes because I had no desire to be in that place. I only wanted to be at church, surrounded by those who were more like me. And though William and I tried to make a difference in school by forming an early morning prayer group with a few friends, my heart continued to long for my friends at Mt. Canaan.

To help me make it through, God blessed me with a special friend at school, one who could identify with me, as she loved the Lord as much as I did. Her name was Patricia Parker, and her pastor, John Lee Jackson, and my dad were friends whose churches fellowshipped together. Together Patricia and I wore our dresses, talked about church, and encouraged one another in the Lord. God also blessed me with a saved boyfriend. His name was Chris Hicks, and not only did we attend the same school, but he and his mom were members of our church. Because we both were receiving the same godly teaching, our relationship stayed strictly holy for the three years we were together. We tried to refrain from doing what comes naturally, such as kissing and petting, as we had been taught that would eventually lead to actions that were unpleasing to God.

Though God had given me these special relationships in high school, there were still those dreaded days. Days where it took everything in me to get out of the car and enter the school building. One morning when Mama dropped me off at school, she yelled at me as I walked toward the building. She had noticed that I was walking with my head down, so before she drove away, she yelled out, "Girl, hold your head up!" At the time, I assumed she was concerned about my safety, as she didn't want me colliding with a pole or a person. But later I found out there was much more meaning in her words.

Mama recognized a spirit of low self-esteem hovering over me because she had experienced it herself during her youth and young adulthood. Therefore, it bothered her to see that same spirit on her daughter.

Today, when I think about my mom's words, "Girl, hold your head up!" I realize not only was she speaking, but also God was speaking through her. He wanted me to hold my head up so that I might glimpse the awesome destiny He had in store for me. He wanted me to hold my head up and be proud of who I was, whose I was, and who I was yet to become. Yes, I might have been *that sanctified girl,* but that was because God had set me apart, making me *His girl.*

Amazingly, my solid stand in the Lord was more powerful than the feelings of low self-esteem that tried to consume me. And God's favor and great mercy shielded me from the temptations of drugs, alcohol, and sex that were all around me, enabling me to graduate high school while still holding on to my innocence and priceless virginity. However, as I stated earlier, going against the grain wasn't always easy. As a matter of fact, the older I got, the harder it got.

4

Mr. Right

> Delight thyself also in the Lord: and he shall give thee the desires of thine heart.
>
> —Psalms 37:4 (KJV)

After graduating high school in June 1987, I was very confused as to what I wanted to do with my life because my heart's desire had always been to marry and have children. I never imagined anything else beyond that. But since there was not a potential husband in my life, as my boyfriend, Chris, and I were no longer dating, I listened to the opinions, suggestions, and counsel of others and gained a few ideas.

I enrolled in a local junior college that fall, and I chose broadcasting as my major. Since I enjoyed reading and writing so much, I tried to envision myself anchoring the six o'clock news. But after discovering the enormous amount of work it would take in order to make it to the news anchor's desk, I changed my major to early childhood development after the first quarter. This subject, though I didn't know it then, would greatly benefit my life in the future.

In college, I discovered a whole new world, which was so very different from my small sheltered world. Although I tried to keep my attention on my studies, I couldn't help but notice the vast amount of fish that were in this new sea. In the back of my mind, I secretly wondered about every guy that I met. *Could he be the one for me?* I mean, let's be real, my flesh was crying out for what it was missing, and believe me, it was not more of Jesus.

Because I had the favor of God on my life, He kept me, even when I didn't want to be kept. Sometimes His favor felt more like a curse because I could not do the things other young people were doing and enjoying. I mean, it was quite frustrating wanting to yield to temptation but being restrained by the Holy Spirit. I always felt like this enormous eyeball was in the sky and was only watching me. And no matter where I went, it was always there. I must admit though, once the temptation had passed, I was glad I didn't yield, and I really appreciated that eyeball.

Though it may have felt like a curse at times, having the favor of God on my life was actually a blessing because God often worked miracles on my behalf that even amazed my parents. For example, after catching rides with friends and the public transit system to and from the junior college that I was attending, I strongly desired to have my own car. However, neither of my parents was financially able to purchase one for me. I remember talking to my dad about the situation, and he encouraged me by saying that whatever I saved up, he would match it and use it to buy me a car. Well, that was all I needed to hear. I started saving every cent that I came across. I saved my paychecks from my college work-study job and the extra monies I had left over from my Pell Grant after purchasing my books. I even had my younger brothers, Dedrick and JaCarlos, helping me save by telling them that every cent they gave me equaled a ride in my new car. They were so excited that every time they found a piece of change, they were running to me with it, and each time I saved up a certain amount, I was running to the bank with it. To my dad's surprise, I saved up $1,200 in a matter of months! He was shocked because he didn't think I'd be coming to him asking for his half so soon. He thought he would have more time to save, so he wasn't ready yet. Nevertheless, he had made me a promise, and he knew I was expecting him to keep it. So, on January 7, 1989, Daddy took me to a used-car dealership where he helped me to purchase my first car. It was a gray 1985 Chevrolet Cavalier that, with my money as a down payment, he would help me pay the notes on it until God blessed me with a good job enabling me to pay the notes myself. Then, about a month or so later, God sent the job.

I worked several jobs during my youth, but they were never the kind of jobs I considered *good* jobs because they were mainly restaurant and daycare assistant positions. However, having the favor of God on my life along with being a good steward over my finances in the area of tithes and offerings, allowed a *good* job with good pay and benefits to find me just before I turned twenty years old! It was a teacher's aide position with the Birmingham Board of Education. God allowed the director of the Child Development Department at the junior college where I was attending to take an interest in me. And when she was asked to recommend one of her students for a wonderful job opportunity as an assistant in a special new program for teen mothers in the Birmingham school system, God led her to choose me.

Though I had been blessed with a car and a good job, it still wasn't enough for me because I wanted to be married. And I didn't want to be married to just any man but I desired a good man, so I spent a brief period on the dating scene hoping to bump into Mr. Right, with no results. Believe it or not, at such a young age, I had already grown tired of dating; my heart's desire and main focus was marriage, therefore I questioned God daily, "Lord, who is he? Lord, where is he?"

I wasn't just looking for any kind of man, as I stated before; I wanted a *good* man. My dad was my best example of how a good man should treat me; therefore, I was well aware of the difference between a good one and a bad one. I wanted a man who was saved, sanctified, Holy Spirit-filled, and who loved and served the Lord just as much as I did. He needed to love and respect his parents and be a good umbrella of protection for me and our family. Bottom line, I wanted a man fashioned by God just for me. And little did I know, that man had been right under my nose all of my life.

One night in the spring of 1989, I remember going up the stairs toward my bedroom and overhearing my mom in her bedroom as she talked on the phone to her best friend, Marilyn. I remember her saying, "Tracy, Marilyn says hi," to which I responded, "Tell her I said hi." Then suddenly I stopped in my tracks, turned around, and said to her to her, "Ask Marilyn to give me Junior's address."

Junior was Marilyn's son. And to this day, I cannot tell you why I suddenly felt the urge to ask for his address, because although I'd known Marilyn and her family forever, I was never ever interested in her son Erskine Daniel Jr.

Erskine and I first met in 1969, while we were still in our mothers' wombs. Then I was born in March, and he followed that June. As babies and toddlers, my brother William and I were his occasional playmates. And, ironically, at my first birthday party, Marilyn mentioned to my dad that she felt her son and I would one day be married. Of course, Daddy laughed it off, thinking those were just playful words.

Erskine and I attended kindergarten, middle school, and high school together, but strangely, we never had an eye for one another. For some reason, although he was in my face, he was still hidden from me. I only saw him as Marilyn's son, nothing more. He just never caught my eye, and I guess I never caught his.

Adding to the irony, after our high school graduation in 1987, our mothers decided to save money by throwing us a combined graduation party. For the party, they ordered a large sheet cake that prophetically stated, *Congratulations Erskine & Tracy*. This was a very innocent coincidence, as Erskine's high school sweetheart was at the party, and so was mine. However, no one in that room, except God Almighty, new those words would have to be repeated four years later.

After graduation, Erskine entered the air force. This surprised me because as smart as he was in high school, I was almost certain he would end up in some renowned college somewhere. I considered him a nerd in high school because he enrolled in all of the tough subjects, such as calculus and trigonometry, and he aced them! He later admitted that he was just tired of school and needed a change of pace, and that's why he entered the air force. After completing his basic training in San Antonio, Texas, he was permanently stationed in Omaha, Nebraska.

I still remember how excited his mom was about giving me his address. You would have thought I was some kind of celebrity. As I stated earlier, I have no idea why I was led to ask her for her son's address. I guess God was supernaturally setting me up with Mr. Right, or better yet, my knight in shining armor.

As I sat down to pen that first letter to Erskine, I really didn't know what to say because, as weird as it may seem, we had never before had a real conversation. I think I ended up writing about school, family, the weather, and other bland subjects. Nevertheless, a few weeks later, I was thrilled to receive a letter from him. Although his letter was just as bland as mine had been, I was still happy to receive it because it proved to me that he was interested. Hoping this would be the start of a new relationship and that it would eventually evolve into much more, I immediately penned him another letter, and this time he followed it up with a phone call. I was on cloud nine!

Not long after we had begun corresponding, Erskine came home on leave, and with him came his best friend, Rodney. I was shocked when he called me late one night during his visit and asked if I was interested in going bowling with them. He said his cousin Angela would be going along with us as a date for Rodney. Although I hated to let him down, I had no choice because I couldn't leave my mom's house at that late of an hour. And although my dad wasn't living in the same house with us, I still respected his rules as well.

As I explained this to Erskine, he laughed it off and said he understood, and I trusted that he did. But once he returned to Nebraska, he stopped calling and writing. In hindsight, I guess I had hurt his ego, but at the time, I had no idea why he cut me off. Pretty soon, the feelings I had of him possibly being *the one* withered away, and I eventually ended up back on the dating scene.

After no luck on the dating scene, out of the blue I received a call from Erskine the following year. I was so happy to hear from him and I didn't bother questioning him about his long absence; we just picked up where we left off. His calls became more frequent, and before long, I was racing home every Sunday night to await a call from my new boyfriend.

As time progressed, he finally explained to me the reason for his disappearance. He said that after he left home and joined the military, he began straying away from the godly teaching that his parents had instilled in him. Therefore, he realized he just wasn't ready for a girl like me who was totally committed to God, as he knew being with me would require him to give up the new lifestyle he had begun to live and he wasn't ready to do that just yet. But one day as he and Rodney were discussing girls and how it was hard to find a good one, he began to tell Rodney more about me. Then Rodney firmly stated to him, "Man, that's just the kind of girl you need!" With that encouragement, Erskine collected the nerve to reach out to me again, with hopes of resuming our paused relationship.

That summer, he came home on leave for two weeks. That was our first face-to-face meeting since our relationship grew over the phone. That first day felt very awkward, especially for him because he could hardly look at me. But as the days passed, we grew more comfortable with one another, so much so that when his two weeks were up, our hearts became extremely heavy because we did not want to separate. Erskine said that he actually cried during most of his drive back to Omaha.

Because of our blossoming relationship, Erskine felt led to rededicate his life to the Lord. He shared with me how one day while alone in his dorm room, he prayed and asked God to save him and cleanse him of his sins. However, God went beyond his request by filling him with the Holy Spirit and giving him the evidence of speaking in tongues.

Days after his rendezvous with God, one of the security officers that guarded the gates at his job begin witnessing to Erskine every day. The officer, whose name was Victor Johnson, and his wife, Deborah, befriended

Tracy O'Neal Daniel Lee

Erskine and invited him to their church near downtown Omaha. During his first visit, Erskine decided to join the church immediately, as he was very happy to have found a church home away from home. In fact, many times, he would be the first to show up for services, nearly an hour before the church doors were opened.

Since our long-distance relationship was so emotionally hard on us, Erskine and I set our minds on not having to go through it for much longer as we seriously began discussing marriage. Through our letters and phone calls, we had become the best of friends, and we knew beyond a shadow of doubt that we wanted to spend the rest of our lives together.

In August 1990, without my knowledge, Erskine made a decision to call my parents on a Sunday morning and ask them for my hand in marriage. I still remember Daddy proudly announcing it to the congregation. And although he was still in Nebraska and I was in Alabama, Erskine didn't allow distance to stop him from claiming what was his as he secretly made plans with his mom to formally propose to me over the phone.

After church, I went by to visit his parents as usual, and while I was there, he called. He asked his mom to put me on the phone, and when I answered, he popped the infamous question, "Will you marry me?" Of course, I said yes, after which his mom surprised me by placing on my finger a small antique engagement ring that had belonged to Erskine's paternal grandmother. There was nothing extravagant about the ring. It was just a tiny diamond centered on a thin gold band. But I wore it proudly, as if it were worth a million dollars because it was his family's heirloom and also it proved to the world that God was in the process of giving me the desire of my heart.

The following year, during the summer of 1991, Erskine came home on another two-week leave of absence, and with a surprise. In his parents' living room on one knee, he proposed to me again. This time he opened a small box to reveal a beautiful, brand-new engagement ring he'd purchased for me in Omaha, Nebraska.

Being a daddy's girl, I made my dad a promise when I was a little girl that I would never leave him, which basically meant that I would never move away when I grew up. In my heart, I just knew I would always be there for him, in ministry and in life. But as we all know, things change. Minds change, people change, situations change. So, now that God had blessed me with a significant other, the thought of leaving Daddy no longer bothered me. But it bothered him.

After noticing Daddy sulking for a few days, I wanted to know why he was treating me so coldly. He finally confessed, "You said you would never leave me." All I could say to that was, "But, Daddy." Then I asked him, "Will you come visit me when I move to Nebraska?" and he teasingly replied, "No, uh uh, because you lied to me." And I responded, "Daddy, are you serious?" After noticing my solemn tone, he stopped joking, turned to me, and said, "I'm just playing. Baby, listen, no matter where you go in this world, if you ever need me, Daddy's gonna be there for you." I held on tightly to those poignant words, tucking them away in my heart, saving them for a day that I would need them in my future.

Two weeks after Erskine returned to Nebraska, I, with my parents' blessings, went to visit him there for about a week. I had the opportunity to meet his pastor, his church family, and his friends. I also visited his job and toured the air force base. This visit was my dad's idea, as he felt it would help me decide whether I was making the right decision for my life. The visit left me with no regrets other than having to part with Erskine once my week was up. When my plane landed back in Birmingham, Alabama, I wasted no time getting busy with the final planning of our November 2 wedding because my dream of happily ever after was only a few months away.

5
Waiting for My Fairy Tale to Begin

> Many are the plans in a person's heart, but it is the Lord's purpose that prevails.
> —Proverbs 19:21 (NIV)

I was so excited; my name was about to change, and so was my life. For the better I hoped. I felt like a princess who was about to be rescued by her knight in shining armor. Erskine was the knight that would rescue me from my painful split-family drama, and I would be joining him in his land of happily ever after. But first, I would have to make it through the extreme frustration of wedding planning.

Wedding planning within itself is a major headache, but in a broken family, it's far worse. This task almost drove me to the crazy house, as it was one of the most stressful times of my life. At one point, to avoid the drama, Erskine and I considered eloping. But in the end, despite the many challenges that arose, our wedding turned out beautiful.

Ms. Teresa Davis
and
Pastor and Mrs. Willie B. O'Neal
request the honor of your presence

at the marriage of their daughter
Tracy Elaine O'Neal
to
Mr. Erskine Nile Daniel, Jr.
son of
Mr. and Mrs. Erskine N. Daniel, Sr.
Saturday, the second of November,
nineteen hundred and ninety-one,
at five o'clock in the afternoon.

"Uh oh," I said under my breath as my mom fastened the last hook on my wedding gown. She was helping me get dressed in a small room near the sanctuary of a North Birmingham church where my wedding was about to take place.

"What?" she asked me in panic.

"Nothing, it's okay," I said.

"No, what is it!" she demanded.

"Well, I have to use the restroom. But don't worry about it. I'll just hold it." I decided to hold my urge to use the restroom because there was not a restroom nearby. And even if there were, I couldn't fathom the thought of using the restroom while dressed in all of that extra fancy wedding gear, as I figured it would pose too much of a problem. So I decided to wait.

However, as my mom's eyes scanned the room wildly, she said to me, "No, you're not going to hold it! I won't be able to rest during the ceremony knowing you have to use the restroom." Then she spotted a large cup across the room, which happened to be filled with ice and belonged to Aleshia, my wedding directress, mentor, and friend. Mama asked someone to hand her Aleshia's cup. Then she poured the ice into a trashcan and, with the assistance of others, she proceeded to pull up my gown, pull down all the stuff I had just struggled to pull up, and made me relieve myself in that cup. It's amazing how a mother's heart works because when I got relief, she got relief.

Our wedding, which was nearly an hour behind schedule, took place at a church that belonged to one of my dad's good friends, Pastor Jessie Mincey. Because Mt. Canaan was in the midst of a million-dollar building project, erecting a brand-new church facility debt free, my dad had to borrow his friend's church for my wedding, as our new building was not complete and our present building was not large enough.

The sanctuary of this borrowed church was full of guests who checked their watches every minute in frustration because nothing was happening yet. Then at last, the moment everyone was waiting for had arrived. The wedding preliminaries began, and our large wedding party, which consisted of ten groomsmen, ten bridesmaids, two flower girls, a ring bearer, a Bible bearer, and a bell ringer, had assembled in the church foyer, preparing to make their grand entrance to the tune of BeBe and CeCe Winans' hit "In the Meantime."

After nearly everyone had entered and the time drew nearer for me to make my entrance, the butterflies that were already in my stomach suddenly increased by a thousand. And as I stole glances of myself in the mirror during my wait, another thousand collected there, as I couldn't believe what I was seeing.

There I stood, at age twenty-two, in my long snow-white wedding gown with an extra long train attached, preparing to watch my dream unfold. This was the day I'd dreamed of my whole life. I couldn't believe it had finally come. I was getting married.

Suddenly, my dad burst into the dressing room, anxious to see me, and when he did, he stood there gasping and staring in amazement. Then after gushing about how beautiful I looked, he lifted my veil and stole a kiss. After the photographer took a few photos of us, Daddy and Aleshia led me to the church foyer where he and I stood arm in arm, awaiting our moment to make our grand entrance.

When the time came, the musician began playing the dramatic intro to the "Wedding March," and the ushers opened the doors of the sanctuary. Then we began to march in.

The congregation, all lit up with smiles, sweetly honored the request written on the programs to remain seated upon my entrance so as not to block the view of others. Experiencing their "oohs" and "aahs" and cameras flashing as we marched truly felt marvelous. But I had one minor issue. It felt as if Daddy was literally dragging me down that aisle. This was because he took great strides when he marched, not realizing that my short legs could hardly keep up with his. Nevertheless, I still felt like a princess. And I assume my dad must have felt like a king because he wore the biggest smile on his face, and his chest stuck out like that of a swollen bodybuilder.

As we marched and admired the beauty of it all, I couldn't help but feel as if we had stepped into a storybook. My fairy-tale wedding had come to pass, and awaiting me at the altar was Prince Charming, my knight in shining armor. He was coming to take me away from my troubled life and take me to a land where we would live happily ever after.

Little did I know, this beautiful wedding was as close to a fairy tale as I would get because the new life I was about to enter would actually come with a great amount of trouble of its own. Trouble that would constantly test my faith. Trouble that my dad's anointed preaching, my mom's praying spirit, and even my stepmom's gift of prophecy could not shield me from. However, the seed that was planted in me during my infancy and watered throughout my youth would be what would sustain me through every trial I'd face in my new life as a wife and mother.

After the wedding, Erskine and I didn't go on a fancy honeymoon. Since we would be moving away to Nebraska in a few days, we just decided to stay about three nights in a local hotel suite. And I must admit the first night of our honeymoon is one of many episodes in my life that will always be embedded in my brain.

Being a virgin, the only thing I had to go on was imagination when it came to knowing what to do on my wedding night. Let me tell you, it was nothing like I imagined, and I do not mean that in a good way. My first experience with my husband was extremely painful for me—*cowboy walk* painful. However, had it not been for the patient, gentle, and loving man God gave me, I'm sure it could have been much worse.

I was taught beforehand that my hymen would break during intercourse and that I should expect a small amount of bleeding. Armed with that bit of information, I assumed I was well prepared for my honeymoon night, but I still wasn't ready. I'm really not sure what in the world happened, but here was no *small amount* of bleeding. There was a heavy gush of blood, which was quite embarrassing to me. I definitely didn't want to be anywhere around the next day when housekeeping arrived to clean our room, so my husband and I left for a few hours. But I've often wondered if, when they saw it, they assumed one of us had killed the other.

A few days after our awkward honeymoon, Erskine and I bid our families goodbye, and we hit the road to Offutt Air Force Base, Nebraska, eagerly anticipating the start of our brand-new life together.

Coming from a broken home, I made a covenant with Erskine to make our marriage work at all cost. Having learned so much by sitting under my dad's ministry as he and my stepmom always taught so emphatically the importance of family and the roles of each spouse, I had great dreams and high expectations for my life with Erskine and our future family. I wanted to be a godly helpmeet for him and a loving, stay-at-home mom for our kids. I wanted my husband and me to continue growing closer to one another as we grew closer to God, and I wanted us to work together at instilling godly values in our children. I would venture to say that my desires were totally against the enemy's plan for my life, as I'm sure it was his desire that I repeat the cycle of divorce that was set before me. So one by one, he sent trials and tribulations our way that would either make us or break us.

Romans 8:28 says, "And we know that all things work together for good to them that love God, to them who are the called according to his purpose" (KJV). All of the trials and tribulations that came our way during our marriage, God allowed them to work out for our good in some way or another, even if it was only to build our faith. Actually, I'm sure God's reason for allowing any of the trials we faced was to build our faith in Him because more faith in Him had been one of my prayer requests since I accepted Him into my heart, and surprisingly, it had been one of Erskine's prayer requests as a youth as well. Therefore, because we both were praying for more faith, God allowed us to endure faith-building trials. We just didn't realize that's what they were at the time.

You see, we had no idea that asking for more faith in Him was the same as asking for problems. Our young minds were not aware of the fact that more faith is obtained through the endurance of troubles and trials. We just assumed that faith was something that we'd miraculously wake up with one day. Needless to say, we gained our faith in Him the good old-fashioned way.

Resulting from a bad financial decision he made just before our wedding, Erskine's direct deposit from the military the month after we married was about three dollars and some odd cents. You heard me right. I didn't say three hundred dollars; I said three dollars. That was devastating. There I was thousands of miles away from home in what I thought was going to be a happily-ever-after marriage, and I was flat broke. I knew it wouldn't be such a good idea to upset my parents with this news, especially my dad, although we really could have used his financial assistance.

Though it was tough, God blessed us to make ends meet as Erskine was also working a part-time job cleaning buildings in the evenings, and we used those tiny paychecks very sparingly. I didn't think I'd be needing the penny-pinching lessons so soon in my marriage, which I had learned from watching both of my moms run their households, but those lessons sure came in handy, and I'm glad I was paying attention.

During our months of scarcity, I obtained an assistant teaching position at a local daycare, and when that ended, I later found a position making sandwiches at a deli on base. Then God sent us supernatural blessings by allowing unexpected monies to locate us. For instance, Erskine's first sergeant discovered by accident that Erskine was due a large refund for monies he was not receiving but should have been receiving due to us living off base. This financial blessing and others are what helped Erskine and me get back on track financially.

In hindsight, I see myself as Dorothy who was searching for the Land of Oz and ended up making a few detours along her way. I, on the other hand, was searching for the Land of Happily Ever After, and though my husband and I ended up on a slightly bumpy detour, I assumed we were now back on track and would be arriving at that happy place very soon. But sadly, the road up ahead only held more detours.

6

My God, Why Have You Forsaken Me?

> My God, my God, why hast thou forsaken me? Why art thou so far from helping me, and from the words of my groaning? O my God, I cry in the daytime, but thou answerest not; and in the night season, and am not silent.
> —Psalms 22:1–2 (ASV)

Before we married, Erskine and I discussed waiting at least a year or two before having children. But strangely, we both began desiring a family right away. So we decided to stop the birth control methods we were using and work on making a baby. But each passing month, when I realized I wasn't pregnant, my heart would break. Then finally, ten months after we wed, we received the news we looked so forward to hearing; we were pregnant!

Up until the time we received that news, we were staying in a top-floor one-bedroom apartment off base while our name was on the list for the next available base housing. However, a few days after discovering that we had a baby on the way, we received word that our name had come up for an available two-bedroom apartment on base. That was perfect timing! That was God's timing. A week or so after receiving the good news, our new pastor and his wife, George and Daty Keys, and our friends Victor and Deborah helped us move in.

God continued moving supernaturally for us when He blessed us with everything we needed for our baby all at one time. Through my friend Deborah, I learned of a young lady who was leaving Omaha and therefore needed to get rid of several baby items that she no longer needed. I called my dad and asked him if he would help us purchase some of her things for our baby, and he sent me a hundred dollars. I went to the lady's house to pick out the things I wanted, and she ended up giving me nearly *all* of her baby items for just that one hundred dollars. I am not talking about small, cheap items but large, quality items such as a baby bed with all the bedding, music mobile, stroller, playpen, highchair, changing table, baby tub, and much more. God blessed us tremendously!

We looked forward to the day when we would have an ultrasound to reveal our baby's gender. Because Erskine was an only son, and his dad was an only son as well, we thought it would be wonderful for us to have a son to continue the Daniel name. When I was about four months along, we had that long-awaited ultrasound, but sadly, that day was bittersweet.

In preparing for the ultrasound, I was instructed to come to my appointment with a full bladder, so I drank large amounts of water all morning. When we arrived, I could barely walk as I tried to hold all that water in, but somehow I managed to make it onto the ultrasound table without wetting myself.

When the technician started moving the probe around my lower abdomen, it took everything in me not to relieve myself all over his exam table. But before long, the beautiful sight of our unborn child made me forget just how uncomfortable I was.

After staring in amazement at the image of our tiny baby on the monitor, the technician finally gave us the news that we were eager to hear, "It's a boy." Wow, God had given us the desire of our heart. But suddenly the room grew quiet as the technician continued to probe my abdomen. The silence became uncomfortable for me, so I tried breaking it by asking the technician, "What are you doing now?" But he wouldn't reply; he just continued staring at the monitor and manipulating the probe over my abdomen so forcefully that I almost wet myself. Erskine and I looked nervously at one another.

The technician suddenly excused himself from the room, leaving us wondering what was going on. Moments later, he returned with a doctor who began probing my abdomen and staring at the monitor as well. Then, in an instant, our good news turned bad. The doctor explained to us that our baby boy appeared to have a birth defect. He had what they called a Duodenal Atresia, which meant a certain part of his intestines was underdeveloped and was not allowing any nourishment to pass through. Because of this, he was not drinking the amniotic fluid as babies in the uterus normally do, which led to me carrying an excessive amount of fluid in my abdomen. The doctor told us that once the baby was born, it was likely that he would have to go immediately into surgery to correct this issue and afterward remain in the hospital for a few days to heal, but after that, he would be fine. The assurance that our baby would be fine after surgery didn't do much to take away the devastation that we were feeling inside. Our unborn baby was sick. Why? It was hard to remain excited about having the son we hoped for after receiving such disheartening news concerning his health. Because of this heartbreaking revelation, my prenatal care was transferred from the base hospital to St. Joseph Hospital in Omaha.

As the days passed, God began to uplift our spirits as we continued to prepare for our son's birth. And because we had no other family with us in Nebraska, our Omaha church family came together and blessed us with a beautiful baby shower to celebrate our baby's highly anticipated arrival.

Although he was due May 13, our son, Brian O'Neal Daniel, made his sudden entrance into the world on April 21, 1993, at 8:40 a.m., giving our families no time to be present for his birth. Now at peace with the news of his intestinal birth defect, Erskine and I felt we were mentally prepared to handle Brian's surgery and his extended hospital stay. But what we were not prepared for was the gut-wrenching news that came later that day.

After laboring with me all night, Erskine waited until I was settled in my hospital room before going home to shower and change. While he was away, two doctors entered my room to talk to me about Brian. To this day, I wonder why they didn't just wait until someone was there with me before giving me the following news. They said that further testing had revealed that our son had been born with a second birth defect, a serious heart disease called Truncus Arteriosus. They explained that in a normal heart, there are two separate arteries keeping the oxygenated blood and the non-oxygenated blood from mixing. Rather than two separate arteries, Brian had one single artery, which allowed the two bloods to mix and flow throughout his body. Because this would eventually cause a number of serious problems, including death, Brian needed major surgery as soon as possible.

When the doctors left my room, I was a basket case as I cried hysterically. I had just given birth to a beautiful baby boy, but my heart wasn't filled with joy as it should have been; it was broken. I couldn't understand what I had done so bad in my life that God would allow me to give birth to such a sick baby. I had tried to be very obedient to my parents and to God all of my life, so why was I being punished?

When the phone rang in my hospital room, I picked it up, but I was unable to speak. All I could do was cry. On the phone was my friend Toni from our church in Omaha. She was calling to congratulate us, but when she heard me crying, she immediately hung up and dialed our friend Deborah. When Deborah called, I still couldn't speak, I just continued to cry, so she hung up and called Pastor Keys. In a matter of minutes (it felt more like seconds), Pastor Keys was there to see about me. Soon afterward, my husband arrived wearing a great big smile and holding a vase of flowers and a balloon, unaware of all that had transpired.

Pastor Keys and I explained to Erskine the new developments concerning our baby, and then the both of them helped me into a wheelchair and we all went to the Neonatal Intensive Care Unit (NICU) to see Brian.

Seeing my baby in that incubator made my heart bleed. I couldn't touch him. I couldn't hold him. I couldn't cuddle him. I couldn't feed him. All I could do was look at him. That was such torture. The next morning, they performed surgery on his intestines, and the following day, he was taken by ambulance to the local children's hospital for a heart catheter then transported back to the hospital were he was born. We later learned that Brian's birth defects were the result of a chromosome defect called DiGeorge syndrome. However, they had no idea which of us had passed the defective chromosome to him.

Three days after giving birth, I was released from the hospital without my baby, and they could not tell me when he would be able to come home. I was beyond hurt, and I told God daily how I felt about it. "Lord, why would You allow me to go through something like this?" "I thought You loved me." "Am I being punished for some reason?" "Please tell me why You're doing this to me." "After spending my life trying to please You, why in the world would You make me to go through such torture?"

Every day we went to the hospital to see Brian. Sometimes even twice a day. Because he was not strong enough to breastfeed, we rented a breast pump from the hospital, and I would pump my milk at home and take it to the hospital to be stored in the NICU freezer. For every feeding, the nurses would thaw his milk and feed it to him through a tube that went through his nose and into his stomach. We were not allowed to hold him for over a week, as his condition was too critical. Many times these restrictions made me want to scream to the top of my lungs. I didn't know what I wanted to say, but I know I just wanted to make the loudest noise I could make. Though I never did it outwardly, I screamed often on the inside. I didn't know what else to do.

Out of all of the teaching I had received in my childhood concerning trials and tribulations, praying, waiting on God, being of good courage, by His stripes we were healed, and so on, none of it felt like it was doing me or my baby a bit of good. Maybe it was because I had never been tested to this extent before. This, I felt, was the ultimate test. My only child, my only son. Could this pain have been the same pain God was feeling when His only Son was dying on that cross? Maybe so, but I wasn't God; I was only human, and I just didn't feel I could bear much more this pain.

Three weeks after Brian's birth, Erskine took a leave of absence in order that we could take our baby home from the hospital and enjoy him a few days before our trip to Ann Arbor, Michigan, where he was scheduled to have open-heart surgery five days later. And though his visit at home was only for a day or two, for the first time since our baby's birth, we were allowed to spend time together at home as a family, just the three of us, without the constant presence of doctors, nurses, and other hospital staff. During this time, Victor, Deborah, Pastor and Sister Keys, and our church family were all great support for us. I really don't know how we would have made it without them.

Being on the plane with our sick baby was very difficult, as he required so much care and attention. Then, arriving in Ann Arbor was awkward because we were in a place where we knew no one. There was not a single familiar face to be found. We felt so alone in the world. It was a good thing Erskine's mom remembered her friend Nate who lived a few miles away in the city of Ypsilanti. She called Nate for us, and he and his sweet wife, Fran, came to our rescue. They were very good to us, as on several occasions, Nate picked us up from C. S. Mott Children's Hospital and took us back to his home, and he and Fran would prepare dinner just for us.

When Erskine and I were allowed to go in and see Brian after his heart surgery, I was not prepared for what my eyes beheld. Our baby, whose last weight before leaving Omaha was a little over four pounds, had nearly doubled in size because of post-surgery swelling. He was very unrecognizable, and I almost fainted when I saw him. His eyes were taped shut, he was on a ventilator, and it seemed lines and tubes were running all over his little body. And to make matters worse, because of the swelling, they could not close his chest after the surgery, so he had a large piece of white tape covering the opening in his chest. Seeing all of this made me weak. It just didn't seem fair for an innocent baby to have to go through such persecution. What did he ever do to deserve such a life?

I couldn't look at him for long. I had to get out of there. And I vowed not to return until he once again looked like *my* baby. When we arrived back at the hotel, Pastor Keys called to check on us, and God used him to encourage me to continue visiting Brian. He even told us to take a picture of him, as this would one day be our testimony. But I just couldn't make myself go back that day, so Erskine went back alone. However, the next day God gave me the strength and courage to go back, and I even took that picture.

I was very desperate to see my baby in his normal state, the way he looked before the heart surgery, so much so that I felt close to hyperventilating because I couldn't remember what he used to look like. No matter how hard I tried, I just couldn't picture him in my mind, and we didn't have any photographs handy for me to look at. Then one day I remembered that the roll of film in our camera had pictures of our baby on it, which we had taken before we arrived in Michigan. After questioning others about a place where we could get film developed in an hour, we discovered that we would have to catch the city bus and go to the mall. It was a good thing I had experienced riding the city bus in Birmingham during my college days because Erskine was unfamiliar with the public transit system, so he was a little hesitant. Nevertheless, we rode that bus and found our way to the one-hour photo shop. And I gained relief as I stared at the photos of my baby for the rest of the evening and the days that followed.

While in Ann Arbor, Erskine's mom and his little sister Karilyn came up from Birmingham to visit with us for a week. They stayed with us in our hotel room, which was adjacent to the hospital. This was our first visit from family since Brian's birth; it felt so refreshing! But on the day that they left us, we were depressed because not only did we hate to see them go, but we were being forced to leave as well.

Our hotel room had become our surrogate home, but our stay in Michigan was growing much longer than anticipated due to Brian's slow progress. Because of this, the grant that was sponsoring our food and shelter would no longer pay the amount we were being charged for our hotel stay. Therefore, we had no other choice but to leave and move a couple of streets over to the Ronald McDonald house for the remainder of our stay in Michigan. So once again we were sent to a strange place where there were no familiar faces. I felt stuck in a bad dream.

One day, the secretary in the office at the Ronald McDonald house called down to our room on the intercom, as there were no phones in the rooms, just a phone in the hall that each family shared. She told us we had a visitor. Erskine and I stared at one other in confusion as we tried to figure out who could be visiting us. We didn't know anyone in Michigan besides Nate. Was it Nate?

When we got off the elevator and turned the corner, my heart immediately skipped a beat when I noticed that our visitor was my dad! He didn't tell us he was coming, as he wanted to surprise us, and boy did he succeed! For me, seeing him sitting there in the lobby was like taking a drink of water in a scorching desert. His presence was like a ray of light in the darkest of night!

Daddy stayed in Michigan with us for about a week. He lodged in a nearby hotel, and he rented a car to get around. Whenever he phoned home, he would joke with family saying that Erskine and I seemed more excited about using his rental car than we were about having him there with us. That wasn't true; we were ecstatic to have him there with us. But at the same time, we were quite happy to have some form of transportation other than our two feet and the city transit system.

My dad's departure sent me into a deeper depression. Not just because he was gone but also because no matter how badly I wanted him to, he wasn't able to fix our situation. Throughout my youth, whenever I ran into any hard problems, all I had to do was call on my dad, and he would try his best to come up with a way to help me solve them. And because he was a preacher, I assumed he had a special connection to God whereby

God would move especially for him. Now that I was a grown-up and experiencing tougher issues, I had to face the fact that whether I liked it or not, Daddy was only human, and all he could do was pray for me. That realization was a bitter pill to swallow. After taking the time to talk to other parents at the Ronald McDonald house who were going through similar situations with their children or worse, my depression seemed to lessen, but it didn't go away.

Approximately one week and three days after my dad left, we were leaving too, heading back to Omaha. This time, Brian could not travel with us, as he was still recuperating from the surgery. So he was transported by helicopter and arrived back at St. Joseph Hospital where he was born, long before we arrived. Once there, we had to get used to an entire new team of doctors and nurses. This had begun to get quite frustrating.

Because our baby had been hospitalized for so long, it started to feel as if he wasn't ours. It felt as if he belonged to the hospital. Nevertheless, we tried to remain hopeful that one day soon he would recover and come home so that we could bond as a family. We were very desperate to become a family. In fact, while Brian was still hospitalized, Erskine and I went out and purchased a van, in hopes that we would use it to take family road trips back home to Birmingham once he was home and strong enough to travel. Then finally, after taking about four weeks to stabilize, and going through bouts of infection and other major issues, Brian was released to come home with us, three months and six days after he was born. And we wasted no time taking him to church and dedicating him back to God.

Now that he was home, we not only had to get used to a baby in the house, but we had to adapt to a special-needs baby in the house. Brian was still on a feeding tube that went through his nose and down into his stomach, but now the tube was attached to a feeding pump that dripped formula into his belly around the clock. He was also on oxygen and several medications. There were several machines in our home for Brian, a machine for this and a machine for that. Naturally, this made us fearful of having him at home, but our desire to have him to ourselves and not feel like he belonged to the hospital outweighed that fear.

Because of his special needs, Brian had nurses who would come by weekly to assess his growth and development. Also, each week we were required to take him to the Children's Hospital to see his heart doctor. For this task, our new van came in handy, as we needed it to transport all of the extra items needed for his care.

I truly dreaded the trips to the doctor, especially since I had to make them alone because Erskine would be working. It was not easy for me having to hold a baby carrier, a diaper bag, and a feeding pump all while pushing an oxygen tank. Many days I felt sorry for myself as I fought to hold back tears. And on other days, just thinking about the situation made me so angry that I just felt like cursing! Loudly! Saying all the bad words I could think of! But I held that urge and just kept screaming on the inside.

The month after Brian's release, one of my best friends, LaTanya Tarver, came out to Nebraska from Birmingham to visit us for a week. Her plan was to come soon after the baby was born, but because of the events surrounding his birth, her trip was delayed. However, now that we had finally begun to settle down as a family, we were delighted to have some company. Her visit brought a little sunshine into our stressful lives, and it gave us a reason to visit the Henry Doorly Zoo and other exciting places we had not yet seen.

As the months passed, Brian was hospitalized once again in order to have a feeding tube permanently inserted into his stomach. This procedure left him with a little flap on his belly (like the air flap on inflatable toys), which we would open up and attach a feeding tube. We would then allow a certain amount of formula to flow into his stomach and then close the flap. This was something he could not get used to, as he had been on the feeding pump for such a long time, and it never allowed him to feel hungry or full, as he was always satisfied. Now, with this new feeding system, he cried often because of the feelings of hunger, and he vomited often when he was full. This was stress on top of stress, but in the midst of it all, we decided to plan a road trip home to Birmingham, Alabama, so that the rest of our family could finally meet our new baby.

Brian's doctor felt his health was stable enough for a trip home. In fact, he encouraged it. He even took him off the oxygen and told us to use it as needed. He thought the trip would be good for Brian and us. So, upon getting his approval, we set a date and began packing.

Our plan was to hit the road on Friday morning, December 3, 1993. My home church was in the midst of Impact, our annual weeklong praise conference that always began the Sunday after Thanksgiving and climaxed the following weekend with a formal banquet held at the Birmingham-Jefferson Civic Center. Though we could not be there for the convention, we at least wanted to make the banquet. After learning that the colors for the affair were black and white, I shopped for outfits for the baby and myself; Erskine would rent a tuxedo when we got home.

The weekend before we were to leave, we wanted to take the baby to Sears to have portraits made in the little outfit I'd purchased for the banquet. He was seven months old, and with the exception of his newborn portraits, we had not taken any other portraits. It was extremely cold and snowing heavily outside, and we kept going back and forth in our minds as to whether or not we should go. Brian didn't make matters any better because he had been fussy all day long. Well, we finally decided to go for it, so I bundled Brian up in his new snowsuit. Then Erskine and I bundled ourselves up, and off we went to weather the storm. When we arrived at Sears, Brian became even more irritable and fussy, especially when we tried to position him for the picture. After several minutes, we were able to calm him down long enough to pose for a few shots, although he didn't feel like smiling. Battling the cold and the snow and laboring to get a decent pose out of Brian would, *three days later*, prove to be one of the best decisions we ever made.

7
It Is Well with My Soul

> When peace like a river, attendeth my way; when sorrows like sea billows roll; whatever my lot, Thou has taught me to say, it is well, it is well with my soul.
> —Horatio G. Spafford, 1873

It was Monday, November 29, 1993, and we had a lot planned for that day and the days ahead in preparation for our road trip coming up that Friday. Brian had been very irritable all weekend, and it started to get worse. While Erskine was at work, I did the packing. In the midst of the packing, I called the doctor's office and informed them of Brian's irritability. They instructed me to bring him in as soon as possible, which meant I had to stop all that I was doing and get Brian and myself dressed to go to the doctor.

When I finished dressing him, my friend Deborah happened to drop by, so she watched him for me while I got dressed. By that time, he had calmed down, and she couldn't understand why I was so worried. He seemed fine to her; he was just sitting in his bouncer chair looking at her as she talked to him.

On the way to the hospital, I began speaking aloud to God concerning this whole seven-month ordeal. I said something like, "Lord, I'm so tired of this; I don't think I can take much more." Those words continued to haunt me years later as the devil often tried to persuade me that they were the cause of the events that followed. However, I now realize those events were predestined, long before I was born.

After signing in at the doctor's office, we had to sit and wait. While waiting, I noticed that Brian was having trouble breathing. I informed the receptionist, and she said that we would be called soon. It felt as if they were not calling us fast enough. My baby couldn't breathe, and his lips were turning really dark. When the nurse finally called us, I told her that he needed oxygen right away because he was gasping for breath. She stated that she could not administer oxygen with out a doctor's approval and she would see about getting him oxygen when she finished his weight and measurements. I watched him get worse and worse by the seconds. She was not going fast enough. Couldn't she see what was going on?

All of a sudden, I saw Brian take his last breath, and then he went limp. I immediately lit that place up with bloodcurdling screams, and everyone came running to see what was going on. Brian's heart doctor and his nurse practitioner happened to be in the conference room nearby, and they heard me screaming as well. When the nurse practitioner looked into the room and saw me, she immediately knew that all the commotion had something to do with Brian. She got the heart doctor, and they rushed Brian to intensive care in a flash.

Through the years, I held extreme bitterness in my heart against that nurse who wouldn't give my baby oxygen. I often wondered if things would have turned out differently if she had only given him oxygen in time. But as I stated earlier, it was predestined. And my dad has taught me repeatedly that nothing happens to us without first passing through God's hands. As a result, I have released the bitterness, realizing that not forgiving that nurse was hurting me more than it was hurting her.

A sweet young receptionist stayed by my side through the entire ordeal because I was there alone. She helped me make all the necessary phone calls to my husband, friends, and family members and even allowed me free use of her personal calling card for my long-distance calls. I may not ever remember her name, but I will never forget what she did for me. When I finished all of my calls, my friend Deborah arrived, and Erskine was not far behind.

Erskine and I stayed at the hospital all day waiting to see our baby. When we finally saw him, it was as if we had taken a step backward in time. Not only was he unconscious, but he was hooked up to several machines. Tubes, wires, and lines were everywhere. He wasn't even breathing on his

God's Girl

own, as there was a ventilator breathing for him. At that moment, we had many feelings running through us all at one time, so we really didn't know how we should feel. And to make matters worse, the many doctors who spoke to us that day all seemed to be saying the same thing, that basically there was no hope.

After going through those seven stressful months, pretty much alone, with a very sick baby, Erskine and I had both reached our breaking point. We could go no further. It felt as if all of our hope, dreams, strength, courage, and willpower had totally run out. When we left the NICU, I made my way over to the phone in the waiting room and called Birmingham. It was Monday evening, November 29, and as I mentioned earlier, Daddy and Mama Trish were in the midst of Impact, Mt. Canaan's annual praise conference. When I called the church, the service was in progress, and my dad was sitting on the pulpit among other ministers.

Uncle D, who was one of the ushers at the time, had answered the church phone. When he realized it was me on other end, he immediately went to get my dad. As soon as Daddy said, "Hello," I reached into my heart and withdrew that promise he gave me two years earlier before Erskine and I married. I said, "Daddy, when I was getting ready to marry, you told me that no matter where I was in this world, if I ever needed you, you would be there for me." He replied, "Do you need me, baby?" I responded, "Daddy, I need you." Without hesitation, he said, "I'm on my way."

After that phone call, Erskine and I decided to leave the hospital because there was nothing else for us to do but pray and wait. When we got on the elevator and the doors shut, I saw a side of my husband that I had never ever seen before; he literally broke down, sobbing. *What should I do?* I wondered. I didn't know whether to cry with him or try to console him. I think I did a bit of both.

The next morning, Daddy arrived in Omaha as he'd promised, and with a surprise. My brother William, who felt like my fraternal twin while growing up, and whom I had not seen in over a year and a half, had accompanied him. Pastor Keys had been so kind as to pick them both up from the airport that morning, and he took them straight to the hospital.

Arriving at the hospital a few minutes after they arrived, I was filled with unspeakable joy when I entered the waiting room and laid eyes on my brother and my dad. The joy in my heart increased upon seeing my pastor and several more of our Omaha church family and friends. Erskine and I no longer felt alone in our trial because we had an awesome support team who was there as strength for us.

I was told that Daddy and William went into the NICU to see Brian before I arrived. They said that when William laid eyes on the baby, he almost fainted, and the nurses had to help him to a chair. He had never experienced anything like that before. I knew exactly how he felt, as that was the feeling I had when I laid eyes on my baby after his heart surgery. It was frightening and overwhelming at the same time.

Jeremiah 29:11 reads, "For I know the plans I have for you, says the Lord. They are plans for good and not for evil, to give you a future and a hope" (The Living Bible). On November 30, 1993, as my baby boy lay in the hospital dying, God decided to speak to me three different times that day concerning His plans for my life. The first time was when we met a young lady there at the hospital who was also trying to cope with an ill baby. The state had taken her baby, claiming his head injuries were caused by child abuse. They believed her husband had done the abusing. She was very distraught as she told us her story. When she was done, Daddy told me to pray for her. *Me?* I thought. *Why me? I'm going through a trial just like she is. Man, you need to be praying for the both of us.* However, though I didn't understand, I obeyed.

I realized God was speaking through my dad that day. God wanted me to know without a doubt that He had given me the gift of intersession, and He wanted me to use it. As a child (and even to this day), God often dropped different people into my spirit. Out of the blue, I would just see

God's Girl

a face in my mind. I remember one day as a teen I mentioned this to my mom, who also has the gift of intercession. She told me, "Whenever that happens, just pray for the person." I've been praying ever since.

The second time God spoke to me, I was walking down the hall of the hospital. As I looked down, I spotted a nice writing pen. I've always loved pens. When I picked it up, I heard God say to me, "Write." Well, I was already a writer and had been since childhood, writing poetry, plays, and a few songs for church. But at this time, I felt God was asking for more. He was urging me to write books for Him, especially this book.

The third time I heard God's voice was after we ate lunch. Pastor Keys had taken all of us out to lunch at a local seafood restaurant. When we were done, Erskine and I wanted Daddy and William to see the church where we attended. So Pastor Keys took us by the church, and he opened the doors, allowing them to look around.

As we were leaving the church, I noticed a beautiful pink rose pendant lying in the street near our van. When I picked it up, I clearly heard God say that my next child would be a girl.

I did not share these supernatural events with anyone for many years. Not wanting to appear as if I was losing my mind, because of all that I was going through at the time, I silently tucked them away in my heart.

After leaving the church, we went home to get some rest because we planned to go back to the hospital later that evening. While Daddy and William slept, Erskine and I just lay on the bed and talked. We were trying to be honest with ourselves about Brian's condition. We knew that our baby really was not there and the only thing keeping him breathing was that ventilator. However, even though we knew these things, it was still hard to let go. I think Erskine was holding on a little tighter than I was, and I assumed it was because he didn't see Brian take his last breath like I did. So he was somewhat in denial.

A few months earlier, while playing with Brian one evening after work, Erskine said to his baby, "Daddy loves you, Brian, and Daddy doesn't know what he would do without you." He even wrote some words in Brian's memory book a few weeks after he was born that were making him feel very helpless now. He had written, "I will never let anything happen to you." Now that Brian was dying, Erskine knew there was nothing in the world he could do to stop it. And believe me, if he could have, he would have.

I, on the other hand, was sad because I didn't get to spend the kind of quality time with Brian as Erskine had. I was always so busy *doing for him,* as he had many needs, that I could not just sit down and *enjoy him.* Whatever God's reason was for giving us this baby and then asking for him back so soon, we'll never know. But one thing we did know, we had to release him. And though it was hard, we stood up and joined hands, and I prayed a prayer for the both of us in which we released Brian back into God's hands, and we asked God to help us deal with the loss.

Amazingly, just as soon as we said, "Amen," the phone rang. It was the NICU calling to say that they needed us to come back to the hospital right away because Brian had taken a turn for the worse. That was the nicest way they could tell us that he had died.

As soon as we arrived at the hospital, a doctor and a nurse immediately took Erskine and me into a small conference room and explained to us that Brian was actually dead but that they needed our consent to take him off the ventilator. We willingly consented.

After all the tubes and wires had been removed from him, we were allowed to go in and see our baby for the last time. With us during those final moments were Daddy and William, Pastor and Sister Keys, and their two young children, Seletha and Jason. Our friends Victor and Deborah were at the hospital, but they were not in the room with us, as they didn't feel they could handle it.

As we held our baby, I could feel the eyes of the doctors and nurses watching us. While we cuddled, kissed, and said our goodbyes, they came over frequently to ask if we were okay. I guess we didn't give them the hysteria they were expecting. That was only because God had prepared us before we arrived. I'm glad He allowed us to willingly release our baby rather than abruptly snatching him away.

Upon leaving the NICU for the last time, we stopped by the waiting

God's Girl

room and Daddy and Pastor Keys used the phone to call and make the necessary arrangements for a funeral home there in Omaha to prepare our baby's body and ship it to a funeral home in Birmingham. Ironically, when we were making plans to go back home to Birmingham for a visit, God had plans for Brian to go home for good.

Though I had remained very calm at the hospital, arriving home was a different story. While preparing for bed, I nervously stole a glance at Brian's car seat and his bouncer chair (he *loved* that chair). My heart broke at the thought that I would never ever see him sitting in those again. That's when I had my meltdown.

Two days later, Daddy and William flew back to Birmingham, and with the help of the Red Cross, Erskine and I were soon to follow. But before we could leave Omaha, we had to make arrangements with the air force concerning Erskine's extended leave of absence and the funeral cost. Without hesitation, Erskine was granted a flexible amount of leave. And it was determined that the air force would pay the cost for the entire funeral. That was another supernatural triumph!

Also, the photos Brian had taken only a few days earlier at Sears were not due back for a number of weeks. But after a few phone calls where I explained our ordeal and the fact that we needed a photo for the obituary, we were assured that the photos would be rush delivered to Erskine's parents' address in Birmingham where we would be staying.

Arriving home without our baby was so painful because we had planned this trip for the purpose of introducing our son to the rest of his family. But rather than a family reunion, we went home to have a funeral. To think that Brian would be dead when the family met him was so painful, and I constantly prayed, "Lord, I need You to help me through this."

The days after we arrived home were very busy for us due to making funeral arrangements. Then on December 7, 1993, God blessed us to have a peaceful home-going celebration for our baby in Mt. Canaan's beautiful new sanctuary. In fact, Brian's was the first funeral held in the new building.

Pastor Keys flew in from Nebraska to do Brian's eulogy. He felt that it was only befitting as he and his family had spent the most time with Brian during his short but impacting life. Not only that, but also Erskine and I had given him and his wife the role as Brian's godparents.

On that day, which in the natural should have been very sad, God gave Erskine and me a supernatural amount of strength and a peace that surpassed all understanding. We were honestly able to say that *it was well with our souls.*

After living eight and a half months in anticipation of a new baby, and another seven in a quest to make him well, we didn't know what to do with ourselves once it was all over. But we did know this; in Nebraska lay the memories of the entire heartbreaking ordeal, and as a result, we didn't feel we could continue living there. We decided to stay in Birmingham clean through Christmas, and then we headed back to Nebraska just to make preparations to go back home to Birmingham for good.

When we returned to Nebraska, our church there held a beautiful memorial service for our baby since they were not able to attend the funeral in Birmingham. The service was so touching and we felt blessed to be surrounded by our entire church family. Also in attendance was Brian's home health nurse, our next door neighbors and even the sweet receptionist from the hospital who had helped me make my long distance calls when Brian was rushed to NICU.

Erskine wasted no time taking the necessary steps to obtain a military discharge. And the military wasted no time honoring his request. We were very anxious to get back home to Birmingham, but our hearts were quite heavy as we realized we would be leaving our friends and surrogate family there in Omaha.

I remember those last few days being very stressful, as everyone wanted to spend time with us before we left, but we didn't have much time left to spend. However, I will never forget the visit we made to Elder and Mother

God's Girl

Relford who were not only the former pastor and first lady at our church there in Omaha but who were like grandparents to us. After sharing with them the ordeal we had been through during the last few months, God suddenly spoke through Mother Relford as she said, "You will never have to go through anything like that again." Her words were so full of power and comfort. I could feel that they had come straight from God, and I always held on to them.

On February 7, 1994, after six and a half years of service, Erskine was granted an honorable discharge based on a hardship, due to the death of our child. This date was also our last day in base housing, and we were required to pass a housing inspection before we left. Because we tried cramming so much activity (spending time with friends, taking care of last-minute business, packing and cleaning) into so little time, when the inspector arrived that morning, we almost didn't pass her inspection. She made us do extra work, cleaning out areas of that place that we didn't even know existed. But though it was tough, we passed. And when the inspector took the keys, we not only left that base house, but we left Omaha, Nebraska, for good.

Normally, the journey from Omaha to Birmingham is approximately thirteen and a half hours; I still cannot believe that it actually took us over two and a half days to get from Omaha to Birmingham. Our families were worried sick about us, and so were we. And my brother William teasingly coined our adventure "The Long Way Home."

We didn't realize we had chosen a bad time of year to take such a road trip. Of course, when we left Omaha, we were aware that there was some snow on the ground, but we figured the further south we traveled, conditions would get better. Surprisingly, that was not the case.

In an effort to get both of our vehicles home, my husband and I had to drive separately. And keep in mind this was 1994, before cell phones were popular, so we purchased CB radios before hitting the road in order to stay in contact with one another. Erskine drove the van, and I drove the car, and each were piled high with the belongings that we didn't send to storage. We looked like a remake of *Sanford and Son*.

When we hit the outskirts of Missouri, that's when our troubles began. And our first problem was not even weather related. It was a vehicular issue. My car began slowing down and making a strange noise. I immediately radioed my husband and told him that we needed to pull over. Once we pulled over, the car stopped and wouldn't start anymore. After just losing a child and now being stranded out in the middle of nowhere, we couldn't even think straight. We talked about just abandoning the car because we didn't know what else to do.

After making room for me in the van, we drove to the nearest rest stop and called my dad. Daddy instructed us to call a tow truck and have them tow the car to their garage. Then he told us to go and have a hitch put on the van so that we would be able to tow the car home. As we began to do these things, we got even more frustrated when we realized that the only place we could find that would install a hitch was several miles away, in the direction that we were headed. This was just too much, but we had no other choice.

When we arrived at the U-Haul place for the hitch, they said they couldn't install it until the next day, so we were forced to stay in that strange little town overnight. We stayed in a little inexpensive motel, which strongly proved to us that you get just what you pay for and no more, but quite possibly less. Conditions in that room were so bad that we had no other choice but to sleep fully dressed. Coats, shoes, and all. Morning couldn't come fast enough for us. At daybreak, we immediately left that place and went to have our hitch installed. Afterward, we backtracked several miles to get our car and had it hitched to the van. By that afternoon, we were on the road again. And that evening, we successfully made it to Kentucky but were totally unprepared for our next escapade.

Because of bad weather, driving conditions in Kentucky were terrible. We didn't know we were driving into an ice storm. The roads were totally covered in ice. At one point, our van swerved a bit on the slick interstate. Then when Erskine regained control, we both breathed a sigh of relief. Suddenly to the left of us, we saw a car facing the wrong way. It was our car! The one we were towing! Evidently, during the swerving, we had not regained total control as we thought. That car forcefully flung us over into the median. It's amazing how no one else on that interstate was affected by our mishap. God supernaturally stopped traffic just for us.

God's Girl

A nice trucker, who saw our CB antenna on the van, radioed us. I remember him saying, "Van, are you all right?" I radioed back, "No, we need some help!" He kindly stopped to help us by trying to pull us out with his 18-wheeler. And though he gave it his all, he was unsuccessful. Later, two men in a car stopped by, and they managed to help Erskine get the van out, but the car we were towing was still stuck. After they left, I got on the CB radio and pleaded with someone to call us a tow truck. We waited several hours before one finally arrived. By the time it arrived and got the car out of the median, it was dark, and we were not about to travel any further.

We found a hotel close by (a much nicer one) and stayed the night. The next day, although ice was still a major threat, we hit the road and just took it extremely slow. We really had no other choice because the money we brought from Omaha was nearly gone. We were so excited about all the money the military had given us for travel expenses, we assumed it would be more than enough, so we planned to put what was left in the bank as soon as we got home. But now all of that money was nearly gone. On the bright side, I thank God that we had it when we needed it most. In fact, I'm sure He knew we would need it and that's why He allowed the military to give it to us.

After driving like a snail on the icy roads and enduring the wildest adventure of our lifetime, God brought Erskine and me safely back home to Birmingham, Alabama, that afternoon.

8

Starting All over Again

> God is not a man, that he should lie, neither the son of man, that he should repent: hath he said, and will he not do it? Or hath he spoken, and will he not make it good?
> —Numbers 23:19 (ASV)

When we finally made it back to Birmingham on February 10, 1994, Erskine and I felt like two poor pitiful souls. We were broke, homeless, jobless, and childless. Being in such a rough predicament was the worst feeling in the world. But our family and friends did not hesitate to stand in the gap for us and sow into our lives. My paternal grandma, Eddie Mae Henderson, whom we call "Grannie," allowed us live with her in her home in Brighton, Alabama, giving us the opportunity to get back on our feet again. And our parents tried tirelessly to help us meet whatever needs we had. My brother William even gave us a hand by helping Erskine obtain a temporary position at the University of Alabama at Birmingham where he worked. And later I found a temporary job with a local insurance agency.

Because we missed our son so much, we were anxious to have another child right away, even though our lives were unstable at the time. At this point, I could truly identify with my mom and dad's feelings after loosing their firstborn and trying to conceive me in order to fill the void.

As the months passed, we tried and tried to have a baby, but it just wasn't happening for us. This was just as devastating as losing Brian had been. Though it was hard, we tried our best to get our minds off it and just focus on getting some stability in our lives.

God's Girl

After staying with my grandma for about five months, we were finally able to acquire a place of our own, and my sister and brother-in-law, John and Triola Crawford, helped us move into our two-bedroom apartment over in Hoover, Alabama. By then, Erskine had found a permanent job doing building maintenance for a notable office building located in downtown Birmingham. Then two months later, God finally allowed us to conceive.

Our new baby was conceived around the time that Daddy and Mama Trish met their good friend Bishop Liston Page Jr. from Paterson, New Jersey. They met this anointed young preacher, who was not yet a bishop then, through one of our church members and decided to invite him to be our guest speaker one Sunday morning. On that day, just before Bishop Page got up to minister, Daddy allowed Erskine and me to address the congregation and share the good news that we were expecting another baby. The church went up in praise, as they were so excited for us. But before we took our seats, I asked Daddy to pray that our new baby would be born healthy; however, he decided to ask the guest preacher to pray for us. After Bishop Page's moving prayer, I had no doubt that our new baby would be born without health issues. However, the enemy still came, as always, to test my faith.

Weeks before I conceived, I accepted a permanent position as a patient care technician at the University of Alabama at Birmingham Hospital. By the time my orientation and training dates rolled around, I was pregnant. During the orientation, I felt extremely ill, but I continued to push myself. However, by the first day of training, I could push no further, so during my lunch break, I called Erskine and asked him if I could let the job go. When he gave me the okay, I left that place immediately and never returned.

The following weeks, my condition worsened, and I developed a severe case of diarrhea that just wouldn't go away. I lost a great amount of weight and became very dehydrated. As a last resort, my doctor put me on a medicine that he felt might help me but could possibly harm our unborn child. That was such a horrible dilemma to be in, as I didn't want to lose another baby. But following the urging of my doctor and my family, I nervously took the medication. However, I didn't have to take it for long because after noticing that the diarrhea was not responding to the medicine, my doctor took me off of the medication and hospitalized me to undergo testing. After spending nearly a week in the hospital, the cause for the diarrhea was never found, but miraculously it began to clear up on its own.

As my pregnancy progressed, I was scheduled to undergo an amniocentesis to make sure that all was well with our new baby. An amniocentesis is a procedure where the doctor inserts a very long needle into the mother's abdomen, and using ultrasound as a guide, he draws out some of the amniotic fluid that surrounds the baby. This fluid is then used for testing.

Erskine and I also had to give blood samples for genetic testing to find out if Brian's illness was something passed on to him from one of us. If it was determined that one of us had passed this defect on to him, we stood the chance of passing it on to our future offspring.

The genetic tests came back negative. Neither Erskine nor I had any chromosome defects that we could have passed to our offspring. Though this was good news, the question remained as to why Brian was born with such a defect. Only God could answer that. But He did give me a revelation to encourage my heart. He said we should view Brian as our first fruit, which we were required to offer back to the Lord. Exodus 13:12 (NIV), "You are to give over to the Lord the first offspring of every womb." And Luke 2:23 (NKJV), "As it is written in the law of the Lord, 'Every male who opens the womb shall be called holy to the Lord.'" So looking at it in that perspective helped me to understand why we had to release our son.

The amniocentesis revealed that there were no health problems with our new baby. It also revealed something else; *we were having a girl!* Wow! This was going to be so exciting and so different. I suddenly remembered the pink rose pin that I found on the day Brian died. God's promise to me concerning it had actually come to pass!

Because Erskine was now the sole provider of our family, our finances were literally stretched to the max. In an act of desperation, we asked our apartment manager for permission to break our lease, and we moved in with my brother William. William's house was actually home for me, as he'd recently purchased, from my mother, the house in Hueytown,

God's Girl

Alabama, that my father had purchased back in 1970 before he and my mom divorced. The house where William and I grew up. After selling William the house, my mom purchased a smaller home for herself and my younger brother Philemon.

Because our little bundle of joy was due soon, we got busy fixing up my old bedroom for her. Then our family and friends threw us a big baby shower that provided an enormous amount of everything we needed for our baby.

On May 3, 1995, a year and 11 days after Brian's birth, our beautiful rainbow baby, Jessica Nicole, entered this world. We were totally engulfed with her. Long before I ever knew whom I would marry, *Jessica* was the name I had chosen to give my first little girl, as I was in love with the way it sounded. And after learning its Hebrew meaning, which is "woman of wealth," I fell in love with the name all over again.

During the first seven months of Jessica's life, I felt as if I had been holding my breath. It was because Brian had died at the age of seven months. However, once she passed her seventh month, and she was still alive and in good health, I felt free to exhale. Then I felt bad for having doubted God because He had already assured me through Mother Relford and Bishop Page that I wouldn't have to go through the pain of losing a child again, yet I still worried.

Though we were living with my brother, our finances were still very tight, and the dream we harbored of being debt free and living happily ever after one day appeared to be just that, only a dream. Whenever Erskine would earn a little extra overtime money in his paychecks, it would all disappear on nonsufficient fund fees or, in other words, fees for bounced checks. We felt if there was such a thing as luck, we surely held the worst of it.

With a desire to move up on his job in order to make more money for his family, Erskine decided to enroll in technical school. Aided by the

Pell Grant and the military GI Bill, he began going to school after work in the evenings, majoring in heating, ventilation, air-conditioning, and refrigeration (HVAC). Those were skills that were sure to help him obtain a higher position on his job.

With Erskine being away for much of the day going to work and school, we missed one other something awful. And many times, I felt like a single parent. But we endured this time apart because we knew that this schooling was one of the main keys to our brighter future. And sure enough, that schooling compiled with the knowledge he gained in the military turned out to be a tremendous blessing for us down the road.

One day, in October 1995, we received an amazing blessing that actually came to us in disguise. There was threat of a severe hurricane, named Opal, which was due to hit Birmingham that day. As Erskine headed back to work from being with us at home on his lunch break, he faced a mad rush in traffic due to the impending hurricane. While driving our van, he was struck forcefully from the side by another vehicle. That impact caused the van to flip over onto its top. Miraculously, Erskine crawled out with only a few minor scratches on his arm, but our van was totaled. And although we'd lost our only means of transportation, we realized that this was indeed a blessing for us, as we decided not to finance another vehicle. Instead, we seized the opportunity to use the extra money to save for a house.

Then, just before 1995 ended, we received a surprise that proved to us that our idea of saving for a house was definitely from God. Six and a half months after giving birth to Jessica, we were expecting again. We had not bothered using birth control because I had learned that breastfeeding was a natural birth control. And since I was breastfeeding Jessica around the clock without any assistance from formula, I just knew that this natural birth control would work for us. But surprisingly it didn't. I guess God wanted to bless us double for our trouble, but ignorantly I couldn't be grateful for this blessing because I was so worried about what others would say concerning us having another baby so soon. I even worried that I wouldn't have enough room in my heart to love another child so fast. I remember talking to my sister Fran about this, as she had been through the exact same situation the year before. Fran assured me that when my baby arrived, my heart would instantly make room for him or her. Seeing how much Fran loved her two children, I took her word for it.

In hindsight, I feel so bad for how I went from begging God for a child to being ashamed of having another child. But thankfully God brought me to my senses when He reminded me that my children were a blessing from Him, as it says in Psalm 127:3 (NLT), "Children are a gift from the Lord; they are a reward from him." I'm so happy God changed my point of view and turned my shame into gratefulness as I became truly grateful for my rewards. However, other people's opinions never bothered my husband, as his thoughts were only of making more money to put us in a home of our own because we were growing fast.

Erskine became discouraged as he began to notice the glass ceiling on his job. Unless someone died or quit, there was no way for him to move up and make more money, and he needed more money for his family's sake. One of his coworkers had pointed this out to him because he himself was searching for a better job and he finally found one with the county board of education. That coworker encouraged Erskine to put in an application with the county as well. Erskine did so, but after a while when he didn't hear any type of response, he continued looking elsewhere for a job.

In February 1996, we saved up enough money to begin searching for a home, and in March, God blessed us to find a small three-bedroom, one-bath starter home. To be honest, we really were not interested in the house because of its outward appearance. We felt it looked a bit old-fashioned. But as the saying goes, "You can't judge a book by its cover." Wanting to turn around and leave just as soon as we drove up to it, I'm so glad we didn't because we would have missed our blessing.

An older couple, who was originally from the north, owned the house, and they had come to Birmingham four years prior in order to retire. Because of their health issues and not having any family in Birmingham to help them, they decided to sell their home and go back north to live with their son. Because they needed to sell so quickly, they were leaving their refrigerator, washer and dryer, their dinning room set, sleeper sofa, window treatments, and many other items. This deal was just too good to pass up because we needed everything they were leaving behind!

Of course, the devil always has to stick his ugly face in the center of a blessing! Just before we closed on the house, the cheap car that we acquired after the van was totaled broke down on us, and again we were without transportation. Then we borrowed a little hit-or-miss car from my dad, just to get from point A to point B. But every week we were throwing money at it, trying to keep it running.

In April, God blessed us to close on our new home, and we moved out of my brother's house and into our own. On the same day that we closed, there was a message for Erskine on the answering machine for a job interview with the area chamber of commerce. After the interview, my husband was left with the impression that he would be making much more money than he was making on his present job, so he accepted the position. He later realized the truth. The figures he had been given included benefits. So his net pay was actually less than what we were used to. Erskine felt like he had made a big mistake because he was trying to move up for his family, and he ended up moving down. Although the benefits were good, his feelings were "You can't eat benefits." In spite of the discouragement, this situation truly allowed us to see the supernatural hand of God in our lives as we miraculously lived off an annual salary of $13,000 while buying a house! How in the world did we survive? On supernatural finances!

We were thankful for that pressure, as it pushed Erskine out into the business world. During that time, as an effort to make a little extra money, he began doing a number of air-conditioning and heating jobs on the side. He was somewhat skeptical at first because all he had to go on was book knowledge, no hands-on experience. And, because of his lack of confidence, when he'd get a call to do a job, he would practically charge pennies or nothing at all. However, because of the seeds he sowed, not only in our consistent tithing but in him freely meeting the needs of others who needed air-conditioning or heating work done, God steadily began building his experience, his knowledge, his confidence, his clientele, and, two years later, his business, which we proudly named We'll Fix It, A/C & Heating Company.

Remarkably, in the midst of our financial crisis, God blessed us to hold steadfast to our integrity. We never missed paying our tithe, our offerings, or our bills. And yes, we paid our bills even if we couldn't buy groceries afterward because, as my grannie used to say, "People will give you something to eat, but nobody is willing to pay your bills for you."

Adding to our discouragement, just after we moved into our new home, our hit-or-miss car wouldn't hit or miss; it just died, allowing us to be without transportation for the third time. Ironically, my brother William was in the same boat we were in, as he had recently lost his car due to an accident. As a result, we all began to share Big Blue. Big Blue was the name my siblings and I had given to the ten-passenger van Daddy and Mama Trish would use to transport all of us when we were younger. Not only was it big and blue but it was an old reliable friend of our family.

On August 14, 1996 the pink rose prophecy struck again as I gave birth to a second beautiful baby girl, little Jasmine Renae. But in the midst of our joy, we were also feeling sorry for ourselves because we had a new house and *no* car, and Erskine had a new job and *no* money. I desperately questioned God, saying, "Lord, why does it have to be either or? Why can't we have the house, the car, the job, and the money?"

I remember sitting in church one Sunday, and as serious as a heart attack, I began asking those sitting around me if they or anyone they knew had a car they wanted to give away. I didn't say sell; I said *give away*. We were desperate. But soon, our dark clouds started to roll away as God began sending blessings in our direction.

On their way to Bible study one evening, Daddy and Mama Trish noticed a nice little blue four-door car for sale in the yard of a home they were passing. After stopping to take a closer look, God placed it on their heart to purchase it for us, allowing us to make small monthly payments to them until we had paid it off.

Then one day in November of that year, as Erskine was reading the classifieds, he came across an interesting job ad. It was for a job in the same field that he was studying in tech school, HVAC. After calling the number listed in the ad, he learned that the job was with the county board of education. He informed them that he already had an application on file with them, and he asked if they could pull it for that particular job. Weeks later, we were thrilled to find out he had been scheduled for an interview, which ended up becoming another one of our supernatural testimonies.

Near the end of the interview, when asked about his licenses that were listed on the resume, Erskine told the interviewers that he didn't have such licenses and that he was only a student. Confused, they questioned the fact that his resume clearly stated that he had them. Surprisingly, as they looked further, they realized that Erskine was not the person to whom that particular resume belonged. The wrong person had been sent in for the interview, and the right person had failed to show up. They said the mistake was easily made because much of the other person's information resembled Erskine's. After the interview, my husband left with a good feeling that he would soon be receiving a call back.

Sure enough, days later he received a call informing him that he had the job and that he would start in January 1997. Erskine was overjoyed that God had allowed him to land such a good job with the county board of education, which not only offered him excellent benefits but much more pay!

In December 1996, when we were concerned about being able to bless our babies for Christmas, God stepped in and saved the day in a most surprising way!

Erskine and I were believing God for supernatural finances for Christmas, as we didn't have any extra money for gifts. We could barely pay our bills; therefore, gifts were not in the budget. The closer Christmas came, the more I prayed, and I even began to involve the children who were only 19 months and 4 months old. Daily, while Erskine was working, my babies and I joined hands and petitioned God heavily for Christmas finances. We would form a small circle on the living room floor and just pray and praise and pray and praise. Now understand this, Erskine and I could have received all the finances we needed from our parents, but we tried not to make that a habit. We realized that we would never get to know the hand of God for ourselves if we were continuously looking toward the hands of our parents.

During that time, I remember telling my husband that I was believing

God for a miracle and that I would be checking the mailbox every day for it. He said to me, "Don't limit God to the mailbox; if He wants to drop it straight from the sky, we'll take that too." So I took the limits off God and just believed Him for a miracle to come any kind of way. Finally, we received our supernatural breakthrough!

It was Christmas Eve, a few hours before the stores would be closing. Because we had not received an answer from the Lord, we decided to go out and put our purchases on a credit card. We figured we could still believe God to pay off the credit card. While getting dressed, the phone rang, and Erskine answered it. It was his cousin Brian Evans. He wanted to know how long we would be home because he really needed to drop by for a minute. Brian had only been to our house one other time in the past, so it wasn't like he was a regular. Therefore, it seemed quite strange when he said that he *needed* to stop by. *For what?* I wondered. Erskine told him he could come by, and I began to pitch a small fit because the stores would be closing soon. I just could not understand why the matter couldn't wait until later.

About fifteen minutes after the phone call, Brian was ringing our doorbell, and he sat down and engaged in small talk with Erskine until I came out of the bedroom, as I was still busy trying to dress the kids. Once I came out, Brian told us his story.

He said for several days God had been showing us to him in a vision. He kept seeing himself coming to our house, and he didn't know why. Then days later God spoke to him about bringing us a certain amount of money, but he procrastinated. Because he was slow moving, God continued speaking to him, and one day God said to him clearly, "Tracy's going to be upset if you don't do this." After finishing his story, Brian then asked, "Can you please tell me what's going on?" I could have passed out! Actually, I did feel a little lightheaded. That was just unbelievable. No one but God and us knew what we were going through. This was proof that God was truly concerned about us. And to hear Brian say that God told him, "Tracy is going to be upset," assured me that God heard every prayer I sent up to Him and that I was indeed His girl.

Of course, we shared our story with Brian after which he reached into his pocket and pulled out our long-awaited blessing. And after several hugs and tears, he went on his way, and we jumped in our car and went shopping!

Almost three years after being back home from Nebraska, life was finally coming together for us. God had promised us in His Word that He would meet our needs, and He did. And when He promised me, by way of the pink rose pendant, that my next child would be a girl, He kept His word, even giving me double for my trouble. He also allowed both girls to be healthy and strong. God also blessed us with a house, a car, my husband's good job, and an awesome church home in Mt. Canaan where we were absorbing the unadulterated, life-changing Word of God. And though we had taken such a long detour, I figured we were now back on the road again, heading toward our long awaited happily-ever-after life. And prayerfully there wouldn't be any more stops or detours along our way, just peaceful cruising ahead.

9
Another Faith Test

> Because you know that the testing of your faith produces perseverance.
> —James 1: 3 (NIV)

Though Erskine and I understood that God's Word says be fruitful and multiply, we were not ready for another baby just yet. So three months after Jasmine's birth, we began trying out different types of birth control, all except the pill because of the negative things we'd heard about it. I had asked God to give me at least a year before I conceived again, and I also asked Him to help me lose weight, as I had baby fat on top of baby fat due to my back-to-back conceptions. God graciously answered both prayers.

The day before our sixth wedding anniversary in November 1997, Erskine's parents kept the girls for us overnight while we went out and celebrated. We dined at a nice restaurant, and then went to see a movie. After returning home, we, quite naturally, planned to top the night off with sweet intimacy. However, I was a bit nervous because I had only asked God for a year, and, you see, my time was up.

Because I've always tried my best to honor to God in every aspect of my life, I didn't feel comfortable considering birth control that night. So before getting into bed, I got on my knees and prayed. I thanked God for giving me the year I asked Him for, and I told Him starting that night we would no longer use the birth control. I expressed to Him that I truly wasn't ready to have another baby just yet, "but nevertheless, let thy will be done."

The following day, which was a Sunday, Erskine and I enjoyed breakfast alone at a little breakfast restaurant and afterward we went to church. When church was over, my friend Rhonda Roscoe asked us to follow her to her car. When we got to the car, she handed us a bag of clothes. They were baby boy clothes that had belonged to our son, Brian. I never expected her to give them back when her son outgrew them. Though it truly baffled us, we shrugged it off, put the bag in our car and went on into the church fellowship hall where my family was preparing to eat dinner.

As we entered the fellowship hall, one of my family members, whom I had not seen in a long time, walked up to us and said, "So ya'll havin' another baby?" I was floored! I had lost so much weight and was looking very well, I might add. So I couldn't understand why he would think I was pregnant. "No!" I exclaimed. "What makes you think that?" He went on to explain that I looked pregnant to him. But because of the scowl on my face and my snappy tone of voice, he quickly apologized. That chain of events turned the wheels in my head. I thought about the baby clothes and the prayer that I had just prayed the night before, and I wondered, *Lord, are you trying to tell me something?*

After dinner, we went to get the girls from Erskine's parents, whom we affectionately call Mama Doll and Paw-Paw. Before we could even mention to them the events that happened earlier, Mama Doll broke out in giggles as she began to tell us that Paw-Paw had dreamed about fish the night before. We knew that a dream about fish in our family was a sure sign that someone in the family was pregnant. Therefore, I knew instantly that God was definitely trying to tell me something.

Two weeks later, when I expected my monthly cycle, it was a no show. After a few more days passed, I went to the doctor for a pregnancy test. I was indeed pregnant. And according to my record keeping, it happened on the night we celebrated our wedding anniversary, when my time was up.

After deciphering this pregnancy message from God, I began to think there was a message in the baby boy clothes as well. And I honestly believed that God had given us another son to replace the one we lost four years earlier. I told all of our family and friends that the child I was carrying would be a boy. I even had a name chosen for him, Matthew O'Neal Daniel. But when the time came for my first ultrasound, the technician confidently announced, "It's a split-tail little girl!" thinking this would

God's Girl

be something I'd be happy to hear. But suddenly I went numb, my heart began to race, and the room began to spin as I thought to myself, *How could this be? Lady, you have got to be wrong!*

After a second ultrasound a few weeks later, the verdict was still the same. I was having a girl. This really confused me, as I thought for sure I had heard from God concerning the sex of my baby. But the pregnancy wasn't over, so I was not going to doubt Him yet. I was willing to believe it until the end, and my sweet husband faithfully believed with me.

I believed it even when my family and others lovingly tried to get me to face reality, and I assured them that if the child was indeed a girl, I would love her no less. I believed it so emphatically that I had no desire to think of little girls' names beforehand. And I believed it up until July 18, 1998 when the baby was pulled out of me and the doctor announced that it was a girl.

The morning after our baby's birth, my husband and I scrambled to think of a name for her and finally decided to name our little blessing Janay Victoria. And just as I vowed, I loved her no less. In fact, I loved her just as if I had known it was *her* all along.

Months after Janay's birth, my mind often fell on a conversation I had with my dad when I received the shock of that first ultrasound. Upon sharing with him how I felt God was about to give me another son and how I would believe it until the child came forth, he said to me, "Baby, if God doesn't do it, just know that He could have done it." I carried those words in my heart for a long time while asking God to reveal to me the meaning of that entire ordeal. I questioned Him because I knew without a doubt that just like there is a season for all things, there is a reason for all things, whether we know the reason or not.

At last, in 2002, four years after Janay's birth, God gave me knowledge concerning my dad's words and that whole situation. He showed me that my faith was being tested. And the test was not in whether I believed He would give us another son, but it was deeper. The test was, would I remain faithful to Him and continue to trust and serve Him even if He never replaced the son we lost? In other words, did I truly love *Him* or did I only love Him for what He could do for me?

As I shared this revelation with Erskine's cousin ReKendra Evans, she likened it to the faith of the Hebrew boys, which was enlightening because

I realized she was right, the faith of the Hebrew boys was the perfect example of the faith God expected of me.

In Daniel 3:17–18 (NIV), Shadrach, Meshach, and Abednego stand up to King Nebuchadnezzar after he gives them the option of bowing to his golden image or being thrown into the fiery furnace. They responded, "If we are thrown into the blazing furnace, the God we serve is able to deliver us from it, and he will deliver us from Your Majesty's hand. <u>But even if he does not</u>, we want you to know, Your Majesty, that we will not serve your gods or worship the image of gold you have set up".

God revealed to me that in my situation my faith needed to be like the faith of those three men. Not only was it important for me to believe He could bless me with another son, just as the men believed He could deliver them from the furnace, but even more so, He wanted me to have the *"But even if He does not"* kind of faith. In other words, I had to have faith in Him regardless, even if He never replaced the son I lost. I had to have a resolve in my spirit that I would remain faithful to Him because of who He is and not just for what He could do for me.

I was happy to have passed that test, because although I was hurt, I still trusted God 100 percent. And I expressed to Him sincerely that if He never did another thing for me, I would follow Him still, and any disappointments, tests, or trials that I may face in the future would never be enough to make me turn my back on Him. But little did I know more difficult test and trials were indeed on the way, and years later, one in particular would be strong enough to make me actually consider turning my back on Him.

10

Trials on Every Hand

> My brethren, count it all joy when ye fall into divers temptations; knowing this, that the trying of your faith worketh patience. But let patience have her perfect work, that ye may be perfect and entire, wanting nothing.
> —James 1:2–4 (KJV)

Until December 1998, I had never heard of such a thing as a nut allergy. But when our daughter Jasmine, who was two at the time, ingested a cookie containing nuts, which caused her to have a life-threatening reaction, I received a crash course on the subject of allergies.

A couple of days before the incident, my husband kept noticing that at certain points during the day, her eyes would look very weird, as if her eyeballs were puffy or swollen. But after putting drops in her eyes and laying her down for a nap, it would eventually subside. Not aware of her nut allergy or the seriousness of it at the time, I understand now that she may have been near someone who had been eating nuts or peanut butter, which caused her eyes to swell.

On the particular night in question, at the home of Erskine's parents, Jasmine ate a cookie that instantly gave her an allergic reaction. Her whole face began to swell, and her eyeballs were puffy again. We all began to panic, and one of us called the paramedics.

When the paramedics arrived, they told us our baby needed to be seen by a doctor as soon as possible because if there was swelling on the outside, then there was possibly swelling on the inside, which could prove fatal.

They gave us the option of taking her to the Children's Hospital ourselves or allowing them to take her by ambulance; we chose to take her.

Hearing the concern in their voices frightened me terribly, and my mind went back to losing my firstborn. I fought those negative thoughts with everything in me as I tried very hard to stand on God's promise that I would never have to go through anything like that again.

The trip to the Children's Hospital turned into an overnight stay because after giving her allergy medicine and steroids, they wanted to keep her for observation. During the night, her swelling went down, and they released her the next day with a prescription for allergy medication, steroids, and an Epi-pen for emergencies. They also made us an appointment to see an allergist.

A few days later at the allergist's office, a round of skin tests revealed that our daughter was highly allergic to all nuts. And though this recent reaction had been treated in sufficient time, it was no guarantee that we would be as fortunate in the future.

From that point on, we worried about our little girl constantly and monitored everything she ate. And we lived in fear of what would happen if we were not around to inform others of her nut allergy should someone offer her anything that contained nuts in our absence. We even considered having T-shirts made for her that read, "I'm Allergic to Nuts," but we never did. We simply stayed diligent about it, always making sure we informed others, especially babysitters, of her allergy. And we rested in the reality that God could watch over her much better than we ever could.

In July 1999, exactly one year after Janay was born, I discovered I was pregnant again. We were shocked because I had been taking birth control pills and still got pregnant. It appeared God's will was being done in our lives whether we approved or not.

When the ultrasound revealed the baby's sex, we could have fainted.

It was another girl. The pink rose prophecy was still in full effect, and we didn't even realize it.

Now that we had a fourth child on the way, we decided to sell our three-bedroom, one-bath home and find a larger one. And after a grueling search, we finally found a home that we really liked. We were approved for a mortgage with no hassle and were ready to finalize the deal, but there was one issue: we couldn't seem to sell the home that we were presently living in. No matter how hard we tried, selling that home just wasn't working out for us. Realizing it must not have been God's timing, we stopped the process and stayed where we were.

As you may recall, when the year 2000 drew closer, there was a great amount of fear and confusion in the world around us. There were even rumors of a major worldwide disaster that was due to happen on January 1, 2000.

Usually, at the end of each year, Erskine and I made a habit of sitting down and discussing the goals that we desired to accomplish for the coming year. But at the time, because of all the uncertainty in the world, we couldn't seem to do that. For us, the future seemed to be a large blur, and no matter how hard we tried to see through the blur, we just couldn't. However, I do remember a brief vision I had a few months earlier where I saw Erskine walk into the house after coming home from work early one day, and in the vision he said to me that he had lost his job. I prayed hard that this vision would not come true, and it didn't. But it was a warning that something just as awful was on the way.

When January 1, 2000, came and passed, we, like the rest of the world, breathed a sigh of relief. All was well, or so we thought. Although the new year didn't come in with the doom everyone had anticipated, for Erskine and me, the doom was just delayed; February and March came in and knocked the wind right out of us!

Allow me to backtrack a little. Four months earlier, Erskine's grandmom, Ernestine Daniel, passed, resulting in him taking a number of days off work to help his parents with her funeral arrangements. The next month, he lost a dear aunt, his mom's sister Joyce Ann Wren Gee, to cancer. He took off a day for her funeral as well. Then the following month, our three girls and I were sick with the flu, and though it appeared Erskine would get by without catching it, a few weeks later, the bug bit him too.

Along with the days he took off for the funerals, Erskine took more days off trying to doctor on himself. Finally, in January, I was able to convince him to go to the doctor, as his symptoms seemed to be getting the best of him, especially a bad, aggravating cough. The doctor diagnosed him with bronchitis and gave him a steroid injection and a prescription for an antibiotic.

In February, Erskine's supervisor reprimanded him for his excessive absences and wrote up an official letter that would go into his file permanently. This upset us to the utmost. Though we could somewhat understand the reason for the action, it still did not rest well with us because the supervisor had no compassion whatsoever. Mama Doll, Erskine's aunt, Elzine Wren Stout, and I encouraged him to fight it and maybe find another job. And even though he seemed to agree with us, for some reason, God wouldn't allow him to deal with it, and he just stood still.

Days after his antibiotics were gone, Erskine still didn't feel any better. And he returned to the doctor's office three more times between February and early March. At each visit, they gave him a steroid injection and a stronger antibiotic. But the cough was still a big issue along with lethargy, as he had zero energy, and he fell asleep often. We knew something just wasn't right.

One day Erskine came home from work complaining of "just feeling bad." That was the only way he could describe what was going on inside of him. He also mentioned that his cough was the result of a funny feeling in the center of his chest that just wouldn't go away. We wondered if his breathing in secondhand smoke at work was the cause of his problem, as his riding partner smoked heavily. We posed this question to the doctor, and he agreed that it was a possible factor. The doctor then ordered an x-ray and blood test. After receiving the results of the blood test, he told us that Erskine's white blood count was doing something weird. Rather than getting better with the antibiotics, his white blood count kept getting worse. The doctor prescribed another antibiotic and an excuse for work that would remove him from the vehicle with his partner who smoked.

After Erskine took all of that medication without any noticeable change, I felt determined to ask the doctor to refer us to a specialist. And ironically, he was already prepared to refer Erskine to a pulmonary specialist. He had his receptionist set up an appointment for us to see a pulmonary doctor that very day. And as the receptionist did this, the doctor decided he would take another x-ray of Erskine's chest for us to present to the new doctor.

When he returned with the x-ray, the doctor told us that he wasn't sure about it, but he thought he saw something questionable in the center of Erskine's chest near his lungs, and he told us to mention it to the new doctor.

After lunch, we went to the hospital to see the pulmonary doctor, and we told him Erskine's dilemma. We also mentioned how the first doctor thought he saw something questionable on the x-ray. After our talk, the doctor sent Erskine to take an episode of breathing tests while he looked at his x-ray. When they returned, the doctor said he didn't see anything out of the ordinary on the x-ray and that the cough could have been related to acid reflux or asthma. He wrote Erskine a prescription for a couple of inhalers and then left the room to get acid reflux medicine samples. While he was away, I asked my husband if I could beg the doctor to take a second look at the x-ray, and he agreed, so when he returned, I did just that. The doctor complied and even had a partner look along with him. This time, he said he did see something out of the ordinary, and he ordered a CAT scan right away, promising to call us the next day with the results.

The next morning, I went to the pharmacy to get Erskine's acid reflux prescriptions filled. While I was out, Erskine called my cell phone saying the doctor had called and he wanted us at the hospital right away. The CAT scans had revealed a large spot in the center of his torso near his lungs. I felt as if I'd been hit in the stomach with a wrecking ball, and I cried so hard that I could hardly see my way back home. *This can't be real! This has got to be a dream!* But it *was* real. Very real.

Because he would need a tissue sample in order to make a diagnosis, the pulmonary doctor had us to meet with the surgeon that he had chosen to perform Erskine's biopsy. The surgeon shared with us that the large tumor in the center of Erskine's chest was hidden between his breastbone and his lungs. He then named a couple of diseases that it could have been, including the one we dreaded most, cancer. We had to schedule a day during that very week for the biopsy. Everything was moving so fast.

Four days after the biopsy, we received the awful verdict; Erskine had cancer. I fearfully accepted this as a death sentence, and I questioned God daily.

"Lord, why are You allowing this?"

"I love this man. Why would You take him from me so soon?"

"Lord why would You make me a widow at such a young age?"

"Are You really going to make me raise these babies by myself?"

"Lord, this new baby inside of me will never get to know her dad if You take him now."

After giving us this awful news, the pulmonary doctor arranged for us to meet with the oncologist and radiologist who would be treating Erskine. During our meeting with the oncologist, he informed us that my husband's type of cancer was called Hodgkin's lymphoma. He said that Hodgkin's had up to a 99 percent survival rate when diagnosed early. He explained his plan for treating the disease, and he shared with us the negative side effects of the treatment, such as hair loss, loss of appetite, weight loss, vomiting, and lethargy.

Because we had recently watched Aunt Joyce battle cancer, those negative side effects were fresh on our brains. But one side effect that we were not familiar with was chemotherapy's ability to make a patient sterile. The doctor said this happens because it kills all fast-growing cells in the body, whether good or bad. This is also the reason for hair loss during chemotherapy.

The doctor gave Erskine the option of freezing some of his sperm just in case we wanted to have more children in the future. At the time, I was eight and a half months pregnant with our fourth daughter. And though my husband and I had previously discussed not having any more children, it broke my heart to imagine not being able to produce more children naturally if we later changed our minds.

After hearing all of that, I couldn't take hearing much more, so I left the room crying and went back to the waiting room with my dad, who had come along with us for support. I felt that if I could just get to him, everything would be all right. But actually, all Daddy could do was cry with me. That was frustrating, and so were the parade of thoughts concerning losing Brian and now possibly Erskine. I was so frustrated that I looked upward and announced, "I feel like somebody up there is picking on me!" I couldn't understand why I had to keep going through such heavy issues in my life. Why couldn't God just give me a break?

The doctor came into the waiting room to talk to me. He wanted to encourage me to be strong for Erskine because he said his healing would be aided by my strength. But as he talked, I silently wondered, *Yeah, you want me to be strong for him, but who is going to be strong for me?*

As the days passed, Erskine went through a series of blood tests, CAT scans, and other testing in preparation for his chemotherapy treatments, which would be starting soon. But he declined to have his sperm frozen because we both agreed that the four children we had were plenty. So we decided to look at the sterilization as a God-given birth control.

For the next nine months, Erskine was off work without pay because he had run out of sick time. He endured five months of chemotherapy and three months of radiation. He was often nauseated and vomited ferociously from his chemo treatments. He went through continuous bouts of fatigue and depression. He was even hospitalized once for severe nausea and dehydration. My husband was trying very hard to get well for the girls and me. And I was just trying hard not to lose my mind.

With this sudden change in our lifestyle, our girls couldn't understand what was going on. There were so many people suddenly in and out of our house. Their dad, whom they normally only saw in the evenings after work, was now at home every day. They often watched him lie on the sofa, lie on the floor, or kneel as he was trying to find some position that would help him feel better. They listened in horror as he vomited uncontrollably during the days after his chemo treatments. And they wondered why suddenly unfamiliar family and friends began coming by to pick them up and spend time with them.

During this ordeal, with occasional help from his family, I took care of my husband as best I could while in my ninth month of pregnancy. Then, on April 22, 2000, I gave birth to our fourth beautiful baby girl, Joycelyn Andrea. We named her after Erskine's aunt, Joyce Ann, who, as I mentioned previously, died of cancer months earlier.

One night, as if we weren't having enough drama already, I found a lump in my right breast after breastfeeding the baby. I first suspected it to be a swollen milk duct. But after having it examined and monitored for a month, I finally had it surgically removed. The doctor said it was sarcoid. I didn't know what that was, but I just thank God it wasn't cancer.

Fatigue, worry, postpartum depression, Erskine's health, and the stress of having five people in the house that totally depended on me made me feel as if I was losing my mind at times. Sometimes I wished I could just walk away from it all. But my loving God held me very close, and He wouldn't let me go. He took care of us as He promised He would in His Word. While we were in the midst of that horrible storm, He covered us and never once allowed us to get wet. During those nine months without a paycheck, God supernaturally kept our utilities on and our house note paid. And He miraculously used family, friends, and even strangers to be ravens for us during our great time of need.

God even revealed to us *one* of the reasons why He never allowed Erskine to react negatively to the reprimand he received for his absences at work. It was because He planned to use the people on his job to bless us tremendously. More than once, while Erskine was off work, they blessed us with boxes and boxes and more boxes full of food and necessities. They even blessed us with finances and much-needed items for our new baby.

Erskine's last chemotherapy treatment was in September 2000.

Amazingly, he never lost much hair, he never lost much weight, and most importantly, he never lost his smile. After the chemo was over, he began three months of radiation treatments. And after that, the doctors ordered another CAT scan, which revealed good news. The tumor was shrinking! Erskine was in remission! My husband was going to live after all!

After spending so much time stuck in the house, going back and forth to the doctor's office, and going so long without a paycheck, Erskine was quite anxious to get back to work. And, in December 2000, he eagerly returned to his job with the county board of education. But for me, just getting through this trial with my mind still intact was a supernatural triumph within itself!

As we entered the year 2001, we felt our future looked much brighter. Erskine was bringing home a paycheck again, and health wise, he was doing wonderfully. We both thought we were about to regain a sense of normalcy in our lives. And I secretly hoped we would continue our journey toward that happily-ever-after place in life. But all of that was so far from the truth.

In May of that year, I was asked to oversee and direct my dad's birthday celebration at church. I worked very hard on the project because I truly wanted to see him blessed. During that time, I lost a lot of weight, but I chalked it up to working so hard and not taking much time to eat. But then I started having night sweats, hot flashes, and trouble catching my breath. I diagnosed my own problem and said that it was just early menopause. The following month, I began to feel something strange in the left side of my abdomen right below my ribs. I tried to ignore it because in the back of my mind I had the fear that one day cancer might hit me. I tried to tell myself that whatever it was it would eventually go away. But it didn't. It only grew larger. I thought, *Is it a tumor? Do I have cancer?*

One Friday afternoon, after discovering the mass had grown larger, I went to the doctor. She told me that what I was actually feeling was my spleen, which was enlarged, and so was my liver. All of a sudden, I felt the room spinning as I thought, *Here we go again.*

The doctor named some of the diseases that would cause the liver and spleen to swell, but without testing, she could not narrow them down to just one. So she took some blood samples and then scheduled me for a CAT scan that following Monday. Needless to say, I had a long wait in the dark.

After the CAT scan on Monday, I waited anxiously by the phone the following day for the doctor's call. When she called, she told me that it appeared I had a rare disease called sarcoidosis.

The doctor said sarcoidosis was not contagious, but it had no known cause and no known cure. The CAT scan showed that the disease was causing severe inflammation in my lungs, spleen, liver, and pelvic area. And though it couldn't be cured, my symptoms could be treated with the widely used corticosteroid known as Prednisone.

I was slightly familiar with sarcoidosis, as my cousin Jackie Sankey Harville was battling that same disease. I then remembered the cyst in my breast, which was removed the year before. The surgeon had said it was sarcoid, short for sarcoidosis.

These new developments weighed heavily on my mind as I thought, *Why, Lord? Haven't we gone through enough already?*

I was referred to a pulmonary doctor who scheduled me for a biopsy in order to find out just how aggressively the disease should be treated. He learned that he needed to place me on a high dosage of Prednisone immediately.

That high dose of Prednisone was extremely hard on me because it carried some very serious side effects. Swelling (especially in my face and abdomen), severe mental confusion, excessive appetite, and personality changes were just a few of the side effects that taunted me. I remember one day trying to stop the medicine cold turkey because I was tired of dealing with those side effects. But when I awoke the next morning, it felt as if I had been beaten with a baseball bat all night long. Every spot on my body ached severely, and I couldn't stand for anyone to touch me. That's when I learned the hard way that I had to be weaned from that medicine. I couldn't just stop taking it abruptly. Those body aches were a symptom of my sudden withdrawal.

After getting back on the medication and learning to deal with its awful side effects, God blessed me to make it through that ordeal much better than I expected. As the inflammation in my lungs and other organs subsided, the doctor weaned me down to a smaller dose of the steroid.

In late August, I returned to the pulmonary doctor and received a great report. My lungs were much clearer, and my liver and spleen seemed to have lost much of their swelling. The doctor then ordered me to take one Prednisone a day just to keep the inflammation down. That was refreshing news. I knew it wasn't just the medicine that had helped me; it was the prayers and encouragement of my family and friends along the way.

11

Nothing's Too Hard for God

> But Jesus beheld them, and said unto them, with men this is impossible; but with God all things are possible.
> —Matthew 19:26 (KJV)

One morning, in October 2001, when it was time for me to get our oldest two girls ready for school, as hard as I tried, I just couldn't get up. It literally took every ounce of energy I could scrape up just for me to sit up on the side of the bed, and as I sat there, I began wondering what in the world was wrong with me. I finally managed to get the kids dressed and fed, but I struggled while driving them to school. When I returned home after dropping them off, I gave my younger girls some cereal, sat them in front of the television, and dove back into bed. Then, after sleeping so long and hard, I finally woke up and tried to diagnose myself. I wondered if my problem was related to the sarcoidosis or if I was coming down with the flu, as I had recently been given a flu shot by my doctor. But something within me told me to check my calendar. When I checked it, I realized that my monthly cycle was over a month late and I had not even realized it. But then the thought hit me, *I can't be pregnant, Erskine is supposed to be sterile.*

After getting used to the idea that we had a permanent birth control due to Erskine's chemo treatments the year before, it was pretty hard to fathom the idea of a possible pregnancy, especially having four children already. I called Erskine at work and told him what I suspected. His tone was very solemn as he said, "All righty then." We were both hoping that my speculations were completely wrong.

I tried waiting until Erskine got home from work before going to buy a pregnancy test. But after a while, I couldn't wait any longer. I needed an answer right away, so I loaded up my toddler and preschooler, and off we went to the store.

I felt so embarrassed buying that pregnancy test. I guess it was because the world has put such a stigma on having more than two children. Although there wasn't a thing wrong with it, as I was a married woman with a great husband who was taking good care of his family, I felt so ashamed for having two little ones in my shopping basket while purchasing such a thing. It was good my other two kids were in school, because if I'd had all four of them with me, I probably would have considered wearing a disguise.

As soon as I returned home, I took the test, and the instructions said to wait three minutes before reading it to give the symbols time to appear. But before I could even finish taking the test, my symbols were crystal clear. I was indeed very pregnant! I couldn't believe it!

After getting past my initial shock, I had to refocus on what had actually taken place. This was *no ordinary pregnancy*. This was *a miracle*. And this miracle was not only proof that Erskine had been healed, but it proved that God was indeed controlling our lives. And God didn't just stop there, as He had more surprises in store for us.

I was extremely tired in the beginning of the pregnancy, my breaths were short, and I had an aggravating pain in my side, which was coming from my enlarged spleen. I knew the sarcoidosis was warring with the pregnancy, and many times the sarcoidosis felt as if it were winning.

I felt absolutely terrible one Sunday as my family and I arrived at my mom's house for dinner. Dealing with the disease and the pregnancy at the same time was a bit much on my body, and I began to bargain with God. I thought about the number of children that I had given birth to, five. Having always heard that the number seven was God's perfect number and that it meant completion, I thought about how badly I wanted completion in our baby making. So, speaking out of fatigue and frustration, I said to my husband, "If God wants me to have His perfect number of seven children (which included our son Brian), then He has to put two babies inside me this time, because after this pregnancy, I'm done! I'm having my tubes tied!" I spoke those words from my heart, as I was dead set on having my tubes tied despite the fact that God's word said, "Be fruitful and multiply." I felt we had done enough multiplying. It was time to put away the calculator for good.

A week later, which was about eight weeks into the pregnancy, my doctor scheduled me for an ultrasound. I had never before had an ultrasound so early in a pregnancy. But because I was seeing a new doctor, I assumed that was his protocol. And since the ultrasound was being done so early, I knew it was too soon to find out the baby's gender, so I didn't bother asking my husband to go with me; I went alone.

As the technician blobbed gel onto my abdomen and began moving her probe over it, the words that fell from her lips will forever be imprinted upon my brain. "Well, honey, I'm glad you're lying down because you have two babies inside of you!"

Her happy-go-lucky personality made me feel she was just teasing with me. So I raised my head up and said, in disbelief, "No I don't," to which she responded, "Yes you do! You want to take a look?"

She then turned the monitor around and pointed to the two little nuggets on the screen. "See, there they are," she said. I was in total shock. All I could do was cry. This made the technician nervous, as she wondered if she had done something wrong by giving me this news while I was alone. After assuring her that I would be all right, I asked her to pinch me so that I could know that this was not dream. She gently obliged.

Not wanting to waste another moment, I asked her to get my cell phone from my purse so that I could call my husband. When I told Erskine the news, there was first a moment of silence. Then he finally responded, saying, "Tracy, stop kidding with me." So I asked the technician to talk to him. She was able to convince him that I wasn't lying, and so together we were both in a state of shock. And after sharing the news with our parents and other family members, they all were in just as much shock as we were.

Every time I thought about it, I just couldn't believe it! God heard my cry, and He actually answered my request! He allowed two babies to form inside of me at one time, giving us seven children, His number of completion. My God never ceases to amaze me!

Considering all of the supernatural events we had experienced during our ten years together, my grannie's reply to our latest news was, "Well, ya'll just full of surprises over there!"

Finding out that we were expecting two more children in addition to the four we already had was quite overwhelming. Just when we'd grown content with the idea of staying in our present home and fixing it up a little, our situation drastically changed. This time we had no choice but to consider moving because the twins were due to share a room with Erskine and me, and they would share a crib with one another.

We not only needed a larger house but also a larger van, two of every baby thing, and above all, more money. We had no idea how we were going to accomplish all of this, but God knew, and He quickly began working on our behalf.

In December 2001, two months after discovering we were expecting twins, God supernaturally blessed Erskine with a higher-paying position on his job. He was promoted to supervisor after only five years at the county. This was surely another reason why God didn't allow him to react to that reprimand he received back in 2000, as he would have destroyed this opportunity that was waiting down the road for him.

Three months later, God enabled us to purchase an eight-passenger van for our soon-to-be eight-member family. And we automatically knew that if God had done these amazing things for us so fast, then the house and everything else that we needed was definitely on the way.

Because this pregnancy was so miraculous, we wondered if God had again decided to give us double for our trouble. In other words, we wondered if He had decided to give us two boys to replace the one we lost? Although we wondered it, we didn't put our hope in it. However, this did not stop many of our family members and friends from proclaiming it. They prayed and confessed that we would have two sons.

Somewhere around my fourth or fifth month, I had an ultrasound, which revealed something shocking. I was carrying two more girls! This was the third shocking moment for us during this pregnancy: 1) Pregnant! 2) Twins! 3) Girls!

I finally remembered that pink rose prophecy. Nine years later, and the words God gave me concerning that rose pendant were still going forth. Six girls! My goodness! No matter how many times I said it or thought about it, I still could not believe it!

As the time drew nearer for the twins' arrival, God began supplying us with everything they needed. In April, our family and our church threw us a beautiful baby shower, and we carried home so much loot that day until, for a while, our living room looked like a small baby boutique. God was steadily proving to us that nothing was too hard for Him.

On May 16, 2002 I gave birth to two lovely angels. Baby "A," Karen Briann, was born at 3:21 p.m., weighing five pounds and three ounces and measuring eighteen and a half inches in length. And baby "B," Kamille Brianna, was born two minutes later, amazingly weighing and measuring the exact same thing.

While looking at the six of my babies together on a photo we took of them at the hospital after the twins were born, I realized that God had blessed me in a very unique way. He had actually bestowed upon me half a dozen pink roses! These girls were my supernatural blessings and my lovely bouquet of roses from God.

While standing in my kitchen staring out of the window at the rotten wood on our back porch one Sunday morning, I found myself becoming increasingly anxious and frustrated because I had grown weary of staying in our tiny deteriorating house. Several factors were causing my frustration. The house was old and in much need of work. I was constantly moving furniture around trying to make more space. We were using every nook and cranny in the house for storage. Our closets were so packed until the doors wouldn't shut. Our new babies didn't have a room of their own. And the need for a second bathroom had strongly presented itself. It all boiled down to my family having outgrown our starter home.

I began speaking to God in my heart. I told Him that I couldn't

God's Girl

understand why so many people around us were being blessed with new homes, and we were not. We were trying our best to live a life that was pleasing to Him, yet we were eight people stuck in a tiny old house. The house had indeed been a great blessing to us when we first moved there, but now it was time to move up.

Having voiced my desire for a new home to others, my faith was a bit shaken by some of the responses I received such as, "My mama raised ten children in a one-bedroom, or a two-bedroom, or this kind of house, or that kind of house." But then I decided to remain steadfast in my faith as I thought, *Good for their mama*. But this mama knew deep inside that my God had so much more in store for my family and me. And considering the many ways He had proven His power to my husband and me through the years, I could not settle for less when I knew He was capable of giving us more.

After allowing me to express my frustrations, God gently whispered Philippians 4:6–7 in my ear, "Be anxious for nothing, but in everything by prayer and supplication, with thanksgiving, let your requests be made known to God; and the peace of God, which surpasses all understanding, will guard your hearts and minds through Christ Jesus" (NKJV). I heard Him loud and clear. And He was letting me know that He heard me too and that He was working on something for us, but I just needed to be patient. As I began to weep, I told God that I was willing to stay right there in that house for as long as He wanted me to, but I would truly need His peace in the midst of it, and He gave it to me instantly.

When we first tried to move, in 1999, our biggest headache was not finding a new home but selling our old one. There was one problem after another with each potential buyer. Then, when the house was appraised, the list of things that needed to be done before we could sell it was just too much for our pocket. Realizing that it was not in God's will for us to move at the time, we just stood still.

Shortly afterward, Erskine was diagnosed with cancer, revealing to us the reason God made us wait. But this time around, in 2002, with the birth of twins, we felt we had no other choice; we definitely needed to move. So once again, we had to face that giant headache of trying to sell our home.

In June, after feeling a *go ahead* in our spirits from the Lord, we decided to put a For Sale by Owner sign in the yard. Although we knew there was much work that needed to be done to our home, we hoped there was someone out there looking for a fixer-upper.

The sign attracted a few people who really seemed interested, but many of them only wanted to rent it. Those who considered buying it could not, because lending institutions would not foot the bill for houses that did not meet inspection. This was so disheartening.

I prayed, "So now what, Lord? We have stepped out into the deep, and we can't turn back." Supernaturally, He began to bless us with extra finances, and little by little, we made home improvements that would hopefully help us sell our home faster. Then one day in late July, God sent us a candidate, and we wrote up a contract that very day! We were so happy and grateful to God because now we could buy us a new house!

———⚜———

We didn't have to search very hard for a new house, as we already knew what house we wanted. During the time that we were trying to sell our old one, we had enough faith to begin looking for a new one. We saw many that we were interested in, but because we didn't have a contract on our old house yet, we didn't feel comfortable putting a contract on any of those, so some of them ended up being sold. But we didn't let that bother us because we knew that whatever God had for us would indeed be for us, and the devil in hell could not change that, no matter how hard he tried. And believe me, he tried.

We came across the house we wanted when we were house hunting one day in the city of Pleasant Grove, AL. During our drive, I spotted an empty house that caught my eye and my spirit. It was on a pleasant little street with a cul-de-sac. Although the house was for sale by owner, as ours was, the owner was working through an agency that was helping him advertise it.

We stopped and looked at the house from the car for a few minutes and wrote down the information from the sign. Then I used my cell phone to call the number, and after entering in an extension, I was able to listen to an automated message that listed the features and price of the house. After the message ended, I screamed to my husband, "That's my house! That's my house!" So we circled the cul-de-sac and passed the house again to take a second look. After we finished looking at that house, my husband decided to drive buy several other houses that were for sale in that city, but my mind was made up, and I didn't want to look at any more houses. I had found our house. However, at the time we still didn't have a contract on our old house, so we couldn't comfortably put one on this one. Therefore, I prayed, "Lord, please don't allow this house to get away from us."

The next day, I called the owner of the house. He informed me that he had stopped showing the house for a while because he and his family were moving into their new house. I was glad to hear that because we needed the extra time anyway. What I was not glad to hear was how many people there were on his waiting list to see the house, ten. We made eleven. As I sadly hung up, my husband encouraged me, saying, "Baby, what God has for us is for us. I don't care how many people are on his list; if God wants us to have that house, then we will have it!"

The next week, after no word from the house owner, I called him to see if he was showing the house again. He said he would be showing it again soon, so he gave us a date and time to come by. He also informed me that he now had eighteen people on his list. I didn't care; that was *our house*.

I accepted an appointment date by faith because at the time we still didn't have a contract on our own house, and I knew that if we got a chance to see this house and liked it, we would want to put a contract on it. I prayed, "Lord, what are we going to do?" And that's when it happened. The day before our appointment to see our new house, God sent us a buyer for the old house. That was awesome timing!

Discouragingly, on our appointment date, after eagerly waiting all day to see the house, the owner had to postpone. Then, on our new scheduled meeting date, he failed to show up. We knew the devil just wanted us to give up, and it was very tempting to do so. However, we also knew we had definitely found our house, so we held on tight.

Though I didn't realize it at the time, I had become just like the persistent widow in Luke, chapter 18. I called the owner of that house quite frequently, and on occasion, I left several messages. Just as the judge in that chapter felt led to move on the woman's behalf because of her persistence, the owner of that house did the same for me. He told me regardless of the eighteen people on his list, he would make sure we were the first to see the house because we seemed the most interested. I confidently told him that we would not only be the first to see it, but we would also be the last because that was our house.

During our new meeting date with the owner, we finally had the opportunity to look around the house. Because it wasn't occupied, there were no lights on, so we had to see the best we could with sunlight. Four bedrooms, two bathrooms, a den, a playroom for our kids, an eat-in kitchen, a living room, a dining room, walk-in closets, a double deck, large, private, fenced-in backyard, and more. The most remarkable thing about it was that it was in our price range! The house we found back in 1999 when we first tried to move couldn't compare to this one! This was another confirmation as to why God had interrupted our first attempt to move, as there was a greater blessing on the other side of our wait.

On the back deck, in the blazing hot sun, Erskine and the owner signed the contract. And as they were signing, the owner's next appointment arrived. But just as I had decreed, we were the first and the last to see the house because he turned them away.

As the days and months passed, there was much headache, frustration, and desperation involved in the process of selling and buying those houses. At one point, we lost our buyer because her mortgage company couldn't approve her for a loan. Then we hired a broker to find us another buyer quickly. After showing the house, about four or five times, the broker wasn't able to find us another buyer in the time span given. During all of this, the owner of the house we were trying to buy kept calling to ask what was taking us so long. It seemed everything was a jumbled-up mess. But we kept the faith.

My dad was so worried about whether this situation would work out in our favor because every time he came to visit us, he would see us living out of boxes month after month in anticipation of our move. Then he'd leave our house grieving for us. But what Daddy didn't realize was, because I grew up watching God move for him in so many awesome ways, especially in the construction of Mt. Canaan's new building, I had no choice but to believe that God would move on our behalf.

I remember how in the 1980s when our church was jam-packed every Sunday and how Daddy had to start holding two services on Sunday mornings in addition to Sunday school. Then one Sunday he announced to the church that God had told him, "Rise up and build and owe nothing to any man except to love him" (Nehemiah 2:18; Romans 13:8). That was his mandate from God to build a new church for Mt. Canaan, and to do it without borrowing.

These orders sounded impossible to Daddy because he knew the meager financial condition of his members, as many were on food stamps, on welfare, and even raising a house full of small children just as he and Mama Trish were. Nevertheless, he stepped out on faith, and God stood with him, anointing him with the ability to raise supernatural finances from such poor people. And rather than complain, the people gave cheerfully and beyond their means, just as the people did in the churches of Macedonia that Paul wrote about in 2 Corinthians 8. And this was not sporadic giving, as these people happily gave to the building fund weekly. And each time they gave, God would breathe upon their sacrifices and increase their faith tremendously.

I watched my dad stand in faith when people all over Birmingham talked about him and laughed at him for taking on the humongous task of building a million-dollar church debt free. I watched him faithfully call on God rather than call on a bank or a loan company when the finances dried up and the building project was halted. And I watched him use his faith to speak many things into existence concerning the project, such as the purchasing, surveying and clearing of the land, the bricks, the roof, each floor, and every piece of furniture and decor that was put inside.

In August 1993, five years after breaking ground, the congregation of Mt. Canaan marched from their tiny deteriorating sanctuary into their brand-new, million-dollar sanctuary, which was built debt free! Because I had such an awesome example set before me, my faith in God was soaring. I could no longer believe God for mediocre when I knew He could do the extraordinary! And because Erskine and I stood firmly in our faith, God began to do the extraordinary in our lives as well.

The mortgage company that was helping us purchase our new home decided to step in and help us sell our old one. They contacted our first buyer and worked diligently to help her fix her finances so that she could purchase our home. And three months later, after so much hard work, patience, and prayer, we happily closed on both homes in the same day.

After living in a home that was so much smaller and older, we could hardly believe God had blessed us with such beauty and space. Our kids were so excited about the extra space that they ran upstairs, downstairs, in and out of rooms, and in and out of closets all day long. Joycelyn, our two-year-old, whom we thought would have the most trouble getting familiar with her new surroundings, loved her new home so much that she told us every day, "Mama, Daddy, I like my new house!"

Then, a few days after closing on our home, God gave us the greatest housewarming gift that we could ever imagine, a house full of beautiful furniture! It was through Erskine's parents that He blessed us. Months earlier, they had inherited a large amount of elegant furniture from a dear friend who lost her battle with cancer. Because their home was not large enough for their inheritance, they put much of it in storage. Then when God blessed us with our new home, they were so happy for us that they tried to fill up every room.

After experiencing God do so many supernatural things for us, Erskine and I made a solid decision to trust Him totally, for the rest of our lives, as there was no need for us to worry about situations or problems that we had no control over. Though it appeared we actually had the perfect reason to worry, because Erskine was the only person in the house working, paying all of the bills and providing food and shelter for eight people, that was actually the perfect reason *not* to worry. We had no reason to worry because we wholeheartedly believed in the teaching we were receiving. Teaching that encouraged us to be faithful in the giving of our tithes, our offerings, and our service to the work of the Lord.

Since I was a child, my parents always taught me the principle of tithing (Malachi 3:10–11). And since then, I've always given God His 10 percent of my earnings, off the top. Having learned this from his parents as well, Erskine gave me no problems when I began tithing from his monthly paychecks after we married. We both understood that was how we would remain blessed. However, I'm reminded of a situation that happened during our time in Nebraska when we came across a financially rough month where we had to explain to Pastor Keys that we would not be able to pay our tithe for that particular month. Though our pastor tried to make us feel better about the situation, it really bothered me because I always took God and His money very seriously. But, as time progressed, we eventually forgot about that missing tithe and simply resumed giving our tithes the following months.

However, two years later, after moving back home to Birmingham and starting life over again, God brought that missing tithe back to my remembrance. And after discussing it with Erskine, we decided to do the right thing and send those tithes plus interest back to Nebraska because we wanted nothing more than to remain in right standing with God and to continue to receive His blessings and favor. By being obedient in that area and many other areas, we witnessed God continuously "rebuke the devourer for our sake" (Malachi 3:11).

Because of our obedience to Him, we noticed how God never ceased to provide everything we needed to take care of our family. For example, each year He appointed numerous families to sow bountifully into our lives, as they willingly supplied us with quality clothing and shoes that their children had outgrown. At one point, we ended up turning one of the bedrooms in our new home into a walk-in closet, just to have a place to store the abundance of blessings God was raining on us for our children.

Although raising our large family could get tough at times, because we basically lived from hand to mouth, we always knew that God would come through for us when we needed Him most. My dad taught us that if God was the one leading our lives, then He was the one responsible for meeting our needs. As long as we remained faithful and obedient to Him, He was obligated to take care of us. So although we may not have had everything we wanted, we had more than enough of everything we needed. And if we didn't have something we needed, God always made a supernatural way for us to get it, as He did with our new home.

Now that we were living in what I considered our dream home, I sincerely believed that this was the start of our happily-ever-after life. We had finally made it!

12

The Goal to Do God's Will

> Wherefore also we make it our aim, whether at home or absent, to be well-pleasing unto him.
> —2 Corinthians 5:9 (ASV)

About a week after settling in our new home, my dad asked us, "So what's next?" He had observed us through the years always working toward some type of goal. There was the goal to have a wedding. The goal to move to Nebraska. The goal to make a baby. The goal to make the baby well. The goal to leave Nebraska. The goal to find a job. The goal to make a new baby. The goal to find a house. The goal to find a vehicle. The goal to find a better job. The goal to get Erskine well. The goal to get Tracy well. The goal to sell our house. And the goal to find a new one. After reaching all of these goals, Daddy wondered what our next goal would be. I had no clue what Erskine thought our next goal should be, but I knew what I wanted it to be, to rest and live happily ever after. I mean, considering all we'd gone through in the eleven short years we'd been together, I figured it was about time we reached our happy place.

Erskine answered my dad's question by saying, "We're going to do whatever God tells us to do." I thought that was a brilliant answer because I was sure God wanted us to relax from our troubles and trials and finally enjoy life. Later, I discovered that God had a laundry list of things for us to do, and the relaxation that I assumed He wanted for us didn't even make His list.

One of the things on His list for me to do was finish the book I'd started writing in 2000, the book He mandated me to write when my baby boy was dying in 1993. During Erskine's battle with cancer and right after I gave birth to our fourth baby girl, I began writing that book. I spent many late nights writing bits and pieces of the many trials and triumphs Erskine and I had experienced since we married. Then, two months after moving into our new home, God revealed to me that it was time to finish and self-publish that book. So, a new goal had presented itself. The goal to publish a book.

As I worked diligently on the book, I asked God questions such as, "Where should the book begin?" "What should I title it?" "Who will want to read it because no one really knows me?" Then God answered my questions saying, "Begin with the day I saved you." "Title it, *Somber Trials but Supernatural Triumphs*!" "And don't worry that no one knows you ... they won't be reading about you; they will be reading all about Me." With that encouragement, I began putting my heart into the project, even praying for my potential readers that their hearts would be touched by my testimony as they read the book.

When I finally finished, I started to worry about how my book would be published. But God gave me peace, saying, "If I told you to write it, then I will make sure it is published." So I stopped worrying about what He had already taken care of.

After finding a self-publishing company online who sent me information on the self-publishing process, I proudly began the process of publishing my book. And as part of the process, I started my own business, which I titled O'Neal-Daniel Productions, as I would need it in order to sell my books. I can hardly explain to you the joy that filled my heart on a beautiful morning in July 2003, when, after working for several months to complete this task, a UPS truck stopped in front of our house and delivered about eight large boxes of books. My books! With my face on the cover and my testimony inside. Finally, my book-writing goal was accomplished, and my obedience to God had given me one of the secret desires of my heart, to become a published author!

Several of our awesome family members and friends helped us to promote and sell the books, which allowed it to reach areas of the United States that I personally have never visited. And in answer to my prayer of the book touching the hearts of my readers, I received several testimonies

God's Girl

by e-mail, US mail, and word of mouth concerning the book's great impact on people's lives.

During this time, President George W. Bush was in office, and I had heard that First Lady Laura Bush was a big reading advocate. With that knowledge, I decided to autograph a copy of my book and send it to the White House. About two weeks later, Erskine raced down the hall to our bedroom early one morning, waving a large yellow envelope he had found stuck in the front door. It was from the White House, and it was addressed to me! First Lady Laura Bush had taken the time to send me a letter thanking me for sending a copy of my book and for "the lovely inscription." She went on to say that she was delighted to know that, with God's help, I and my husband had triumphed over some very difficult challenges and that she and President Bush wanted to congratulate me on the publication of the book and they wished me much success. Wow! Not only was my book touching people's lives across the United States, but it had also made it to the White House! I felt super blessed!

A couple of months after publishing my book, I felt the Lord calling me into ministry. Just as He had called my dad, my stepmom, and even my brother William, He was now calling me. But I hesitated because I had no desire to stand before a congregation to preach. That was not what I signed up for when I wrote that book. I simply wrote it to share my testimony. I was no preacher. At least I didn't think so. I actually felt like Moses; my speech wasn't eloquent enough. I couldn't imagine myself ministering before an audience unless I wrote the message down and read it word for word. I told God, "Lord, just let me write for you." However, in spite if my bargaining, He didn't change His mind, so I gave in, telling Him I was willing to be used by Him in whatever capacity He needed me.

I received e-mails daily from readers who wanted to praise the book and share their own testimonies with me. I enjoyed receiving the e-mails so much that I started to get a little disappointed whenever they would slow down. Then one night in October 2003, God said to me, "The way to get mail is to send mail." And He gave me an encouraging word to send to all of those in my e-mail contact list.

Because it was rather late when I sent the message, I knew it would be morning before many people received it, so I wrote "Good Morning Saints!" in the subject line. The message was so well received that I was encouraged to continue sending messages daily. Each day God gave me more encouraging words to send, and I sent each message with the same subject title, *Good Morning Saints!*

After about a week of doing this, I realized I had walked into my calling. The ministry to which God had called me wasn't limited to standing in a pulpit preaching, it encompassed my books, email, the web and social media as a way to reach, encourage and rescue His people. Eventually my tech savvy husband created me a website that we titled *Good Morning Saints!* And those who were touched by the book and the e-mail ministry connected on the website.

The GMS website featured my daily words of encouragement. It also promoted other ministries and enabled people near and far to encourage and pray for one another. It became very comforting to know that we had prayer partners all across the United States helping us to bombard heaven concerning our individual and corporate prayer request.

In speaking of prayer request (and I know I'm going down a rabbit trail, but I promise I'll be back), it was during this era in my life that I witnessed God answer a prayer request of my mom's that she waited eighteen long years to receive. When her second marriage, to my brother Philemon's father, ended in divorce, Mama spent many years trying to find her Mr. Right with a number of failed marriages. However, after eighteen years of singleness, desperately praying, and believing God for a good man to enter her life, God finally sent Mr. Right in 2003 in the form of my lovable stepdad Dewey Murray.

Dewey's cousin, who was a friend of my mom's supervisor at work, introduced the two. While living in Florida at the time, Dewey talked to my mom on the phone for about three months before actually meeting her

God's Girl

in person. Then when he finally arrived in Alabama for their first meeting, he came bearing a trunk load of gifts and a beautiful diamond ring, and he proposed to her on the spot. They had a lovely wedding ceremony in March 2004, after which I nicknamed my new stepdad "Papa Dewey."

Papa Dewey spoke some heartfelt words to me one day that I have always carried in my heart. He told me I was the best preacher's daughter he'd ever met. He said I was unlike others he knew who were actually embarrassments to their parents, but I was a PK who made my parents proud. Those were humbling words for me, and I knew I couldn't take any credit for it because it was all God.

After reading my book from cover to cover, Papa Dewey was so blessed by it that he mailed several copies to his family members in other states. I was happy to make him proud.

God had sent Papa Dewey into our lives at the perfect time, as six months before he and my mom wed, Erskine lost his dad, Erskine Sr., with whom he was very close. But God saw fit not to leave my husband fatherless, as not only was my dad a father to him, but Papa Dewey also became a father to him and a friend.

In June 2004, Erskine joined me in writing for the GMS website when God placed some words of encouragement on his heart that he was eager to share. His profound article entitled "Never Let Satan See You Sweat" encouraged readers never to allow negative words to escape their lips during tough situations. They needed only to stand still in those situations and trust God because He would always bring them through.

After receiving so much positive feedback from the messages that we shared via GMS, I decided to take the advice of several of my message recipients and put the messages together in a book. So, in 2004, the year after publishing my first book, Erskine and I published a second book, which we titled *Good Morning Saints! A Ministry of Godly Encouragement for Your Soul*.

It really felt good being used by God, as I've always wanted nothing more than to please Him with my life. It also felt great to be working in ministry with my husband, as it wasn't long after I accepted my calling into the ministry that he accepted his. He said he'd always known there was a calling on his life, but he tried so hard to ignore it. Now that I had accepted my call, it motivated him to accept his.

I figured if working in ministry was what our happily ever after consisted of, then that was fine with me because it wasn't so bad at all. I eagerly accepted this new ministry endeavor as another goal … the goal to do God's will.

Daddy and Mama, junior prom, 1967

Mama and Daddy, high school graduation, 1968

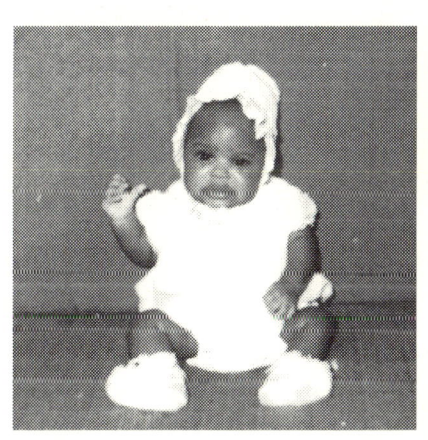

Me as a baby, 1969

Me and my brother William, 1971

Daddy and Mama Trish (early 1970s)

Me and siblings on dad's side (early 1980s)
Back: Franchesca, William, Tracy
Front: Dedrick, Triola, Chop, JaCarlos

Me and siblings on my mom's side.
William and Philemon (circa 1989)

Mt. Canaan's first building (circa 1980)

*Daddy and Mama Trish
(circa 1978)
Pastor and First Lady
of Mt. Canaan*

*William, Fran, and me at church
singing a song I wrote (mid-1980s)*

*My high school senior
picture taken in 1986*

*The Daniel Family
Erskine Sr., Marilyn, Erskine Jr., and
Karilyn aka Nikki (circa 1986)*

Our ironic graduation party, June 1987

Our first official photo together, June 1990

Marching down the aisle with Daddy, 1991

Wedding picture with our parents, 1991

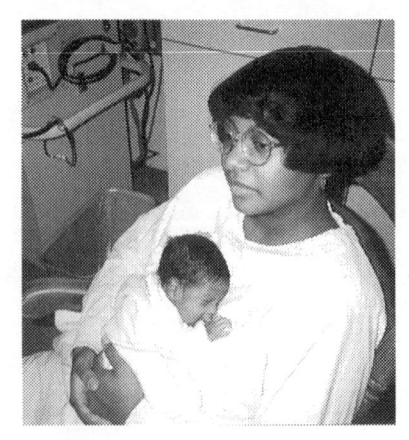

Me and my son, Brian, 1993

Erskine and Nikki, 1993

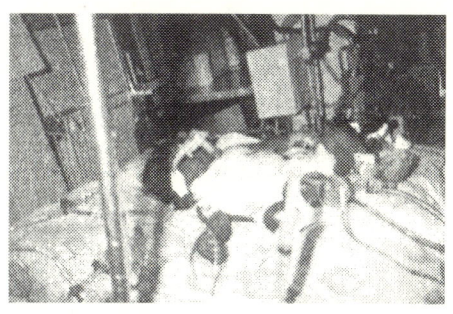

Brian, the day after heart surgery, 1993

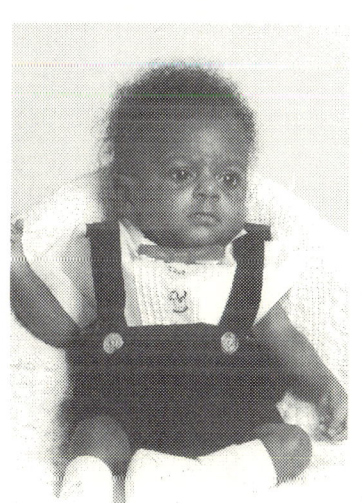

Brian at seven months, 1993

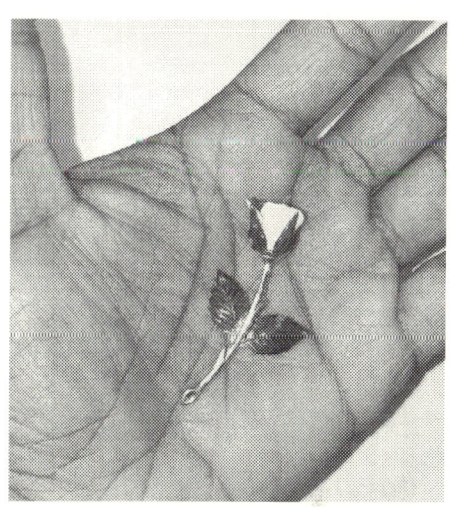

The pink rose pendant I found, 1993

Erskine and me with Pastor George Keys, 1994

Mt. Canaan's new debt-free building, 1994

Janay (on right) and Joycelyn, 2001

Jessica (in back) and Jasmine, 1997

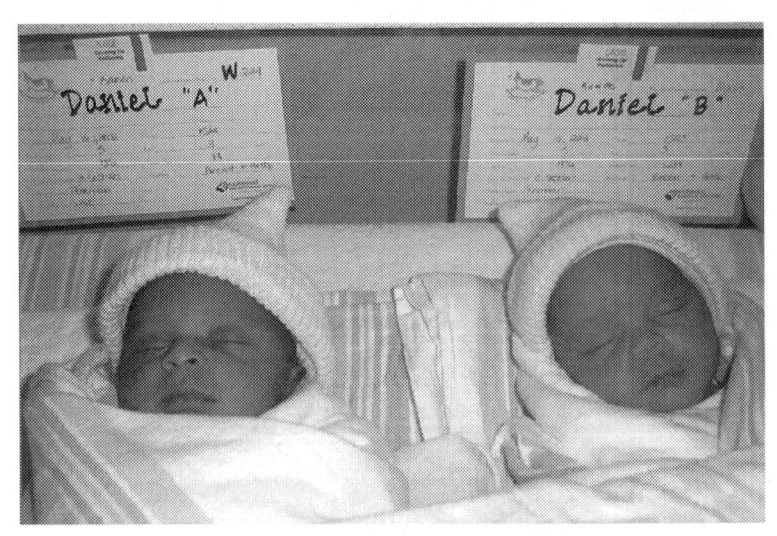

Twins, Karen and Kamille, 2002

Me and my roses, 2002

Me and Daddy with my first book, 2003

Good Morning Saints book, 2004

Mom and Papa Dewey, 2003

13

Busy Working for the Lord

> May the favor of the Lord our God rest on us; establish the work of our hands for us—yes, establish the work of our hands.
>
> —Psalm 90:17 (NIV)

I've worked in ministry all of my life. The choir, the usher board, the drama department, the television ministry, and more. And when I married, God blessed me with a husband who not only gave me the freedom to continue working in ministry but who also joined me in it. In Omaha, Nebraska, we both were members of the choir. And when I wrote and directed a couple of holiday dramas for our church there, Erskine was my right hand, aiding with production.

Upon moving back to Birmingham in 1994, Erskine joined, and I rejoined, Mt. Canaan. Soon after completing new members classes, we were eager to become active in the church once again, so we both joined the choir, and Erskine even joined the maintenance department, as God had bestowed troubleshooting and technical skills upon him, which he enjoyed using.

A year later, the media ministry recruited Erskine to help with the audio recording of Sunday services, and I was busy writing and directing a few holiday dramas for the drama ministry.

Erskine continued with the audio department for several years, also giving assistance to the in-house sound team and the video department.

God's Girl

But when I became full-term with our first daughter, I went on a long hiatus and stayed home to care for our growing family.

In 1999, four years after my hiatus, I decided to volunteer in the media ministry a few days a week as assistant editor of our church's television broadcast. But after a few months, I ended up back at home dealing with morning sickness from the pregnancy of our fourth daughter. It wasn't long before Erskine was joining me at home due to his diagnosis of Hodgkin's lymphoma in March 2000.

By November 2000, Erskine anxiously returned to light ministry work, and by 2004, he was the all-around technician at Mt. Canaan, helping to maintain every aspect of the media ministry. In addition, after creating our *Good Morning Saints* website, the church recruited both of us to revamp and maintain their website. During this time, Erskine was still working with the church's maintenance department, strictly dealing with the air-conditioning and heating aspect of it. Then, in late 2004, two years after the birth of our twins, I returned to the media ministry with him, aiding in media production and sales. These events lead to Erskine and me being appointed Mt. Canaan's media ministry directors in 2005, a position we held for seven years.

Erskine and I put our minds, hearts, and souls into the operation of Mt. Canaan's media ministry. Together we encompassed a spirit of excellence that was evident in everything we put our hands to. He was the technical mind behind the department, and I was the creative mind, and together, along with our faithful team of volunteers, we did awesome works for the Lord.

There were many duties that Erskine and I were responsible for performing or overseeing as the directors of the media ministry. They included the editing of my dad's Sunday morning sermons for broadcast on Mt. Canaan's *Spirit-Filled Life* television and radio broadcasts. Transferring edited video and audio to DVDs and CDs. Creating thirty- and sixty-second commercials advertising church events for television, radio, and in-house, maintaining a weekly work schedule for twenty-plus volunteer workers in video and audio production, directing camera operators in finding and taking camera shots for recording during services, and so much more.

At home, I created flyers and other paraphernalia for the church that advertised monthly events and special services. And while performing these tasks for our church, a few other churches and businesses took notice of our work and employed us to do small jobs for them. As a result, we began using O'Neal-Daniel Productions for more than just book production, as we began creating websites, videos, flyers, business cards, and other marketing tools for the public. However, the busier we became working for Mt. Canaan and ODP, the less time we put into our GMS web ministry, as it was hard trying to balance them all.

Because a representative from the media ministry was required to attend every church function, as most of the services required the assistance of microphones and many times video recording, our new position became very tasking on us. This was because many of our volunteers would only show up on Sunday mornings, leaving the faithful few of us to attend all the other church functions.

It was especially tasking because I tried to do all of this while caring for my large family, and Erskine suffered through it while having his primary job at the county to be present for each morning. But amazingly, we never quit because our hearts and minds were set on pleasing God, and everyone recognized this, even the devil. Thus, he sent more dark trials our way.

14

Staying Alive

For it is God who works in you to will and to act in order to fulfill his good purpose.

—Philippians 2:13 (NIV)

At some point in the later part of 2004, the sarcoidosis disease that I'd been diagnosed with started to flair up again. I would become breathless just walking very short distances, such as from the bedroom to the bathroom, which was adjacent to our bedroom. Therefore, I was always out of breath.

I remember once after returning home from picking up my oldest two daughters from school (ages six and seven), I didn't have enough energy to get my twin toddlers and two preschoolers out of their car seats and into the house, as was my daily ritual in the morning and afternoon.

On this particular day, I literally felt like a rag doll. When I pulled into the driveway, I got out of the van while telling my oldest girls to help their younger sisters into the house. They had never done this by themselves before, but I had no other choice but to allow them to try because I felt very close to passing out.

God enabled me to pull myself up two flights of stairs and into my bed, and I knew then that I had to make a doctor's appointment as soon as possible because I needed to stay alive for my children.

I spent a few months hopping from doctor to doctor trying to find someone who could get the disease under control without throwing more and more steroids at me. I finally met an Asian doctor, Dr. Chen, who was a devout Christian, and after explaining my difficulty in finding someone that could really help me, he kindly responded, "Let me try." Those words were so comforting to me.

Dr. Chen told me how he'd been successful at helping others with the disease and that he was sure he could help me. He was also concerned about the length of time I had been on steroids, explaining that he wanted to wean me off them, as they were known for having adverse affects on the bones and heart.

In January 2005, after our church's annual fast and with Dr. Chen's help, God did something miraculous for me. Not only was I weaned off the steroids, but also the inflammation in my lungs had greatly decreased, putting the sarcoidosis in remission.

I mentioned the church's annual fast because that year my dad decided to change our annual fast to the Daniel fast, which was derived from the book of Daniel in the Bible and involved eating only fruits, vegetables, and grains and drinking only 100 percent fruit juices and water for about three weeks. Today, I attribute my supernatural healing not only to the methods of my new doctor but also to the Daniel fast. Combined with the godly wisdom of my doctor, this yearly cleansing of my system with pure foods and liquids gave me another start at life. And despite some permanent scarring in my lungs, which limits my overall air capacity, I haven't had any new sarcoid flare-ups since 2005.

When we first moved into our new home in 2002, Erskine was bringing in extra income from his air-conditioning and heating business, which supplemented his paycheck and kept us afloat. But by 2004, he was working his business less and less, as he said it was wearing him out and he really didn't have a desire to do it anymore. A year later, it felt like we were literally drowning in debt because Erskine had completely stopped doing any side work, and we were relying on credit cards for almost everything, including food, gas, Christmas toys, and more. Though I constantly prayed that God would help us get out of debt, it felt as if we were only sinking deeper.

My husband wanted to be out of debt as much as I did, but he couldn't feel the sting of it the way I felt it because I was the one who kept the budget book, and I knew what our figures looked like. I even started feeling guilty, as if our debt was my fault because I kept the checkbook and I did all of the shopping for the family. However, everything I purchased was based on need and not greed, so it was really out of my hands. But regardless, I kept this information from Erskine for as long as possible, trying not to stress him. Then when I couldn't hold it any longer, we finally sat down and talked about it, afterward we both got on our knees, and my husband took the opportunity to talk to God from a sincere heart. That's when our situation began to change. If I had known God would answer my husband's request so quickly, I would have told him about the issue much sooner.

Early one morning, a bill collector called our home in an effort to collect a credit card payment. I explained to him our dilemma, and because he recognized our past credit history was good, he suggested a solution to our problem. He gave me the number to a credit counseling service that could help us get out of debt. When I called the counseling service, they explained to me that if we joined their program and diligently made the required monthly payments, we could be debt free in five years, but only if we did not make any new debt during our time in the program. That was music to my ears. Erskine and I joined the program and experienced much relief by having a tentative date in which we would reach our goal of being debt free. We set our eyes on the prize and faithfully made our payments, and we were not very worried about the temptation to form new debt because, by now, we were sick of debt.

The only concern I had was the temptation every now and then to use a credit card for food or gas if we felt we had no other choice. But Erskine made a declaration by faith that from that point on, no matter how tempting it was, we would only use our debit card for food and gas, and not a credit card. He also declared that the money we needed would always be in our bank account and we would never have to use a credit card for such purchases again. God miraculously backed him up!

As the months passed, Erskine grew tired and breathless and there was a lot of swelling in his face and abdomen. Then he started having a weird feeling in his chest. He said it reminded him of the feeling he had when he was first diagnosed with cancer. That frightened us. He made an appointment to see his oncologist, and after being examined, there was good news and bad news. The doctor said his cancer was still in remission, but there was something going on with his heart. So the receptionist made him an appointment to see a cardiologist. In June 2005, about the same time that we were appointed as directors over the church's media ministry, we received disheartening news from the cardiologist concerning Erskine's heart. He was in congestive heart failure, and it was due to one of the chemotherapy medicines he had received for the Hodgkin's lymphoma back in 2000. It seemed the same medicine that healed his cancer had damaged his heart.

His ejection fraction, which is the measure of the heart's ability to pump, was between 20 and 25 percent. Normal is 50 percent. The doctor told us that although medicine could help his heart, his heart would not get better, only worse. He said that eventually Erskine would have to find an easier job or come home on disability. But Erskine was only thirty-six years old. He didn't want to think about being disabled at such a young age. He had a wife and six children to provide for. He wasn't ready to retire yet; he was too busy working for God and working toward a goal of debt freedom. This news was hurtful to us, but by now we had grown accustomed to receiving such news, so we did what we knew best: we put our trust in God and tried to go on with life.

In 2006, our church began offering a minister's training class whereby those who felt the call of God upon their life could obtain nine months of training. Erskine and I not only joined this class because of the calling we felt on our lives, but as the directors of the media ministry, we were required to video it for future reference. So in 2007, twenty years after graduating high school together, he and I graduated the minister's training class together, complete with caps, gowns, and diplomas. The class of 1987 was now the class of 2007.

Later that fall, our twins started kindergarten. They were the last of the Daniel clan to leave the nest for seven hours a day, and they attended the same elementary school their sisters attended. Because my life had been absorbed with caring for my girls since 1995 when Jessica first made her debut into the world, I was not very sure about what to do with myself at this new point in life. But by the spring of 2008, I made up my mind to go back to college and finish the early childhood development degree that I was working on before I married. So I got up one morning and drove half an hour to the community college that I used to attend and inquired about what steps I needed to take for reenrollment.

After running into a few stumbling blocks that made me question whether or not I should go forward with my plan, I jumped back into my van and embarked upon my thirty-minute journey home, questioning God as to what He would have me to do. As I drove, I thought about how far the college was located from the city where my kids attended school. I didn't feel very comfortable being a half hour away from them in case their teacher were to ever call saying they were sick or something. But at the same time, I really desired to do something productive with my life now that I wasn't needed at home as much. I really needed God to tell me what I should do.

Having had no major problems with my van leading up to this day, about three minutes before my freeway exit, it started smoking unexpectedly. And as soon as I pulled it over to the side of the road, it gave up and died, and we had to have it towed to a mechanic, who said we needed a brand-new motor. Rather than become angry about this misfortune, I decided to accept it as God's answer to my prayer. Reenrolling at this school to finish my early childhood development degree was not His will for me. His will for me included ministry.

Never having had any formally training in the television editing work that I performed weekly for Mt. Canaan, I felt God leading me to enroll in the radio and television broadcasting short certificate program at Lawson State Community College, which was only twenty minutes away from my kids' school. Because I only had watch-and-do training from my husband, my friend Joyce, and my brother Dedrick, I was excited about receiving formal training from this college, which I hoped would enable me to do even more for the ministry.

Going to Lawson State turned out to be one of the best decisions I'd ever made, as I was blessed to gain knowledge in television production, radio production, and even filmmaking, which sharpened the skills I already had. And just before graduating in May 2009 with a 4.0 grade point average, my professor surprised me with the Radio and Television Broadcasting Producer Award.

After driving my dad's car back and forth to school for the entire year due to our van breaking down, we finally acquired a new vehicle just before I graduated. We purchased a beautiful, fully equipped, eight-passenger SUV that I happily accepted as a graduation gift from God.

In 2007, Erskine received a good report from his doctor concerning his heart. This was surprising because, as I mentioned earlier, he was originally told that his heart condition couldn't be cured and that it would get progressively worse. Now the doctor was baffled because all of a sudden Erskine's heart was back to normal, resulting in the doctor taking him off some of his heart medications. That was wonderful news! But then, one night after dinner, our hope of healing turned frightful.

After eating a deli sandwich late one evening, Erskine went to use the bathroom before retiring for the evening. In distress he began calling my name and asking me to bring him a wastebasket. I jumped up from the bed, snatched up my bedroom wastebasket, opened the bathroom door, and sat the wastebasket in front of him. As soon as I shut the door and walked away, I heard a loud thump. I panicked as I ran back to the door and when I opened it I saw him lying on the floor unconscious.

After screaming his name and not getting a response, I had a brief moment of confusion as I tried to figure out whether to try to get him up or call 911. I ended up calling 911, and as I was speaking to them, he started waking up. By the time the ambulance arrived, he was fully awake, and we were discussing what happened.

He said he asked for the wastebasket because he suddenly felt nauseous

God's Girl

and thought he would have to throw up in it. But as soon as he leaned over to do so, he became lightheaded, and then everything went black.

After taking his vital signs, the paramedics left and I took him to the emergency room. But after spending a couple of hours there, they couldn't give us a valid reason for his nausea and fainting spell other than it must have been something he ate. Not knowing why this had happened, for several weeks afterward I watched my husband closely, all the while praying that it would never happen again. Erskine was just as nervous as I was, and for a while, he stopped eating deli sandwiches out of fear. But I truly believe that fainting spell had nothing to do with the deli sandwich and everything to do with his heart.

Sure enough, in 2008, the year after receiving a good report about his heart, Erskine received another bad report. For the second time, he was in congestive heart failure. This time the doctor decided to run tests to determine whether there was a blockage because he couldn't figure out why Erskine had suddenly taken a turn for the worse. When they found no blockage, they put him back on all of the heart medicines they had previously stopped.

Erskine was very torn by this, and he fought many mental battles trying not to become angry or bitter with God. One day I told him, "God is not going to give you a healing and then turn around and take it back. He is not that kind of God." Those words seemed to lift his spirits, and together we began recalling the many times the devil had tried to take his life and how God had delivered him from every snare.

To begin with, he grew up with severe asthma. I was told that his asthma attacks were so severe that he nearly died each time.

Then the doctor who was treating his asthma put him on a strong medicine called Theophylline that, known for its adverse side effects, grew to a toxic level in Erskine's bloodstream and almost destroyed his kidneys.

Then there was the chicken pox virus that almost turned deadly because of his weak immune system. Thick, clustered blisters had formed in his head, mouth, and throat, requiring his maternal grandma, Fannie Wren, whom we affectionately called Grandma Fannie, to scrap scabs from his throat and mouth daily in an effort to help him swallow.

And as I mentioned in an earlier chapter, in October 1995, Erskine was in a bad accident during Hurricane Opal that flipped the van he was driving. The van was totaled, but amazingly, he crawled out with only a few scratches on his arm.

Lastly, in 2000, God delivered him from the Hodgkin's lymphoma cancer that had invaded his body. So, we felt that if God had allowed him to live through all of these mishaps, surely He could deliver him from heart disease. Armed with that encouragement, Erskine cheered up and continued believing God for the healing of his heart.

Erskine and I both felt that our obedience in giving our tithes and offerings, as well as the sowing of our gifts, talents, and time into the ministry were what was keeping us alive. While he was dealing with the heart disease and cancer remission, I dealt with the limited airflow in my lungs and the sarcoidosis remission. But thankfully, though we both had underlying health issues, neither of us really looked like what we were going through. We actually looked like a picture of health. That was all God.

Not taking our call into ministry nor our position as directors of the church's media ministry lightly, we never allowed our physical problems to hinder the jobs we were required to perform for God. For instance, we not only showed up for nearly every church service to perform media duties, but we spent many personal hours in the church's media room creating promotional videos to advertise the church's monthly events. This, many times, resulted in us pulling all-nighters at the church. We'd pack food and bring the kids, and they would bring their toys or homework to keep them busy. And when they were sleepy, they'd lie on the pews, cover themselves with prayer cloths, and go to sleep. In our efforts to be faithful to God and His work, the church had literally become our second home.

As if we were not already doing enough, the itch to write another book came upon me, as I had not written one since the GMS book in 2004. However, I didn't know what I should write about, so I asked God to show me. One day, He brought back to my remembrance a desire of mine from years ago when my oldest daughters were very young. At that time, I had a desire to write a children's book.

Back then, my oldest sister, Triola, gave me the idea of taking my girls to the library to sign them up for the summer reading program. We would check out lots of books then bring them home, and I'd read each book to them. I enjoyed reading to them just as much as they enjoyed hearing me read. I enjoyed it so much that I tried to write a children's book of my own during that time, but there was one issue: I couldn't find an illustrator.

But in 2010, after sharing my most recent book idea with my girls and mentioning that I needed an illustrator, one of my eight-year-old twins, Karen, who had been drawing since she was three, asked, "Mama, can I do it?" I thought that was a brilliant idea, and I felt so blessed that God had given me another opportunity to accomplish my heart's desire, and He even allowed me to birth my own illustrator.

Beginning our project in the summer of 2010, Karen and I titled our book *God Made You Special*. It would be a book filled with encouraging words, illustrations, and scriptures to help all children discover just how special they were to God. During every free moment, we worked on the book, and any illustration I requested from Karen, she proudly produced. We made an awesome mother-daughter team for the Lord!

The gifts and talents Erskine harnessed gave him the ability to work in many different capacities within Mt. Canaan. Basically, he worked all over the place. For instance, on a Sunday morning, you might see him in the media room recording a service, duplicating discs, or troubleshooting a piece of equipment. And later, you might catch him setting up one of the television cameras or giving pointers to another camera operator. Before long, you might find him outside working on an air-conditioning unit, after which, you might run across him in the fellowship hall, sweating profusely while giving some type of audio assistance to the youth ministry. Then he might head upstairs and stop by the main office to troubleshoot a problem with one of the secretaries' computers or the office printer. And before you know it, he'll be up in the balcony again, aiding the sanctuary audio team with the sanctuary sound, just before he heads into the media room to start the process all over again. That's what a typical Sunday morning looked like for my husband, and it had been many years since the two of us and our children had actually sat down together as a family during a church service, as sitting still for too long was uncomfortable for him. He was all about work.

Erskine spent nearly seven days a week at the church fixing something, as he couldn't resist a challenge, especially one that someone else may have deemed impossible. Our friend Chrys McDaniel gave him a befitting nickname, *The Church MacGyver*. But I called him *Mr. Millionaire* because as busy as he stayed for the Lord, I had no doubt that God would one day bless him with abundant finances, especially since he worked so hard to take care of his large family while in poor health, which proved very difficult for him at times.

Erskine and I worked very well together because we gave each other purpose. My creative gifts and talents gave purpose to his technical gifts and talents, and together we used them in the ministry. The more we worked for God, the more our vision increased as we were filled with visions of doing even greater works for God in the future. We also envisioned ourselves as future philanthropists, spreading funds wherever there was a need. We lived by the principle that if we took care of God's business, God would take care of ours, and God always kept His end of the bargain. That's why we remained so close to Him, because He remained close to us.

As you can imagine, our lives were very busy and had become all work and no play. Thank God, none of that busyness tore us apart. It actually made us closer. But I must be honest. We did begin to grow weary of the load that was upon us in the media ministry. And it became increasingly difficult to be thrilled about going to church every Sunday because, for us, church meant work. However, we hung in there, all the while working and praying, hoping that God would hear our prayers and bring about a change that would give us some relief.

God's Girl

In 2010, life started looking up for us financially as we completed the credit-counseling program. But we didn't feel as debt free as we thought we would because other needs had surfaced.

Not only were we paying on the new SUV, but after my graduation from Lawson's Radio and Television certificate program in 2009, we were both excited about me putting my skills to use in our business. So Erskine purchased for me a high-quality camera, computer, and editing software in an effort to take O'Neal-Daniel Productions to the next level.

Then, because he was feeling better physically due to his body adjusting to the heart meds, he started working his We'll Fix It, A/C and Heating business again. But by this time, he no longer had his work van because we had given it away to a friend, so he weighed down the trunk and backseat of his car with the heavy tools of his trade. After hearing him mention his desperate need for a truck repeatedly, I began searching the Internet, hoping to find one we could afford that would not set us back. After about two weeks of searching, God blessed us to find a great deal on a black, four-door pickup truck. To Erskine, it was like Christmas in July, and he spent months customizing it, trying to get it exactly the way he wanted. It blessed me tremendously to see my husband so happy. And in my heart, I felt this truck was one of God's ways of rewarding him for his deep devotion to the ministry. But sadly, in the midst of our happiness, there was a terrible storm brewing on the horizon.

15

What's Going On?

> But know this, that in the last days grievous times shall come.
> —2 Timothy 3:1 (ASV)

"Living under an open Heaven in 2011" was the new year slogan my dad suggested for the New Year's Eve service that would usher in 2011. Daddy had a habit of coming up with slogans for each coming year as a way to excite and encourage his congregation. But this time, his words were more than just a catchy slogan, as they actually became sheer prophecy.

And speaking of prophecy, about a week after the New Year's Eve service, Dr. Pat McKinstry from Toledo, Ohio, visited our church and delivered to us a profound word from God. At the start of her anointed message, she explained to us the biblical representation of the number eleven, stating that it represented confusion. I had never heard of this, and to be honest, I questioned her words. But it wasn't too many days after her visit that those words began to manifest, making me aware that Dr. McKinstry had been sent by God to prophetically warn us that confusion, tragedy, and calamity were indeed on the way.

Just before the close of our 11:00 a.m. church service on Sunday, January 23, 2011, my dad asked everyone to remain seated, as he had something heavy on his heart that he needed to share with us. Daddy explained how he'd felt the spirit of death hovering and how he had a strong urge to pray over us. Some of my siblings and I assumed the spirit Daddy was referring to resulted from the severe illness of our sister Triola.

God's Girl

Tree had suffered from years of high blood pressure and even had a heart attack back in 2004, which resulted in a quadruple bypass. She later developed severe kidney failure, which resulted in a diagnosis of a rare and deadly disease called Calciphylaxis. This disease, which derived from an excessive build-up of calcium in her blood, caused her to have extremely large skin ulcers on her legs. Though she fought this disease as hard as she could, many times it seemed she would lose the fight, and by January 2011, many of us had given up hope, as we felt it was only a matter of time before she would make her transition to glory.

The day after Daddy's prayer, Monday, January 24, the spirit of death actually struck, but it shocked us all because it didn't come in the direction that we were looking.

That Monday morning began as any normal day for my brother Dedrick and his family. Dedrick went to his job as a truck driver, and his wife, Evette, went to her job as a high school science teacher. But just before the end of her workday, Evette, who was a beautiful picture of health, suddenly collapsed and was rushed to the nearest hospital where she died the following day, sadly leaving behind two young sons, Evann Bruce O'Neal and Isaiah Tinker ages one and ten. And just as Dr. Pat McKinstry had predicted, there was definitely confusion in the air.

This tragedy left my brother and everyone who loved Evette terribly distraught as we tried to make sense of her shocking death. And what was even more shocking was how, weeks earlier, she had posted my dad's words, "Living under an open Heaven in 2011" on the wall of her classroom, and now it seemed that *open heaven* had invited her in.

Less than a month later, we were grieving another death. A well-known music minister in the city of Birmingham, Minister Dewayne Davis, who was a great friend to my dad and stepmom and the family of Mt. Canaan as a whole, had been invited into that open heaven as well. Then, a month later, death struck again.

Deacon Glenn Johnson and his wife, JoAnn, who were like an uncle and aunt to my siblings and me, were faithful and well-loved members of Mt. Canaan for over thirty years. Though we all knew Deacon Glenn was experiencing a few health challenges, he never carried himself as if his life were in jeopardy. So it took the entire body of Mt. Canaan by surprise when on Thursday morning, March 31, we received word that he had passed away.

The next month, the death cycle continued as news spread concerning the unexpected death of Frank "Bozo" Myers, a well-known sound engineer in the city of Birmingham. Having performed hundreds of sound jobs for Mt. Canaan and several other churches and businesses within the area, the impact of this young man's death was felt heavily throughout Birmingham. However, nothing could have prepared us for the tragedy that erupted four days later.

I dropped my girls off at their schools on the morning of April 27, and the climate was rather warm and humid, which was a sure sign of an impending tornado. Not long after I returned home, I received calls from several of the girls saying their schools had no power. Because of to the lack of power and the tornado threat, the kids were released early, and by midday, Erskine had been sent home early as well.

We kept an eye on the news for much of the day, hoping that the tornado would just pass over us. I remember my mom had cooked a pot of pinto beans for my family that day, and two of my girls and I went over to her house to pick them up. We had no fear of being caught in the storm because the weather was still calm, and we assumed it would all be over shortly.

However, while at my mom's house, we noticed it was getting very windy outside, and the girls and I made jokes of eating pinto beans and watching the tornado go by. But minutes later, it was no joking matter as the sky started turning dark and the wind grew even stronger while knocking around the furniture in my mom and pop's backyard. So we got our beans and hurried home.

Not long after arriving home, we heard the weatherman on TV say the tornado was in Tuscaloosa, Alabama, and that it was headed our way. As I watched the live footage of that massive tornado ripping through Tuscaloosa, I began yelling to my husband and kids, "Let's go! Let's go!

It's coming!" So we all ran and took cover in the basement. My mom and pop must have packed up to leave their house just as soon as we left them because when we took cover in the basement, they were ringing our doorbell. Then other family members started calling our phones trying to warn us that the tornado had been spotted in our area. A few seconds later, we heard the weatherman announce that the tornado was near us and for us to take shelter immediately. Suddenly, the power went out.

As the majority of us took shelter in the basement, strangely, Erskine, Papa Dewey, and Janay, stood outside trying to get a glimpse of the tornado. They didn't get their glimpse, but they did hear a strange whishing noise in the distance, and Erskine said his ears started to pop. Realizing that this was probably the tornado, they ran inside.

When the storm passed, the sun returned, shinning so bright as if nothing had ever happened. And on our street, all was well, except for the power outage and some fallen debris. Parents came out of their homes to assess the damage, and kids began playing in the street as usual. We all assumed the tornado had passed over us and that life was about to go back to normal. But that was far from the truth.

In the distance, we began to hear siren after siren. We heard so many sirens until we grew worried. Without power, we had no televisions or radios to receive updates, so we had no clue as to what was going on. After my mom and pop went back home, Erskine and the girls and I jumped in the SUV and followed the noise of the sirens to see what was going on.

We could only get about a mile and a half up the road before we realized the police had blocked off several roads. We went to a nearby store parking lot where we saw people congregating. After spotting someone we knew, we questioned her about what was going on. She shared with us the catastrophic things she had heard, and we left the parking lot totally distraught. Some of our girls were in tears. Not wanting to go back home to a dark house, we headed to Mama Doll's house just to find out they were in the dark as well.

Throughout the rest of the evening, we received disturbing reports of people who had been terribly injured or killed or who had lost their homes in the storm. And we worried about friends and family whom we had not heard from that we knew lived in those severely affected areas. When we finally returned home from Mama Doll's, the girls were too afraid to sleep in their own bedrooms, so they slept on the floor in our bedroom, as we all feared that more storms would come during the night.

Power in our area was out for about three to four days, making an already troubling situation even more difficult, and the severity of damage in our city gave way to looting. As a result of the looting, the National Guard was called in to help. Residents were required to show proper ID in order to enter the city, and we were under a strict curfew. Our lives were disrupted for such a long period. Even the schools took awhile to resume, at least two weeks or more.

According to WBRC.com, several deadly tornadoes ripped through a number of Alabama cities that day. The storm also tore through six other states, but Alabama was hit the hardest with the largest tornado categorized as an F4. Hundreds of deaths and injuries were reported from this massive outbreak of storms. And this tragedy was just another manifestation of the confusion we had been warned about at the beginning of 2011.

Our daughter, Jessica, was about to turn sixteen the first week in May. And before the storm, I had been in the midst of planning her formal sweet sixteen birthday celebration. However, after the storm, I wasn't sure if I should continue with the party, as so many people's lives had been disrupted by the storm and I felt they may not be in a party mood. But my friend Lisa Woodall, whose home had been destroyed by the storm, encouraged me to continue with my plans because she felt it would bring some needed sunshine into her and her daughter's dark situation. So on Friday, May 6, we took a few moments to separate ourselves from the problems at hand and made time for eating, laughing, dancing, and fellowshipping. But a month later, the confusion returned.

Due to complications of a 2004 gastric bypass surgery, Erskine's only sibling, Karilyn Nichole Daniel, affectionately known as "Nikki", was admitted into the hospital in June 2011 in very poor condition. At thirty-two years of age, Nikki was suffering from Pellagra. Pellagra, which is

God's Girl

known as the "disease of the four Ds," diarrhea, dermatitis, dementia, and death, according to MedicineNet.com, is caused by the deficiency of niacin, which is a B-complex vitamin. Nikki's body was no longer able to absorb this or any other nutrients. Food literally went right through her. As a result, her health began declining rapidly.

Then in June, while at church working in the media room, Erskine and I received a phone call from Mama Doll informing us of the sudden death of her sister-in-law Sandra Jean Wren. Aunt Jean was the wife of Erskine's uncle General M. Wren. They were the ones who graciously paid our house note when Erskine was sick in 2000. We always admired Uncle Mac and Aunt Jean's relationship because though they had been married for nearly fifty years, they still showed the same love and affection for one another as if they were young lovebirds. Our hearts were so heavy for Uncle Mac.

A week or so later, in early July, Nikki was rushed to the ER where she coded three times and eventually fell into a coma that lasted a little over a week. Seeing his sister in this dreadful state took a toll on my husband, as I remember opening the door to the restroom in the ICU waiting room and finding him sitting on the floor sobbing.

After spending nearly a month and a half in the hospital suffering from infection, kidney complications, and other life-threatening issues, Nikki passed away at the age of thirty-two on August 17, leaving behind three beautiful young daughters, Joelle, Kadejah, and Jori Daniel, ages ten, nine and five. During her sickness, Erskine and I promised Nikki that we'd do our best to look after her babies.

On September 27, the death cycle continued as we received news of yet another unexpected death in the body of Mt. Canaan. It was our good friend Anthony "Bookie" Young. Bookie had been killed instantly in a motorcycle accident during the night, and our hearts ached deeply for his wife, Tracey, and their two young sons. After Bookie's death, nearly everyone in our church had the same unspoken thought. *Who will be next?*

In October, death visited my side of the family once again when my Grannie lost her sister, Thelma Harris. Aunt Thelma was my grannie's best friend and last living sister. She and Grannie had helped raise each other's children, so, to my dad and his siblings, Aunt Thelma was much more than an aunt; she was a second mom. Having fought cancer much longer than doctors had anticipated, Aunt Thelma gracefully bowed out on October 28, 2011.

On November 10, our phones rang again with another report of death among our church members. Patricia Tate, one of our dedicated ushers and faithful members who had also been a member of Mt. Canaan for over thirty years, lost her battle with cancer. During her illness, Sister Tate never allowed cancer to keep her from church. And she even continued to wear her beautiful smile regardless of how she may have been feeling. This is why we were greatly taken aback upon hearing of her sudden passing because she never looked like what she was going through.

As the end of 2011 approached, we desperately hoped that the spirit of death and mass confusion would be exiting with it.

The end of November ushered in the kick-off of Impact 2011. And during the second night of the service, my dad felt compelled to ask his entire family to stand before the congregation with him. Grateful to still be alive, well, and standing together as a family, considering all we'd gone through that year, he asked us to give God a great praise as the musicians played.

As everyone broke out in his or her own style of praise, Erskine began jumping straight up. And with each jump, it seemed he went a little higher and a little higher until he was jumping higher than I've ever seen him jump before. In fact, I had never seen him jump before, so this was very surprising, especially considering he had heart disease.

That was an unforgettable rendezvous Erskine had with the Lord that night. But I don't know if it had something to do with losing his sister or if his spirit sensed what was lying up ahead for us as the confusion that we were wishing away actually continued the following year.

16

Something's Coming

> Surely the Sovereign Lord does nothing without revealing his plan to his servants the prophets.
> —Amos 3:7 (NIV)

In His Word, God often used prophecy, dreams, and visions to reveal His plan for the lives of His people. It is only in hindsight that I've realized God had been revealing the life-altering plan he had for my family via prophecies, dreams, and visions throughout the years. It was a plan that would begin to unfold at the beginning of 2012 and by the end of the year would reach its startling climax.

God's first efforts of revealing His upcoming plan were through a prophetess back in the summer of 1995. Mt. Canaan hosted a youth conference in which Dr. Angel Smith from Detroit, Michigan, was the guest minister. During the service, Dr. Smith had a prayer line that Erskine and I stood in as he held our daughter Jessica. As we approached her, Dr. Smith looked at our little family and said, "God says He can trust you." Then she anointed and prayed for us. Those words stuck with me for many years, as it made me proud that God said He could trust us. But I assumed He meant He could trust us in the area of paying our tithe and offering and just living a life that was pleasing to Him. I had no idea His trust in us would include so much more.

Dr. Todd Hall, a prophet from Orlando, Florida, who has spoken at several of our church's annual Impact conferences, decided to have an impromptu two-day revival at our church during the first week of January 2010. On this trip, he brought along his daughter, Chelaé Cummings, who was visiting our church for the first time, as she was his product manager.

On the first night of service, Chelaé made her way into the media room and introduced herself to my husband and me. Then she questioned us about the methods of video editing and graphics we used. The next morning, as I went to do some editing at the church, she stopped by to see me, and we continued our discussion of video editing, graphics, and more as she had an interest because she was also her dad's video editor. I shared with her all the information I could and even gave her some of our graphic animation software and after our long conversation where we even discussed personal issues, we exchanged contact information in an effort to stay in touch. I guess this young lady felt I had done something very special for her because Prophet Hall later mentioned our meeting in his message that evening.

That night would be Prophet Hall's last service. Erskine had to work late and therefore was too tired to come, so the kids and I went to church without him. During the service, the prophet broke away from his message and asked my dad "Where's your daughter who's been helping my daughter?" Of course I was working in the media room, which was located in the balcony, so my dad yelled for me to step out of the room for a minute, and I came out and stood in one of the balcony aisles. Prophet Hall then said to me, "I want to first say thank you for helping my daughter, and I know she said she shared some things with you, but you blessed her. And out of all of the churches we've been to, she's never said this, but she could have gotten help out of all of them, but I think you and her talked together better, that's all. I think she started talking better and got better results. But you helped my daughter, and the Lord told me to tell you this, because you did: 'Tell her stay encouraged cause I'm about to give her, her own cable network.'"

After the congregation gave a thunderous applause, the prophet told me, "The Lord said it's going to start on the Internet first, and then it's going to grow." At that moment, I was lost in praise, and the prophet encouraged those around me to help me. Then he continued with his prophecy. "That's right. Watch and see. It's going to look like professional Internet television. That's where you are going to be first. And then a cable network is going to call and say, 'Who does this job?' The Lord says, 'She's been trying, and she's been testing.' But the Lord says, 'I'm about to make her tap into something. The phone is going to ring.' The Lord says, as happy as you are and love your father, 'You were getting tired.' You didn't even want to say it, but you were getting real, real tired."

Prophet Hall saw me nodding my head several times when he mentioned how tired I was. I did so because his words were true. I was very tired. In fact, that was my and Erskine's main topic of discussion lately, how tired we both were and how we needed God to work something out where we would not be doing this job forever. Then he said to me, "But the Lord said, 'I gotcha. You are about to turn into favorville.'"

After another thunderous applause from the congregation, the prophet began speaking more words to me, which left a greater impression on me than his previous words. He said, "And you know what? I'm laughing and this is going to sound like I'm a false prophet because the Lord is taking me back somewhere I don't want to go. He said to tell you regardless. I don't know you, whether you are married or not, but God said, 'The one who should have married you missed a millioneiress.'"

It wasn't the prophet's words about me being a millioneiress that stuck with me, but rather it was the words, "The one who should have married you." And I began wondering immediately, *Who is he referring to? Who was it that should have married me?*

To be spotlighted and given those overwhelming words of prophecy that night was truly a humbling experience, and I immediately shared it with my husband when I arrived home. But, being the deep thinker that I am, I had many questions about the prophecy as time progressed. For instance, why would God choose the night that my husband was absent to give me such a word? Erskine rarely missed a service. And even more, he and I were a team. We worked together for God. And we both had grown weary of the load that was upon us, so shouldn't God be considering rewarding us both? Yet the prophet talked only to me and never once mentioned my husband. And he even went as far as saying, "I don't know you, whether you are married or not." God knew I was married. Why didn't He tell the prophet? Why did He inform him of those other things but skipped that important piece of information?

And concerning the prophet's words about the one who should have married me, I still wanted to know who the man was in my past to which he had referred. For the rest of the night, I flipped through the pages of my mind, trying to figure out who that could have been. I searched my brain thoroughly, trying to recall all of the boyfriends I had before I married Erskine. There weren't many. And out of those few, I don't ever recall seriously discussing marriage with either of them. Then I wondered if he could have been referring to my high school sweetheart, Chris Hicks, because that was the longest relationship I'd had before Erskine. But Chris and I were only kids, and therefore we had a long way to go before considering marriage. I was stumped. Who in the world was God speaking of?

I knew Prophet Hall was not a false prophet because I'd witnessed too many of his prophecies manifest in the lives of others. Also, I trusted that my dad would not bring in a false prophet year after year to lie to God's people. So, with that assurance, I stopped torturing myself with the questions and just tried to focus on God's promise, knowing that the answers would be revealed in His time.

On another night in 2010, I was abruptly awakened out of my sleep by fear. For some strange reason, a heavy spirit of fear had gripped me, and I couldn't go back to sleep. I don't remember having a bad dream or anything; I just woke up afraid.

Strangely, I started to worry that someone might break into our home while we slept. However, no one had ever broken into our home before, so I couldn't understand why I felt the need to worry about such a thing. But I couldn't stop worrying, and I grew increasingly fearful by the minute.

During all of this, I never once bothered my sleeping husband. I just lay there beside him tossing and turning in deep anxiety.

I finally asked God to remove the spirit of fear that was trying to control my mind. I prayed that He would give me peace and help me go back to sleep. Then suddenly, He gave me a vision. He allowed me to see an aerial view of our home. Encamped around our home were angels, very tall angels who were posted on each side of the house. Seeing them gave me a peace that rocked me back to sleep. But in the days that followed, I often wondered about the fearful spirit that had suddenly gripped me. Even while laying next to my husband, the strong man of our house, the protector of our family, I was still fearful, and I wanted to know why. But that was another question that God would eventually answer in His timing.

Along with the confusion that erupted in 2011 came a number of foretelling dreams and visions among my girls and me. Strangely, at different times during that year, my oldest two daughters and I had dreams where we saw ourselves taking care of a baby. I couldn't understand why we were all dreaming about babies because there was no way I could conceive another child as I'd recently had a partial hysterectomy, whereby my uterus was removed in December 2010 due to fibroid tumors and sarcoid nodules. And I had no reason to suspect either of my girls was pregnant. So what was God trying tell us?

Also, my daughter Jasmine had a dream where she saw the eight of us sitting at the dining room table eating dinner when all of a sudden her dad passed out, falling out of his chair and onto the floor. She said she and her sisters panicked, but I stayed calm, reassuring them that their dad would be okay. She said the part of the dream that really stood out to her was how amazingly calm I had remained.

At another point during that year, I had a vision of my husband coming home early from work saying he didn't feel very well. It reminded me of the vision I had back in late 1999 or early 2000, just before we found out he had cancer, when I saw him come home early from work telling me he'd lost his job. I hoped that this would not be a similar situation.

Then in October, I had a dream that stayed on my mind for several months. In the dream, I saw a doctor in a white lab coat standing alongside Erskine and me. It appeared we were taking a photo while holding a poster-sized check for $100,000. I wanted so badly to know the meaning behind that dream. After sharing it with Mama Doll, we both concluded that it probably had something to do with the Karilyn's death and a potential lawsuit, as she had just died two months earlier from complications of a gastric bypass surgery. Though I wasn't 100 percent convinced, I accepted that explanation as the dream's meaning for lack of any other explanation.

Lastly, as I mentioned several chapters back, ever since I was a child, I unexpectedly saw random people's faces in my mind. After sharing this with my mom one day, she told me, "Whenever that happens, just pray for the person," which I then made a habit of doing. Well, one day while lying across the bed in December 2011, it happened again. There was a face before me, and this time it frightened me because the face was mine. I had never had that to happen. Quite naturally, I prayed for myself, but at the same time I wondered, *Why am I praying for me? What's about to happen to me?* Well, God would later reveal this to me along with the answers to all of my other questions, in 2012.

17
Blindsided

Have mercy on me, my God, have mercy on me, for in you I take refuge. I will take refuge in the shadow of your wings until the disaster has passed.

—Psalm 57:1 (NIV)

January 2012–May 2012

During the second week of January 2012, our church embarked on its annual consecration with the Daniel fast. Fasting from meat, starches, sweets, and processed foods for three weeks was not always very easy, but we never failed to make this yearly sacrifice because of our sincere love and appreciation for God.

Usually, by the end of the second week, Erskine would become very grumpy and easily agitated, as he would begin missing his meat. But this year was different. Surprisingly, he entered the third week of the fast like a champion, never complaining about what he couldn't eat and even remaining in a pleasant mood. I told him I was so proud of him. However, toward the end of that week, rather than complaining about what he couldn't eat, he began complaining of an aggravating pain in his back that wouldn't go away. The following words are his account of that awful experience.

"This time, coming off of our annual fast at Mt. Canaan Full Gospel Church (in January 2012) was different. One day while at the church, I was finishing some work and was getting ready to go home when one of the secretaries offered me a package of almonds to eat. We were about to finish a three-week fast of eating nothing but fruits, vegetables, and nuts. When I was almost home, I got a severe pain in my back under my shoulder blade that I thought was gas pain, and I thought that it maybe came from the almonds. When I got home, the pain was still there, and I took some medicine to make it go away, but it didn't. I also noticed that when I would lie on my right side, my back would hurt, and there would be a vibrating feeling coming from my right lung. I thought to myself, *Lord, what is going on with my body?* But through all of this, I continued to press on, day by day."

Throughout the distractions of 2011, Karen and I finally finished our children's book and looked forward to promoting it in 2012. In February 2012, we began doing book signings at our church. I also researched other ways to promote the book, eventually landing a spot on a local television morning talk show called *Talk of Alabama* where Karen and I discussed our book.

Then, Mr. Jacks, the elementary school principal, allowed us to set up a table and sell the books during a couple of school events. And rather than hoard all of the proceeds for ourselves, we gave a percentage of every book we sold to the American Cancer Society and the Cystic Fibrosis Foundation in honor of our family members who'd battled these diseases. But it wouldn't be long before all book promotion ceased as something major was about to surface.

Erskine continued pushing himself to go to work daily and even continued working at the church. In fact, Mt. Canaan had recently begun a new set of classes called Pastoral Care, which started the first Saturday in February and would continue every Saturday for a number of weeks. Because the classes needed to be recorded for future reference, we, being the media team, were required to attend. Erskine and I attended the first two classes, but days before the third class was to begin, he had an increase in symptoms that couldn't be ignored. He would awaken during the night drenched in sweat, and he noticed that while at work, he was having difficulty breathing whenever he exerted himself. One day while at work, he called and asked me to make him an appointment to see his primary care physician. He was afraid he was going into congestive heart failure again.

The day before Erskine's doctor appointment was Valentine's Day, and out of our twenty-plus years of marriage, he had never before surprised me for this special day of love as he did this year. He brought home a huge heart-shaped balloon and a large vase full of roses with a touching card attached. The card, written in his own sweet words, read, "Tracy, I love you more than you could ever imagine! I never thought that I could love someone so much! You have shown me what true love is all about! Happy Valentine's Day!" He caught me totally caught off guard with this beautiful surprise, and I loved it!

Later that evening, Erskine decided to take our girls, his mom, his nieces, and me out to dinner to celebrate Valentine's Day. He'd never done that before. And at the end of the evening, just before leaving the restaurant, he asked for our attention because he had something very important he needed to say. When everyone was quiet and eagerly awaiting his words, he said, "I just wanted ya'll to know I love ya'll. I really do." After our replies of, "We love you too," his mom and I secretly wondered why he felt so compelled to say that to us. I even considered the surprise he'd given me earlier, and I wondered why my unromantic, workaholic husband was being so unusually soft and sentimental? Was there something going on that he was not telling us?

———

At his doctor's appointment the next day, the doctor performed several tests and took an x-ray. He later came back to the room saying that the x-ray showed some fluffiness in Erskine's lungs, so he prescribed acid reflux medicine and cough syrup, and he increased the daily dosage of one of Erskine's heart medications. Then he told him that if he did not feel better within five days to come back and see him.

Three days later, on a Saturday morning, Erskine and I decided that he needed a second opinion because there was not even a hint of improvement in his condition. So, rather than attend the Pastoral Care class, we went to the emergency room. The following words are Erskine's own.

"When we got to the ER, because of my symptoms, they immediately started to look at my heart, but after several tests, they found my heart to be just fine. What they did find was fluid around my right lung, but they did not know why it was there. The doctor decided to do a CAT scan to see where the fluid was coming from, and that's when the world as I knew it changed! After the doctor returned with the results, he stated that my right lung was filled with about one-third of fluid and that they saw what they believed was a new mass. In 2000, I was diagnosed with Hodgkin's lymphoma, which God totally cured me from, so this is why the doctor said a 'new mass.' To tell the truth, it all felt like a bad dream. But one thing I did know is that my God was in control!"

I was not in the room when the doctor gave Erskine this news because after he left the room for his CAT scan, I stepped out into the lobby to return phone calls. As other people in the lobby watched Whitney Houston's televised funeral, due to her drowning in a hotel bathtub the week before, I sat in a corner chair and called home to check on my kids, who happened to be engrossed in the same. As the girls questioned me about what was going on with their dad, I tried to remain cheerful for them, and I told them we didn't know yet but to just keep praying.

After talking to the girls, I returned the calls of our parents, who were trying to get an update. While speaking to my dad, he informed me that the church's executive directors had prayed for Erskine early that morning before the Pastoral Care class began. Hearing that gave me peace, but sadly, the peace didn't last long.

When I arrived back to Erskine's room, he solemnly shared with me the doctor's findings. I can still feel the sinking feeling in my stomach that I felt that day. When he finished giving me the terrible news, I immediately left the room to find the doctor, as I wanted to hear it straight from him. The doctor and I returned to Erskine's room, and he explained again the results of the CAT scan. Then he encouraged us to contact Erskine's oncologist on Monday morning.

As we left the ER, we both were in total shock. We couldn't believe we were going through the same stuff we went through twelve years ago. As soon as I climbed into the SUV, I sent out a mass text to several of our church members, family members, and friends who I knew would pray fervently for my husband and our family. Almost immediately, I began receiving encouraging replies and prayers from everyone.

Before going home, we went by to see Grandma Fannie, the grandma who took care of Erskine and nursed him back to health when he suffered that bad case of chicken pox I mentioned in an earlier chapter. When Mama Doll informed her of his newest health scare, Grandma Fannie wanted to be the first to lay hands on him. After instructing him to have a seat in her favorite recliner, she then had Erskine to open his shirt, and then she placed her hand in the area of his right lung and prayed a fervent prayer for her beloved grandson.

I dreaded having to tell our children this frightening news about their dad. The last time their dad went through such a thing, we only had the four oldest girls who were ages five, four, two, and newborn, and they really didn't understand what was going on. This time they were highly intelligent sixteen-, fifteen-, thirteen-, eleven-, and nine-year-olds.

When we arrived home, I called the girls into the living room for a family meeting. After sharing with them the doctor's findings, I reminded them of Isaac Caree's latest single, "In the Middle of It," which we heard often on the radio. I told them that we were going to praise God in the middle of this trial and not allow the enemy to make us worry or fear. I told them that their dad was going to be okay and that we would continue to believe God for his healing, regardless of the scary things we had heard.

I also told them how when the doctor gave us the news, I instantly felt in my spirit that God would be disappointed in me if I allowed even the smallest amount of doubt to enter my mind. This was not the time to doubt. This was the time to recall the many somber trials of our past and every supernatural way God had brought us through them. And we needed to remember that if He did it before, He could surely do it again. So no matter how bad things looked, we had no other choice but to keep the faith.

The next day, which was Sunday, my dad updated the congregations in both the 8:00 a.m. service and the 11:00 a.m. service of Erskine's dilemma, and they prayed mightily for us!

On Monday, we called Erskine's oncologist as the ER doctor had instructed us, and we hoped they would be able to fit him in that day because we were anxious for answers. But they had no available appointments, so they scheduled him for Wednesday, which gave us a frustrating two-day wait.

Though it was nice to see Dr. B again, we hated that it had to be under such conditions. After explaining to him Erskine's symptoms, he encouraged us to go back to the other hospital, get a copy of the CAT scan disk, and bring it back to him. Then he scheduled Erskine for another scan called a PET scan, which checks for diseases in the body.

On Thursday, after the PET scan, Erskine came home and gave Jasmine, our second oldest daughter, her first driving lesson. Jasmine, who was in the eleventh grade and enrolled in driver's education at school, had been very persistent about us teaching her how to drive. And though her dad wasn't feeling his best, he didn't disappoint her, as he knew I did not have the nerves to teach anyone how to drive.

That following Monday, Erskine had a biopsy in which they took a tissue sample and a liter of fluid from his right lung. After having these tests done, we anxiously waited for the doctor to call us with the diagnosis, but after waiting all day Wednesday for his call, we didn't hear anything until that evening. And even then, he only called to say that he didn't have the report yet and we would have to wait five more days. All that waiting was such torture.

On Monday, March 5, we waited all day again for Dr. B's call, but he didn't call until 7:00 p.m. And when he called, Erskine wasn't home because he was working at the church, so the doctor said he would call back later. Erskine had actually gone straight to the church after work to keep his mind occupied because he was so worried about what the doctor would say. I called and told him that he needed to come home right away because the doctor only wanted to speak with him. So he came home, and we waited for Dr. B to call again. Because he was so nervous, Erskine called our friends David and JaQuita Davis to come over and be with us when we received the doctor's call. He felt we needed them there for strength.

David and JaQuita were a young couple who were members of our church. It was only recently that our relationship with them had grown closer because they had just moved across the street from us after losing their home in the 2011 tornado. It seemed God used that tornado to blow them closer to us. On that night, they talked with us, encouraged us, and prayed with us. But evidently, God didn't want them there when the doctor called because he actually didn't call back until 10:48 p.m., long after our friends were gone and we had gone to bed.

Because it was so late, we didn't expected Dr. B to call back; we figured he would just wait till morning. However, when he called, Erskine put him on speakerphone, allowing me to hear both ends of their conversation. And when the doctor revealed Erskine's test results, we both were horrified. Twelve years after being healed of Hodgkin's lymphoma, Erskine had another cancer.

I later realized that this is why fear had gripped me late that night back in 2010. My spirit had sensed that the strong man of our house had been bound. "No man can enter into a strong man's house, and spoil his goods, except he will first bind the strong man; and then he will spoil his house" (Mark 3:26–28 KJV). However, God allowed me to see those angels standing around our house to give me His assurance that even though our strong man had been bound, we as a family were still protected.

Before ending his call, Dr. B instructed us to call his office the following morning and set up an appointment to discuss the next steps, one of which was more testing to find out what type of cancer Erskine had.

Not being able to sleep all night due to this devastating news, I arose very early that morning and sent out a mass e-mail to our friends and family requesting their prayers. I even sent an e-mail to Jay Jacks, the elementary school principal. About an hour later, Mr. Jacks sent back a most touching response.

Tracy,

You can definitely count on the prayers for your husband. I will pray for God's divine intervention in the healing of him from cancer. I will also be praying for all of your girls. I know that there will be tough times, but God will see you through. In fact, think of it as running with the Giants.

I look at your girls' ages as a blessing this time around. Many years ago, they were dependent on you. Now, they can also be encouragers for you, your husband, and each other. They can also be some serious prayer warriors. I encourage you all to select a time of day best for you all and stand around your husband praying over him daily. Pray aloud over him. Speak life over him.

Please know that I will help you and the girls any way I can … just let me know. Please keep me in touch. Thanks for the e-mail. It is special to me.

Mr. Jacks's words were calming encouragement for me, and they gave me great peace. I took to heart everything he said, believing that as I placed healing scriptures on nearly every wall in our home and gathered the girls each evening to pray and speak God's word over their dad that God would hear our prayers and heal His son.

After receiving such depressing news the night before, surprisingly Erskine got up that morning and went to work. And after I finished sending my e-mails and taking the girls to school, I went to work at the church.

Later, during his lunch break, Erskine came by the church to see me. He was going through some serious mental challenges that made it hard for him to concentrate on his job. He came up to the media room where I was working and sat down next to me. Then he laid his head on the desk and began to cry. My husband was a nervous wreck. He worried about dying, and he worried whether he had lived a life pleasing enough to God to be allowed into heaven if he died. After encouraging him as much as I could, I talked him into coming with me into the sanctuary where Mama Trish and my sister Triola happened to be sitting.

Triola was dealing with her own health challenges, as I described to you in an earlier chapter, and she had recently witnessed the hand of God supernaturally change her situation by allowing her to walk again when all odds were against her. My sister began encouraging Erskine with her own testimony. And Mama Trish, who had been her caregiver during the lowest part of her sickness, chimed in with words of encouragement as well. This gave Erskine enough strength to go back to work and finish for the day. But in the back of his mind, he still worried about the meeting with Dr. B, which was scheduled for the next morning.

My dad, Mama Doll, and Erskine's aunt Elzine Stout accompanied us to the appointment with Dr. B. We all listened attentively and took notes as Dr. B spoke with us about Erskine's condition. But before he could tell us exactly what kind of cancer Erskine was battling, he said he needed to schedule him for yet another biopsy. This one would be performed by one of Birmingham's top thoracic surgeons the following week.

During this time, Erskine thought a lot about his many family members who had passed away from terminal illnesses, such as two of his aunts, an uncle, his sister, and his dad to name a few. His dad, Erskine Sr., had been a dialysis patient for well over thirty years and had bravely endured his battle with kidney disease. From a very young child, Erskine watched his dad suffer through this illness, and, ironically, he said he often prayed that he would never have to suffer any such illness during his own lifetime.

When we left the doctor's office after our meeting with Dr. B and entered the parking deck, Erskine had an emotional outburst as he began jumping, crying, and praising God. When he finally calmed down, he shared with us that he was relieved because the doctor never said his cancer was terminal, as that had been his greatest fear.

With so many doctor appointments, Erskine was missing an extreme number of days from work, so by mid-March he had to take a medical leave of absence. After that, everything began moving so fast. Tuesday, March 13 was his official last day of work, and on Wednesday, in preparation for his biopsy, he had to endure a stress test that literally took all day. On Thursday, we met with the surgeon, and then on Friday, the biopsy was performed.

We were hopeful that the biopsy would give his oncologist the information he was looking for so that he would know what kind of cancer Erskine had and how to treat it. I was hopeful that he would be on the road to a speedy recovery soon, just as he was in 2000. But it didn't quite work out that way.

Erskine's surgery, which was scheduled for 5:45 a.m., was way behind schedule and didn't start until well in the afternoon. And after waiting with us for several hours that morning, my dad had to leave before the surgery began, as he had a prior out-of-town engagement.

As I sat alone in the waiting room waiting for Erskine's surgery to be over, a receptionist called my name and instructed me to go to the conference room where I would have a meeting with the surgeon. Because I worried that I wouldn't remember everything he'd say to me, I set up my tablet to record him. I also called Mama Doll and tried to put her on speakerphone, but for some reason, that didn't work out, as she could barely hear what was being said.

The surgeon, who entered the room with two other doctors, had no desire to feed me any false hope, so he cut through the chase and delivered the most depressing news I'd heard since 1993 when I received that terrible report about my baby boy's condition.

Back in April 1993, two doctors entered my hospital room after Erskine had gone home to freshen up after being with me all night during the birth of our son. The lead doctor spoke to me bluntly about my new baby's condition, regardless of the fact that I was alone at the time. Now, nineteen years later, it was like déjà vu as this was happening to me all over again. But this time the terrible news was about my husband. I guess God knew He had made me much stronger than I ever thought I was.

The following is a portion of the conversation between Dr. C and me.

Dr. C: "There could be cancer not just in the lung but also on the pleura space. The pleura is the space between the lung and the ribs. There's a lining there. So we made one small incision, and through that we did multiple biopsies, and actually Dr. H and I were able to get tissue that showed squamous cell cancer."

Tracy: "What does that mean?"

Dr. C: "That means the cancer has spread. It's not in the lung. It's in the pleura, which means it's stage 4. Cancer goes 1, 2, 2A, 2B, 3, 3A, 3B, 4. This is the final stage of cancer. Now, that doesn't mean he can't do all right. That's up to the good Lord, and we have great faith in that His plan may be very different than what we think His plan is. And we're praying and hoping for that. But I have to tell you that this is advanced disease."

Basically, the doctor was telling me that my husband was dying. But at the time, I couldn't come to grips with that. And though I held up fairly well during the meeting, afterward I was so distraught that I called my dad. Daddy and Mama Trish were on the road headed out of town. When I expressed to Daddy how I could no longer handle this by myself, he called our friend David Davis, who came to the hospital immediately to be by my side.

Later, when Erskine was assigned a hospital room, David's wife, JaQuita, joined us along with two other members of our church, Pastor Victor Hill and Rozita Smith, because my dad had sent them in his stead. Having them there gave me strength because I was very worried about breaking the surgeon's news to Erskine. I tried to do it in the most delicate way possible, as I assumed he would take it very hard. But surprisingly, he handled it far better than I expected, as he simply responded, "Well, God's got it." At that moment, his great faith was uplift to mine because I was a total wreck inside and, every now and then, on the outside.

Mama and Papa Dewey spent the night at our house with the girls, allowing me to spend the night at the hospital with Erskine. And during that season of our lives, my dad and my pop became a team in helping to transport our girls to and from school. Daddy was there in the mornings to take them, and Papa Dewey was at the school in the afternoons to pick them up.

With the number of doctor visits we were making, expenses such as co pays, gasoline, parking fees, and fast food were draining us. But miraculously God used our family and even our church family to reach out to us financially. It was amazing how freely they were giving to us, never realizing they were actually helping to sustain us. One person in particular was my uncle Irving Newell who lives in Virginia. When my mom told him about the issue we were facing with Erskine's health, he immediately went to Western Union and wired us one thousand dollars! This was very unexpected as Erskine and I had not asked anyone for anything. We just prayed about everything and watched God work. If I never knew the importance of family before, I had a crash course during this season of my life.

Erskine and I discussed writing a book together about this newest trial we were facing because, in spite of the negative outlook, we were not going to stop believing God for his healing. In fact, he actually started on the book without me by writing bits and pieces of his story whenever he had a good day and felt like writing, such as the pieces you've read so far.

Per our annual tradition, we made an appointment to take family portraits for my birthday in March. He and the girls and I, dressed up in jeans and different shades of orange tops then visited a portrait studio across town. Though the pictures were for my birthday, we were also taking them for our book, and we even took one specifically for the book's cover with Erskine standing out front and the girls and I standing in the background.

When we were about to complete our photo session, I came up with the idea of having Erskine sit, and all the girls stand around him and plant kisses all over his head and face. The shot turned out beautiful, but it made him a little uncomfortable because he said we were carrying on as if he was about to die. After our photo session, we ate dinner and then went to church for the Institute in Basic Life Principles video seminar.

As I mentioned near the beginning of this book, many years ago my dad was introduced to the seminar teachings of Minister William "Bill" Gothard Jr., founder of the nondenominational organization, Institute in Basic Life Principles. This seminar enlightened him on such things as God's structure of the family, His principles of finance, and other godly principles of life. My dad's life was so touched by these teachings that he introduced them to his family and his church, sending his members to these seminars yearly.

Now, decades later, the seminar videos were made available for church use, and my dad featured them periodically in special services to those who were interested in learning these godly principals. Erskine didn't allow his health issues to keep us from the seminar that night, as he desired more of God for all of us. And it was his desire that his girls be raised with the same godly principles that I had learned as a young girl.

On the third night of the seminar, during a video break, God allowed several different church members to speak spontaneous words of prophecy into Erskine's life. The atmosphere became so spiritual and very emotional for us, as each prophecy basically gave the same inspiring message, that Erskine's sickness was not unto death. This impromptu supernatural moment gave us the strength we needed to keep the faith regardless of Erskine growing weaker and short of breath.

In spite of how bad he felt, Jasmine was able to encourage her dad to give her another driving lesson, and he allowed her to drive home after a visit to his mom's house. I couldn't help but wonder if God was allowing these lessons because Erskine was steadily becoming too weak to drive; therefore, God was raising up another driver in the family to help me.

The next day, which was Sunday, Erskine pressed his way to church, but he said he felt terrible, and I could tell that he needed to see a doctor. But after not being able to get a call through to the doctor's office on Monday morning, we decided to wait until Tuesday since he was scheduled for a CAT scan on that day. We figured we'd stop by the doctor's office after the scan.

Our unscheduled visit to Dr. B's office led to an impromptu meeting about Erskine's most recent test results. In the meeting, Dr. B disclosed Erskine's final diagnosis. The type of cancer he was dealing with was called Mesothelioma. It was the lung disease that we always heard about in television commercials. The terrible disease that comes from exposure to asbestos. The disease that requires the assistance of lawyers for personal injury or wrongful death compensation. Yes, that horrible disease.

As Dr. B encouraged us to get a lawyer, Erskine sat there with the most pitiful look on his face. I felt so sorry for my husband. We couldn't understand how this could have happened to him. At what point in his life did he breathe in asbestos? And when did it erupt into this deadly disease?

Erskine wrote the following words six days after receiving this news.

"In March 2000, I was diagnosed with cancer, Hodgkin's lymphoma. After chemo and radiation treatment, I was considered cancer-free in November 2000. In 2004, I was diagnosed with cardiomyopthy (weak heart muscle), which was caused by one of the chemo drugs they gave me for the Hodgkin's lymphoma. Recently, I have been diagnosed with stage 4 lung cancer, Mesothelioma. My doctor feels that it was caused by my having come in contact with asbestos at some point in my past due to the type of work I do. And because I have never smoked, he feels it developed into cancer because of the radiation treatments I received for the Hodgkin's lymphoma."

When Erskine and I were so happy about him being cured of the Hodgkin's lymphoma, we had no idea that the methods that they used to cure him would create new diseases down the road.

After our meeting with Dr. B, I immediately called our parents and asked them to pray because I knew this news was tearing away at Erskine's mind. And I told our parents that no matter what we were going to continue to believe God for Erskine's healing.

Trusting God through tough situations was all I'd ever known to do.

I didn't know anything else to do. And I definitely wasn't going to give up on my husband, so my only other option was to fight with faith. During this season, I became Erskine's loudest cheerleader and strongest motivator. I cheered him through his struggles and motivated him to keep the faith in his weakness.

I later realized this was what Jasmine's dream was about when she said she saw her dad pass out as we were having dinner. She said she was amazed at how calm I had remained in the dream, telling her and her sisters that their dad would be fine. God was showing her my faith.

As I shared earlier, in the beginning of this ordeal, I felt God would be highly disappointed in me if I allowed doubt to enter my mind. With all He had done for us, there was no way I was going to allow the devil to trick me into doubting Him. So I was very adamant about keeping the faith until the end, just as I had done during my pregnancy with our third daughter, Janay whom I thought would be our son.

The next morning, I did as Dr. B encouraged us to do; I contacted a local law firm who specialized in asbestos cases. Once I got that ball rolling, I took Erskine to have his very first chemotherapy treatment, which he was scheduled to have every three weeks afterward.

He and I worried that he would have adverse reactions to the chemo medicine, such as vomiting or loss of appetite, but we were pleasantly surprised when everything seemed to go well. He even sent me a text during his treatment saying, "I'm hungry." It felt good to know he still had an appetite.

The following day was all about taking care of business. We filled out forms for medical disability, Social Security disability, and a cancer grant. Then a legal aide from the law firm we hired came to our house with even more paperwork for us to sign.

April started very busy for us, as we were still filling out paperwork. There were forms for this and forms for that, and they all needed our immediate attention. Then on the morning of April 3, we received some good news from the lawyers. They said they had already located monies for us, $26,000 to be exact, with much more to come in the future. That money would be a great blessing because we knew it would enable us to get closer to our goal of being debt free. But this news was actually bittersweet because though we would be closer to reaching our goal, it was at the expense of Erskine's health.

In the midst of all of the busy work, Erskine began having severe symptoms from the chemotherapy. I not only had to deal with his issues, but our oldest twin, Karen, seemed to be having asthma issues around the same time. This was a lot on me as a mother, a caregiver, a homemaker, a chauffer, a secretary, a record keeper, and everything else in between. I must admit, as I look back, I can truly see the hand of God holding me up during that era in my life as I was ridiculously pulled in several different directions at once and on a daily basis. That's why I'm truly grateful for the many helpful people God placed in our lives during that time, as it could have been much worse. God not only had people in place to take our kids back and forth to school but also to church and anywhere else they needed to go. And there were other people who gave us finances, cooked us meals, bought us groceries, helped our kids with homework, ran errands for us, did our hair, cut our grass, washed our vehicles, gave us words of encouragement, prayed for us, and so much more. These special people, too many to name, helped to make our very heavy ordeal a little lighter to bear.

Because of nausea and lack of appetite, Erskine had not eaten in a few days, and he was dealing with severe bouts of vomiting. On this particular day, April 3, he had grown extremely weak, but he managed to make his way to the bathroom where he began vomiting in a most horrendous way. It truly looked like a scene straight out of a horror movie. Because the bathroom door was open, I could see all of this from my bedroom.

Then, as if in slow motion, he fell against the wall with a loud thump and started going down. I jumped up instantly and ran to catch him. God gave me supernatural strength as I managed to keep him upright, supporting him as we struggled back to the bed. After sitting him down, I checked his blood pressure and noticed it had dropped severely. I immediately called his doctor and was instructed to bring him in right away. I then had to figure out how I was going to dress this grown man who was too weak to dress himself. After trying to get in touch with someone who could come quickly to help me, I remembered a couple of Erskine's work partners who would probably be working near by. I managed to contact his work partner, Cory Lawson, who agreed to come, and as he was en route, I called Mama Doll and asked her to have someone bring her by to pick up Karen. Then I began dressing Erskine as best I could.

By the time Cory arrived, I only needed his help with putting Erskine's shoes on and getting him to the car. But I'll never forget the look on Cory's face when he saw Erskine. It had been several weeks since he'd seen his friend, and it was under better conditions, as Erskine was much healthier then. But seeing his now frail, sickly condition made it hard for Cory to hide the pain he was feeling inside, as it showed all over his face.

When we arrived at the hospital where Dr. B's office was located, I allowed the valet to park my vehicle and I requested a wheelchair for Erskine. As I helped my husband into the wheelchair and wheeled him away to the doctor's office, I could feel God holding me up supernaturally.

In the doctor's office, they gave him IV fluids, which seemed to help him feel a little better. And after we were released, it felt really good to see Rodreecas Brown, our friend from church, sitting there in the lobby waiting to assist me with Erskine.

The following day, I took Karen to the pediatrician where she was diagnosed with walking pneumonia. Then I returned home to discover Erskine was still not doing well. I took his blood pressure and noticed it had dropped even lower than the day before, so I called his uncle Nazoma Stout, who rushed us to the ER. This time Erskine was admitted. And this would be the second of about seven hospital stays he would have to endure.

Since I wasn't prepared to spend the night with Erskine, I went back home to our girls, and I promised him that I would come by to see him after seeing the girls off to school the next morning.

The following day, I was at the hospital as I'd promised, and my husband and I were so happy to see one another. The IV fluids they were giving him not only made him feel better, but they were giving him an appetite and putting the color back into his big beautiful cheeks. I stayed with him all day until it was almost time to pick up the girls from school. Then I promised him that all of us would come by and see him after school the next day.

The girls and I went straight to the hospital after school the following day to see their dad. Not long after we arrived, Dr. B, who was making his rounds, came by Erskine's room and was thrilled to meet our girls. He was especially interested in the twins whom he dubbed *his twins* because he was the doctor that told us Erskine probably would not be able to have any more children due to the chemotherapy he received back in 2000. Ironically, we were surprised with the twins two years after he told us that. After meeting and taking pictures with Dr. B, the girls and I went to eat dinner in the hospital cafeteria.

While sitting there as the girls ate, I had a few minutes to reflect. I began thinking about how my life felt so out of control. I'd always been a person who liked order. I hated chaos, and it felt that was exactly what I was living in. I also dreaded the pressure of having to be Superwoman for my family because it was becoming increasingly stressful. I though about how even though Erskine was tolerating my absence, I could tell he really wanted me to spend the night at the hospital with him. And I really wanted to be there for him, but at the same time, I felt I needed to be at home with our children. For the second time in my life, I began to wonder who was going to be strong for me while I was being strong for everyone else.

Before I could sink any deeper into my feelings, God pulled me out, reminding me that this was no time for a pity party. He was my strength and had always been my strength. He was more than enough for me.

When we returned to Erskine's room, a nurse was there who was preparing to give him blood. She didn't know why, but she said for some reason his blood was very low. This blood refill would have to be repeated

God's Girl

several more times in the following months, as he was constantly losing blood.

The next week, Erskine had his second chemo treatment, and for several days afterward, he had no problems other than the normal weakness and pain that stemmed from the disease itself, and he was learning to deal with that. Surprisingly, he felt good enough to cook breakfast for the family a week later when the girls were out of school for the memorial of the 2011 tornado. We assumed the chemo must have been doing its job and his complete healing would be coming soon.

A week later, Erskine had outpatient surgery in order to have a port installed for the remainder of his chemo treatments. This port, which was a small, round disc that was installed under the skin of his left upper breast and attached by catheter to a large vein, was suppose to be better than using a normal IV in the arm for giving him his treatments. The following week, he had his third chemo treatment, which also seemed to go well. Although he spent the majority of his time in a reclined position, either in the bed or in his lounge chair, over all, Erskine seemed to be doing well with his chemo treatments. And the week after his third treatment, we found out why, as we received from Dr. B the results of another CAT scan.

Dr. B told us that the cancer seemed to be responding well to the chemotherapy because it was shrinking as he hoped it would. Then, after giving us extended details of the report, he ended the meeting by declaring, "Today is a good day." Erskine and I were overjoyed, and I sent out a mass text to all of our family and prayer partners, sharing with them Erskine's good news.

Our daughter Jasmine has special memories of the happiness she felt when she received my text while at school. She said after sharing the news with her friends, they began celebrating with her.

Because he had begun missing his work partners and other county school employees that he was used to seeing daily, Erskine decided he felt good enough to go by one of the schools where he knew they would be working and pay them a visit. When we arrived, everyone was so excited to see him and his infamous smile. After posing for a few pictures, he, in true Erskine style, talked, and talked, and talked, because he was so happy to be feeling well and he was thrilled to be back among his friends.

Since things seemed to be looking up for my husband, I just knew in my heart that we were about to make it over this bump in the road as we had in the past, and pretty soon we would be on the road again headed to our happily-ever-after destiny.

18

The Good Wife and Mom

> Her children arise and call her blessed; her husband also, and he praises her: "Many women do noble things, but you surpass them all." Charm is deceptive, and beauty is fleeting; but a woman who fears the Lord is to be praised.
> —Proverbs 31:28–30 (NIV)

June 2012–October 2012

My husband was having good days and bad days. But because I never knew which day would be good or bad, I decided to search for a place that our youngest four girls could go every day in order to keep the house quiet for him during the summer break. Our oldest two daughters were already attending the Trio Upward Bound Program at Lawson State Community College for the summer, but the younger girls were not old enough for that program. So after learning about summer camp at the YMCA, I placed them there for a few weeks.

With Erskine being sick, I was the only driver in the house at the time. And because I didn't want to keep bothering other people, I stayed busy ripping and running all over the place. I'd take the girls to each program in the mornings, then pick them up at different times of day. I'd take Erskine back and forth to the doctor, pick up his medicines from the pharmacy, go grocery shopping, and more. But I didn't complain during all of this because I just wanted my husband well, and if this is what it took to make that happen, then so be it.

I didn't care for leaving Erskine at home alone ever since that scary bathroom episode, and I tried to stay close to him as much as possible because of his breathlessness. Talking too much or too loudly tired him out quickly, so I had to be close enough to know when he needed me. And I always tried not to stay anywhere too long because he would be watching the clock, eagerly awaiting my return, as he hated me to leave his side.

While out running my morning errands, I'd always stop and get us some breakfast. If he ate it, I knew he was having a good day, but if he didn't, well, you know. And after arriving back home, I'd always do exactly what I knew he wanted me to do. I'd climb back into bed with him, and together we would eat our breakfast and watch television and afterward, sleep. I would stay in bed with him all day until it was time to run another errand or get the kids out of school because that was what he always wanted.

Because my husband no longer felt comfortable driving, I became the full-time family chauffer and errand girl. And because I wasn't used to doing so much driving, the calf muscle on my right leg began aching something awful around that time. It took me awhile to realize that the pain was from my new exercise of constantly pressing on the gas and the brake pedals.

Erskine started paying attention to all of the ripping and running I was doing, and as a result, he began feeling sorry for me and apologized often. I assured him that I was fine and just wanted him to focus on getting well. Then one day he said, "You know what the devil keeps telling me?" I said, "What?" He answered, "He said the reason you have to do all the running and handling of our business is because you're being prepared for when I die." I replied, "Yes, that was the devil talking because you are not going to die."

One day after dropping the girls off at the Upward Bound program and the YMCA, I remembered that I needed to make a quick stop by the grocery store before I headed back home to be with Erskine. As I walked out of the store toward my SUV, I noticed my right back tire was flatter than a pancake. I couldn't understand how that had happened so fast because it didn't feel like I'd been driving on a flat tire when I arrived at the store. Regardless, it needed to be changed in order for me to get home.

I wanted to cry because all I could think about was getting back home to Erskine as soon as possible. And since I didn't know how to change a flat, I tried my best to think of someone close by who could come quickly and help me. I remembered he had coworkers who worked at the school down the street, so I tried to get in touch with them, but they weren't there. And after trying to contact a few other people with no success, in desperation I called my husband.

I was used to being able to call him for anything. No matter what mechanical or technical problem I ran into, all I had to do was call him, and he wouldn't stop until he fixed it. Air-conditioning, heating, appliances, computers, drains, car issues, you name it. And if he couldn't fix it, he would find someone that could. So quite naturally, I called him about my flat tire, but I soon regretted making that call.

When he arrived, I could tell he had used most of his energy just walking from the house to his truck. As he struggled to loosen the bolts on the tire, he fussed the whole time saying, "I'm not supposed to be doing this." Then suddenly, God sent a Good Samaritan to aid us. He took a tool from his trunk and loosened all of the tire's bolts, making it easier for Erskine to remove it. I did my best to help him finish the job, as I felt so sorry for him. I had never seen him that vulnerable. He was the man that everyone called on to fix almost anything, but now those skills were steadily fading away.

Around this time, due to the poor quality of his health, Erskine medically retired from his fifteen-year career at the county board of education. Just to think that at forty-three years of age he was already retiring was unbelievable. We always assumed he'd be well into his sixties before he retired from his job. But I didn't mind it because I was looking forward to the day when he would beat cancer and become stronger. Then we would spend each day finally living happily ever after.

While taking care of Erskine, I was also planning a large sweet sixteen birthday party for Jasmine, who would be turning sixteen in August. Along with that, I was helping Jessica, our oldest daughter, with her senior year preparations as she was about to be a high school senior in the fall.

Erskine tried to help me with the sweet sixteen party planning. He listened as I ran ideas by him, even giving his input at times, and he went with me to view the inside of the buildings that I was considering for the event. However, because he couldn't stand up for very long, he would take a seat and allow me to look around.

To be honest, the fact that he couldn't stand up long started to worry Jasmine and me because, per the tradition we started with Jessica, he would have to escort her into her party. But since it was July and the party wasn't until August, we hoped he'd be a little better by then and able to stand by his baby's side.

One morning during that summer, our youngest twin, Kamille, woke up from a dream, which she nervously shared with me. In the dream, she saw her dad in a coffin, which made her assume that he was going to die. I assured her that it was just a bad dream and that her dad was going to be okay. I believed this with all my heart, and I made sure she believed it too. Amazingly, God kept me strong for my girls and for Erskine because, for some reason, they all seemed to be taking their cues from me. If I worried, we all worried, and if I was strong, we all were strong. And no matter how bad my husband felt, if I told him that he was going to make it, he believed he would make it.

I continued sending out text messages requesting prayers for Erskine and giving updates of his health because the encouraging replies from our prayer partners were a tremendous help in keeping us afloat. Also, the girls and I continued to encircle their dad nearly every night, with each person, even Erskine, reciting a memorized healing scripture. And we designated a person each evening to say the prayer.

Before school in the mornings, we would form a circle in the living room, and the designated person for that morning would say a prayer of protection for the family. Our girls really learned how to pray during this season of our lives. In fact, whenever my dad took them to school, he was always astounded by their ability to pray like seasoned adults.

The girls were not only a big help in praying, but they were a great help to me in taking care of their dad. For instance, every night they took turns changing his vaporizer water. And Karen, the oldest twin, would set up and administer his breathing treatments each evening because she had asthma and therefore was familiar with administering her own breathing treatments. Jasmine, the second oldest, would massage his legs, arms, and back because it seemed to relax him. And the rest of the girls would help in many other ways. The girls even took turns keeping their dad company when I was busy doing other things in the house. My oldest girls and I realized this was the meaning of our baby dreams, as the baby we saw ourselves caring for turned out to be their dad.

We were now working with out-of-town lawyers for Erskine's Mesothelioma case. Because of his young age as well as his past occupations, they said it was not possible to pinpoint a definite place where he could have breathed in the asbestos. There were a number of places from his childhood to adulthood where he could have been exposed to this deadly material. As a result, our new lawyers began the long, drawn-out process of researching materials from every possible place that Erskine could have received asbestos exposure. This led to Erskine filling out and signing mounds of paperwork and being scheduled to give a deposition that would be video recorded.

During the last week of July, Erskine and I met with the out-of-town lawyers in the conference room of a local upscale hotel for the deposition.

The elevator ride and lengthy walk to the conference room nearly wore him out.

Upon arriving at our destination, I felt so overwhelmed because I was not expecting what my eyes beheld. The room was set up like a television press conference. There were several lawyers there representing different companies, and those who were not present were on a telephone conference line, which was placed in the middle of the table.

I was allowed to sit through a portion of the deposition, but at a certain point during their questioning, they decided I should no longer be present, so I was escorted out.

Because I was so sure that my husband would be healed of this disease, it didn't dawn on me that this video was being taken of him for trial use, after his death. Because Mesothelioma patients normally have a short life expectancy, the lawyers were preparing for Erskine's sworn testimony to live on, long after he had expired.

Erskine had a constant cough that we had grown accustomed to, but we started to notice that it had gotten progressively worse. He also appeared to be much weaker and more out of breath than normal. He had become so weak that when I took him in for his seventh chemo treatment around the first part of August, I had to get another wheelchair and push him to his doctor's office, as he couldn't even stand up for a few seconds. It seemed his condition was deteriorating.

During this time, I was still making party preparations, as Jasmine's sixteenth birthday party was only a couple of days away. Then, the night before the party, Erskine was in such bad shape that he labored for every breath he took. The girls and I literally had to beg him to go to the hospital because by now he had grown to hate hospitals. He also didn't want to go because he didn't want to spoil Jasmine's big day by not being present. But she assured him that she would be more hurt if he didn't go to the hospital than she would be if he missed her party. He finally agreed, but he worried about who would escort her into her party in his absence. So I called my dad and my pop and told them that Erskine wanted them both to be Jasmine's escorts in his stead, one on each arm. They were honored.

Early the next morning, I took Erskine to the ER while the girls stayed home preparing for the party. We were there for several hours before they finally put him in a room. After helping him settle into his room, then answering all of the nurses' questions and promising that I would see him the next morning, I rushed back home as fast as I could, as I only had a few hours before the party would begin.

At the party, I took the microphone and facilitated the evening, but I made sure to explain Erskine's absence and requested the prayers of our guest. I tried to be a good party host, but the only thing on my mind the entire night was getting it over and done with so that I could go and see about my husband. Though I kept a smile on my face, I was very distraught on the inside. Then, while standing before the people facilitating one of the party games, Erskine rang my cell phone, so I stepped off to the side and spoke with him.

After asking how the party was going, he told me, "They found out what's wrong with me." And I asked, "What?" He replied, "I have blood clots in my lungs." At that moment, I did all I could to keep myself from falling face forward onto the floor because I knew I needed to remain as calm as possible for my children and our guests.

I went on with the rest of the night in supernatural grace, as if all was well. But in reality, I was wishing I could just tell everyone to get out immediately because I was ready to go. After the games, dinner, roasting, and cake cutting, some people left while others began to dance. But while they were dancing, it started to storm outside, so much so that the lights went out. That was my way of escape! Everyone stopped dancing and began working together to clean up in the dark, and we were out of there in a flash!

The next morning, the girls and I rushed to the hospital to see their dad. He told me that the doctor had put him on blood-thinning medication to break up the clots in his lungs. But the drawback to that was a severe bleeding risk if he were ever to hurt himself in such a way that would cause him to bleed. That was frightening to me, but since he didn't do anything but lie down every day, I figured there should be nothing to worry about.

Erskine came home four days after he was admitted. And because that day happened to be Jasmine's actual birthday, he took that opportunity to celebrate her since he didn't make it to her party. He and the girls and I gathered in the living room, and as we presented her with small gifts, Erskine sweetly expressed his love and appreciation for her.

The following week, he received his eighth chemo treatment, and he seemed to do well with it because days later he joined me in grocery shopping and cooking dinner. And the next week, we all ate dinner at Mama Doll's house, which he really seemed to enjoy, not realizing that it would be his last meal for a long while.

Four days after the dinner at Mama Doll's house, I had to rush Erskine to the ER again for dehydration. He had not eaten anything since that meal at his mom's, and he had basically vomited out everything that was in him. I knew they would admit him, so I came prepared to spend the night, as he had grown weary of hospital stays, and like a fearful child, he no longer wanted to be there alone.

Staying with him was somewhat stressful for me because although our girls were old enough, I felt very bad for having to leave them home alone for several days at a time. Sometimes it seemed being a good wife and a good mother clashed because it was so hard to do both at the same time. I wanted to be there for my children just as badly as I wanted to be there for my husband, but I was only one person. I thank God that we were living in the age of cell phones because they were a big help in my staying in constant contact with the girls. And when the hospital visits began to grow longer, making us spend even more time away from our girls, God sent two beautiful souls to watch over them for us.

During Erskine's hospital stay, I received a call from the nurse at the elementary school concerning our youngest daughter, Kamille, who was having pain in one of her ears. I really didn't know what to do because I couldn't leave the hospital at that moment, and my parents were not in pocket. This was one of those moments where I felt so overwhelmed with having to care for my husband and my children simultaneously. Then suddenly, God reminded me of Zambia.

God's Girl

Zambia Harris was a young lady who attended our church. She was also a schoolteacher at the middle school, which was located right next to the elementary school. I contacted her at work with a large and desperate request. I asked if she could leave her job for a few minutes, go to the nearest store, pick up a bottle of eardrops, then go to the elementary school and administer them to Kamille. Zambia quickly agreed, never once making me feel as if I were asking too much of her. This day marked the beginning of an amazing friendship between us.

My mom told me about Andrea MacArthur, a cousin of ours who had been inquiring about my family and wondering how she could be of assistance to us. Well, because I couldn't think of anything I needed her to do, I never responded to Andrea's request to help. But my cousin was adamant. She continued to contact my mom and my dad because she desperately wanted to know in what manner she could serve us. Finally, during Erskine's most recent hospital stay, I realized I needed her. I called my cousin and asked if she could take food to the house for our girls, as I didn't have a chance to buy groceries beforehand and I knew the girls would need something to eat while we were away. Not only did Andrea take plenty of groceries to our house that day, but also she and Zambia teamed up and went beyond the call of duty to meet the needs of our girls.

The two of them took it upon themselves to go by our house every day and spend the evening with our girls, becoming an awesome support system for them in our absence. They even brought their own children with them, and together all nine kids would eat, play, do homework and fellowship with one another. This system helped our girls get their minds off their dad's sickness and our long absence.

While in the hospital, Erskine began having nosebleeds due to his nostrils becoming dry from the oxygen tubing in his nose. One day, when Uncle D came to the hospital to see us, he agreed to sit with Erskine while I ran home to see the kids and get more clothes. But before I left, Erskine was having a nosebleed that the nurses were working hard to stop, as it was difficult because of the blood-thinning medication he had been taking. Though I was greatly concerned, I went ahead and left, assuming there was no cause for alarm because he was in the hospital; they would know how to take care of it.

When I arrived home, Uncle D called me in distress saying Erskine was hemorrhaging and choking on blood, and they couldn't get it to stop. That was the moment I broke. I had been so strong for my family from the beginning when we first learned of the mass on his lung. Then we learned it was cancer. Then there was the Mesothelioma diagnosis. Then the lung clots. And now an unstoppable nosebleed. Was God really going to allow him to bleed to death?

After calling our parents and giving them the update, I called my girls into my bedroom so that we could call on God. After telling them, through tears, what was going on with their dad, we all fell on our knees around my king-sized bed, and I cried out to God. I really can't remember what I said in that prayer, but I just remember praying and crying all at the same time. And because, as I stated earlier, my kids took their cues from me, they were crying as well. They assumed that if Mama was crying, then something was terribly wrong.

I packed my bags in a hurry, and the girls and I rushed back to the hospital. Uncle D was still there, and Mama Doll had arrived minutes before we did. By then, the bleeding was under control because an ear, nose, and throat specialist had been called to handle the situation. He had stopped the bleeding by pushing some kind of large balloon apparatus up into Erskine's nose, which went pretty far inside his head. It was very uncomfortable as he complained often of the pressure, but he tried his best to deal with it for fear of another bloodbath.

During this hospital stay, other health issues were exposed. Erskine was found to have hypothyroid disease, so the doctor added a new medicine to the laundry list of medications he was already taking. Also, he began having more issues with his heart, so they put a cardiologist on his case.

It was a few hours after the big nosebleed when a doctor in a white lab coat walked into Erskine's room. After introducing himself as Dr. H from cardiology, he began to ask several questions in order to learn more about Erskine and his heart condition. He was a very nice man with a great personality and bedside manner. As we talked, something about him seemed very familiar to me. And at one point while talking to us, he abruptly stopped and said to me, "I feel like I've seen you before." And I replied, "That's what I was just sitting here thinking about you."

After the doctor's visit, I continued to ponder on where I'd seen him. Then it dawned on me; he was the doctor I saw in my dream back in 2011. In the dream, he was dressed in his white lab coat and standing next to Erskine and me while we held a poster-sized check written for a large sum of money. And the weird thing about it was, I not only recognized him, but he recognized me! I finally understood that dream. It was a foretelling of Erskine's sickness and his Mesothelioma lawsuit.

Because of the new health issues that had surfaced, Erskine had become very discouraged and confused and was once again fighting serious mind battles. One day, as I sat there in the hospital room with him, I took a marker and several pieces of notebook paper and began to print several of the same healing scriptures we had on our walls at home. Then I taped them to the closet doors that stood directly in front of his bed, as I wanted God's promises to remain constantly in his eyesight. The girls continued our nightly prayer regimen as they called us each night during his hospital stay, and I put them on speakerphone to pray and recite their scriptures over him.

Because of the mind battles, Erskine needed lots of encouragement and inspiration to help him fight. I tried my best to give him everything he needed. I was a listening ear, a shoulder to cry on, a cheerleader, and a motivator. Even late at night when he was wide awake and needed to talk, I would fight sleep in an effort to listen and encourage. At times when my words weren't enough, he'd ask me to call my dad. Erskine loved talking to my dad, especially during this season in his life. Doing so seemed to give him a sense of peace. I guess, to him, being in the presence of his pastor was as close as he could get to God here on earth.

My dad tried to make himself available to Erskine as much as possible. Whether at our house or at the hospital, he would come often to talk and pray with him. Many times Erskine would repeat the same things he'd talked about the previous days, but my dad would listen as if he was hearing it for the first time and simply reiterate the same encouraging words he'd already given him.

When Daddy came to the hospital to see us during Erskine's most recent stay, he decided to do something that had not even crossed our minds. With it being such a beautiful day, he helped Erskine into a wheelchair and rolled him outside for a few minutes of fresh air. I think I needed that breath of fresh air just as much as Erskine did. Pausing a minute to soak in the beauty of the day brought a bit of calm into our stressful situation. At least for me it did.

I was actually feeling imprisoned in that hospital room. Like I was being held hostage. Some days I thought I would go crazy as I wanted so badly to break free, but my love and devotion to my husband wouldn't allow me to go anywhere.

The day I married Erskine, I spoke every single word of those vows from my heart. And I was not only making the vows to him, but I was making them to God. I promised to be by this man's side for better, for worse, for richer, for poorer, in sickness and health until death do us part. And no matter how tough our situation became, I was never ever going to give up on him.

After eight days in the hospital, Erskine was released, but he was still having issues because a new ailment had begun to surface, a severe pain in his back. Three days later, he was due to have chemo, but he put it off until the following week because he was too weak and in too much pain to go anywhere. Dr. B suggested that I bring him in the office for IV fluids, which gave him a little more strength and enabled him keep his next chemo appointment. But his back pain had become excruciating, so Dr. B made him an appointment to see a neurosurgeon, and the neurosurgeon sent him to have a CAT scan.

God's Girl

I was now having to valet park and request a wheelchair every time we went to Erskine's doctor's appointments because he was just too weak to walk and his back pain made moving around very tormenting for him. His life had taken a turn for the worse.

Since he could no longer get into the bathtub, I began giving him sponge baths in the bedroom as he reclined in his chair. One day as I washed his legs and feet, he watched me with tears in his eyes. When I asked him why he was crying, he said it was because he had been sick for much of our marriage and I was always having to take care of him. I assured him that I had no problem with taking care of him because that was my job as his wife. Then he told me how much he wanted God to heal him so that he could spend the rest of his life making me happy and showing me just how much he loved and appreciated me for sticking with him and taking care of him. By then, we were both wiping away tears.

Erskine had not eaten in several weeks, as he no longer had an appetite. His aunt, Gale Wren Evans, came to our house one day and tried her best to encourage him to eat, even spoon feeding him a little soup in hopes that she could wake up his appetite. However, her efforts failed because he only ate those few spoonfuls that she fed him and nothing else. In the days that followed Erskine was constantly nauseous, which led to vomiting, dehydration, and finally another hospital stay. This would be his fifth hospital stay in nine months.

These hospital stays not only tortured Erskine and me, but they tortured our girls as well because they were beginning to see less and less of us as each hospital stay grew increasingly longer. But in hindsight, I realize this was just a part of the girls' growing up process, as being without us helped them to grow independent because they were forced to do things for themselves and for each other that I had often done for them all.

Erskine's situation was critical. During this newest hospital stay, there were several doctors assigned to his case. Along with the oncologist, there was a gastroenterologist assigned to examine his stomach to see why he wasn't eating, a nephrologist to treat his kidneys, a pulmonary doctor to treat his lungs, and the cardiologist that I mentioned previously was treating his heart.

I sent out a mass text message to our family and prayer partners requesting their prayers because Erskine was in desperate need of them. Not only did we receive loving replies, but we also received many visits and phone calls from those who wanted to encourage and love on him. My big sister Triola, whom God had literally raised from a near-death experience and who was now doing amazingly well, had also come with her husband, John, and son, John Jr. Tree wanted to help Erskine and me keep the faith and to remember that if God healed her, He could heal him.

Though we tried our best to keep the faith, the devil kept hitting us with blows to the head that made us almost lose it on several occasions. For instance, Dr. B came in one day and told us that the CAT scan the neurosurgeon had sent Erskine to take had shown bone spots, meaning the cancer had spread to his bones, mainly his spine, which was the reason for his pain.

A few days later, a nurse told us that they were considering catheterizing Erskine because of his low urine output. She also, said that the doctor had mentioned dialysis. This really frightened my husband as he was totally against both. He wanted no parts of the life that he grew up watching his dad suffer.

When the nurse left the room after giving us this awful news, Erskine cried like a baby. And I felt so helpless because I wanted so badly to fix this problem for him, but all I could do was pray. So pray is what I did. And mightily.

I prayed so hard for him that night that I began speaking in a heavenly language I'd never heard myself speak before. And there was a spirit of boldness that arose in me that I'd never felt before. I tried to pray heaven down for my husband that night, decreeing and declaring that his kidneys would began to function as they should and that he would not have to go on dialysis. That prayer alone gave my husband peace, and he had no doubt that God would intervene on his behalf. But then came another blow.

In an effort to find out if there was a problem in Erskine's stomach that was hindering his eating, he was wheeled off to a gastrointestinal doctor on another floor of the hospital. The doctor put a scope down Erskine's throat and into his stomach to look for any abnormalities. The good news was there were no abnormalities, but the bad news was the scope had irritated his stomach to the point that he had to be put on a morphine pump for the pain.

Though the morphine may have helped his stomach pain, his back pain was still excruciating, making him very uncomfortable. And he constantly begged me to massage his back and neck and to adjust his pillows all throughout the day and night, but there was still no relief.

In the midst of the turmoil, I worried about my children who were calling me daily, wanting to know when we would be coming home. I guess they were growing tired of being home without us. I was too. I knew they were in good hands, but I just felt sorry for them because they had to put up with our constant absence. I didn't want them to feel like orphans.

Very early one morning as they were preparing for school, I received a call from our eleventh grader, Jasmine, reminding me that she needed a certain book for school and it was due that day. With everything that was going on with her dad, I had totally forgotten about it. Because I was at the hospital with Erskine and I couldn't leave him, I really didn't know what to do. Then the Holy Spirit dropped Erskine's coworker, Cory Lawson, in my spirit. So I immediately called him and explained our dilemma. Before I could finish explaining, Cory agreed to take care of it, and before Jasmine's literature class began, he made sure she was in possession of the book she needed. God was always doing amazing things like that for us. I saw it as His way of assuring us that He was taking care of our business because we always tried to take care of His.

Aunt Gale called me one day and said she was coming to the hospital to relieve me for a few hours. I didn't ask her to; she just offered, as she knew I'd been cooped up in that hospital room for several days, taking care of her nephew, and she wanted to give me a break. I was happy because I'd been longing to go home, even if only for a few minutes, just to lay eyes on my girls, to meet whatever needs they may have had, and to briefly see a different environment other than the four walls of that hospital room.

But when I told Erskine that his aunt was coming to relieve me, he immediately shot down my happiness as he said, "Please don't leave me. And don't let her talk you into leaving me either." At that moment, I felt tears welling up in my eyes, so I hurried into the restroom to keep from crying in front of him.

I was so frustrated and confused. And I was tired of that hospital. I started crying out to God inwardly, saying, "Lord, please help me. I can't take this anymore. Erskine needs me, my children need me, and I just don't know what to do. Lord, this is just too much!" I truly felt like screaming. I thought I was going out of my mind. But after taking those few moments to release that pent-up frustration, I dried my eyes and went back into the room with my husband with a new determination to help him get out of that hospital as soon as possible, because I knew my freedom was attached to his.

After learning from one of the nurses that Erskine couldn't be released until his urine output and kidneys looked better, I began the quest of helping to make that happen. In addition to praying, I gave him water and juice around the clock to increase his urination. It seemed to work, and we were both excited each time he felt the urge to go.

My friend Rose Greene from church came to the hospital to visit Erskine, and she brought along a CD of Dr. Creflo Dollar reciting healing scriptures and a CD player on which to play it. Her mom had recently passed, and she wanted to share with us the healing scriptures she had listened to daily. I thought that was an outstanding idea to have God's Word spoken into the atmosphere repeatedly. I hoped it would help to put Erskine's mind battles to rest. But my mind battles were just beginning.

That weekend, a good friend of my dad and stepmom's, Pastor Mamie Harris-Smith from Georgia, came by the hospital to see us and pray with us. When she was about to leave, she suddenly turned to me and said that she had just heard the word "communion" in her spirit. She then asked me if anyone had administered communion to Erskine recently and I told her no. So she encouraged me to have someone come and do that for him.

After she left, I thought about her words, and I wondered if she felt that communion would be the key to Erskine's healing. Then I thought about it again and realized that taking communion would actually signify that he was preparing to die, so I decided against it. I was trying to keep the faith for him, and I was going to continue to believe God for his healing until God personally told me otherwise.

Test results proved that my prayers and efforts concerning Erskine's kidneys and urine output had worked. Just as I'd prayed, he didn't have to be catheterized, nor did he have to dialyze because his kidney function started to improve. And three days after those test results, he was released to go home, though he was still not eating very well.

While hospitalized, Erskine noticed that having the oxygen tubing in his nose made breathing less difficult for him. So we asked if he could be sent home with oxygen. I also requested a wheelchair because walking more than a few steps was no longer possible for him. They assigned us a social worker who helped to get everything he needed. She called a local medical supply company who sent a representative to the hospital with a wheelchair and an oxygen tank before Erskine was discharged. And they delivered a large electric oxygen machine with extra-long tubing to our house for home use.

My brother Dedrick was at our house waiting to help Erskine inside when we arrived. After getting him safely into our bedroom, my brother made a statement to me on his way out that did not sit well with me at the time. He said, "Well, Tracy, at least you are getting a chance to say goodbye. I didn't get that chance when Evette died."

I didn't care for Dedrick's words because I didn't want to accept that Erskine was dying. I was trying to have faith that God would heal him, and I wanted others to believe with me. But my brother's words told me that he had already given up on Erskine's healing because he had looked death in the eye before and knew exactly what it looked like. But I didn't.

Erskine was due to have chemo three days after his discharge, but he and I had a long talk about how he felt the chemo had done him more harm than good. He knew the disease was a factor in his health declining, but he also felt that the chemo was the largest factor in the sudden breakdown of his body, so he refused to have any more. I called his doctor's office to let them know that he was done with chemo, and his oncologist agreed, saying that he had been feeling the same way about it.

After being out of church for so long due to his illness, Erskine and I desperately wanted to go back, as we felt a deep need to be in the midst of the saints, so we planned to go to church the following Sunday.

Upon our arrival, my dad made sure that some of the men were outside waiting to help us, as I would require assistance getting my husband into the church. I could tell that many people were shocked to see just how sick Erskine was. And looking at him made several of them very sad. He was in his wheelchair, he had the oxygen tubing in his nose, and he was very frail and weak. He could hardly hold his head up. This was not the Erskine they were used to seeing.

During the service, my dad had us come before the church to receive prayer. But just before they prayed for us, Erskine and I shared a few words with the congregation, mainly thanking them for all of their prayers and support. After they prayed for us, one by one they were led to bless us with financial offerings. It was such a humbling experience. And though others may have predicted it, I had no idea that day would be Erskine's last Sunday sitting in church with us.

Erskine had been fighting some upper respiratory issues that had begun to get worse, and in addition, he was experiencing hearing loss in his left ear, so I took him to our family ENT doctor, Dr. Jack Dabbs. Dr.

God's Girl

Dabbs verified what Erskine and I had suspected; chemo was the culprit for his hearing loss. Now we wished we had stopped it sooner.

Surprisingly, Erskine's appetite had begun to wake up that morning because before going to the doctor he desired to eat a few chunks of honeydew melon. Then after leaving the doctor, he asked me to buy him a hamburger on the way home. Though he couldn't eat the bun, he did eat the bacon and the meat-patty from the burger. And he even sipped on a milkshake. The girls and I celebrated this milestone because he actually kept his food down this time. The next day, he ate a sandwich and kept it down. We celebrated that too.

Because Erskine had been more comfortable in the recliner at the hospital than in the bed, I bought him a recliner one day that Daddy and Dedrick put together for us. From that day forward, Erskine lived in that chair, day and night, as he said it took pressure off his back.

Since he was doing so well keeping his food down, the next day after a scheduled PET scan, he and I went out to eat lunch at Chili's. That was our first time eating out together since his birthday in June. I had no idea it would be our last. And since our twenty-first wedding anniversary was two weeks away, we considered the lunch an early anniversary celebration.

The following day, Erskine had an appointment with Dr. B. While helping him get dressed for his appointment, I noticed the skin around his waist had turned almost black, and it felt like leather. This was very disturbing. Since he could not turn his head to see what I was so upset about, I took a picture of both sides of his torso and showed it to him. We knew immediately that this was also a result of chemo, and we realized yet again that we made the right decision in stopping it.

At Dr. B's office, he talked to us about a new drug he wanted to use to treat the cancer in Erskine's bones. The drug was called Zometa, and before starting it, he said Erskine would have to have all required dental work done because after starting this new drug he could never have dental work again without experiencing serious jawbone issues.

Because of another bout with low blood, on Friday, October 19, I took Erskine to the cancer center for another blood transfusion. I knew it would take awhile, so I left him there and went back home. As I was leaving home to go back to the cancer center to pick him up, my cell phone rang. It was my dad, who was out of town at the time, as he and Mama Trish were in Chicago on a ministry assignment. Daddy was calling to find out if I had heard the news that they had just heard. When I said I hadn't, he informed me that my sister Triola was dead. I couldn't believe it. Dead? What? Why?

God had healed my sister, and she was doing very well. No longer bedridden, she was up and about, happy, vibrant, and enjoying life again. Why would she be dead? Daddy was just as shocked as I was. And though he and Mama Trish wished they had not been so far away when it happened, they rested in the thought of knowing that God had allowed it. Amazingly, God gave Mama Trish a tremendous amount of peace while dealing with the sudden loss of her oldest child.

But what played repeatedly in my mind was how when many of us thought Triola would die during her grave illness, she shocked us all and lived through it. Even using her highly diseased legs to walk again just as she proclaimed she would. And when we thought she was doing great and had many more years of life to live, she shocked us again when she died from a massive heart attack at the age of forty-five.

I shared the news with Erskine on the way home from the cancer center, and he was just as heartbroken as I was. Tree had been so instrumental in encouraging him through his sickness. And she had recently visited him in the hospital a few weeks earlier. It was so hard to believe she was gone.

Erskine decided he wanted to be the one to break the news to our girls, as we knew hearing about their aunt's death would only make them worry even more about him. He wanted to reassure them that they didn't need to worry about him because he was going to be just fine.

When I picked the girls up from school and returned home, I told them to meet us in our bedroom where their dad was sitting because he wanted to talk to them. The thought of this impending meeting frightened them, as they dreaded family meetings nowadays because lately they seemed to entail frightening news. And some of the girls actually assumed their dad was about to tell them he was dying.

Erskine broke the sad news to them about their aunt Triola, and it put

God's Girl

a heavy damper in the air. And regardless of his insisting that they not worry about him, his struggle to breathe and talk to them at the same time only increased their worries.

Later that week, I took Erskine to an appointment with Dr. D, the radiologist, because Dr. D wanted to speak with us about trying a new procedure on him called Cyberknife. This was a more intense and direct form of radiation that he wanted to perform on the tumors in Erskine's spine. The only issue was Erskine would be required to lay flat on his back and remain very still for several minutes during the procedure. Erskine didn't think he would be able to do this, but we decided to leave it in God's hands and wait and see what happens. Dr. D scheduled the first dose for the following week.

That weekend, as we gathered for my sister's funeral, the simple task of walking from our car into my dad's house to wait for the motor processional to the church proved to be too much for Erskine. When we arrived inside, he could hardly catch his breath and suddenly began to vomit. This frightened many of our family members, and seeing Erskine in such a weak and frail state, while throwing up so violently, only increased everyone's grief.

When we arrived at the church, my dad had someone immediately escort Erskine into the sanctuary and sit him down on a pew near the front, as Daddy knew he was not strong enough to endure the family's processional into the church. Though his demise may have been evident to others, especially as they watched him sitting on that pew looking twice his age, it was not so evident to me because I was trying to keep the faith. In my mind's eye, I saw him coming out of this and looking much better, just like Brother Kenny.

Kenny Cunningham, Sr. was one of our longtime church members who, just a few years earlier, had been healed of cancer. I remember hearing about how faithful his wife, Debra, had been, staying by his side as a caregiver, encourager, and motivator. And she would not allow just anyone to visit her husband, only those whom she felt were strong in their faith, as she wanted no doubters in husband's presence.

When Brother Kenny finally returned to church after being out sick for so long, he literally looked like a dead man walking. He had lost all of his hair and nearly all of his weight. He was so frail and fragile. It was hard to look at him every week without feeling a lump in my throat or tears welling up in my eyes because he was not the same man I once knew. But as the weeks turned into months, and the months turned into years, we all watched Brother Kenny transform back into the healthy and handsome man of God we were used to. So, I was not going to be moved by my husband's looks because I felt, if God could do it for Brother Kenny, He could surely do it for Erskine!

Erskine was scheduled for a dental assessment the following week to determine whether he needed any dental work done prior to starting the Zometa. That visit to the dentist office was very scary for my husband because he worried about me not being able to accompany him in the exam room, and he worried about having to lie too far back in the exam chair, which would be tormenting for him. But after speaking with the dental assistant and explaining his dilemma, they allowed me to stay in the room, and they tried very hard not to make him too uncomfortable. After the assessment, it was determined that Erskine needed a permanent crown put on a tooth in which he had a previous root canal, so they set an appointment to start on this the following week.

19

Too Tired to Cry

> I can do all this through him who gives me strength.
> —Philippians 4:13 (NIV)

November 2012

The second of November was our twenty-first wedding anniversary, and to give us some time alone, our friend Melanie Alexander from church came to pick up our oldest four girls and allowed them to spend the night with her. The twins spent the night with Mama Doll and their cousins.

We didn't do anything special for our anniversary because there wasn't much we could do with Erskine being sick. And I don't remember what was for dinner because he was still not eating, so whatever it was, I ate it alone.

Normally, the night of our anniversary would be topped off with a sweet night of intimacy, but for this anniversary, we simply enjoyed a quiet house together, as the intimate part of our marriage had ended two months earlier. Even hugs between us were scarce. Because of the restriction in his lungs, my husband would have a look of fright if it appeared I was trying to give him a hug. A kiss was okay, but a hug was torture. I really missed the affection we once shared, and I longed for the day when it would return.

I took the opportunity on this kid-free night to work on a project in our small kitchen. I started laminating the floor with squares of sticky-back laminate. Erskine would have been pleased with me just lying down next to him all night, but for some reason I had no desire to lie down. I wanted to do something productive.

Since the kitchen was only two doors away from our bedroom, I could look out into the hall and see him in the bedroom. So, to keep him company, I talked to him and checked on him as I worked. But he wanted to know what I was doing in the kitchen so badly that, before I knew it, he had gotten up and shuffled his way into the kitchen. It felt so good to see him standing because that had become an uncommon sight. But he was only there for a few seconds before he began shuffling back down the hallway to the bedroom, dragging his extra-long oxygen tubing behind him.

Election Day was a few days after our wedding anniversary, and President Barack Obama was running for his second term. But, before we could go vote, I had to take Erskine to the dentist for his temporary crown. He was just as nervous as he was during his previous visit, reiterating that he wanted me in the room with him. I had no idea what difference my being in the room with him was making, but he wasn't having it any other way. I guess my presence was some form of security for him. Anyway, just as the last visit, the dentist allowed me to sit as close as possible to him while he worked in his mouth. After leaving the dentist, we headed to our polling place, where I helped him into his wheelchair and rolled him into the building to cast our votes.

In mid-November, Dr. B gave Erskine his first dose of the bone drug Zometa and an appointment to receive his second dose a month later. This drug was given to him intravenously, pretty much like chemotherapy. A week later, I took him to his last dental visit to have his permanent crown installed.

Erskine's back pain had intensified, and his pain medicines were no longer working for him. When I tried increasing his dosage of Lortab, he would get nauseous and begin vomiting. And though the Tylenol 3 seemed strong enough to hold back his pain, it wore off before it was safe enough to take another dose. I called Dr. B's office and asked if they could give him something more effective, and Dr. B phoned him in a prescription for Oxycodone.

The next morning, which was Thanksgiving, after having taken the Oxycodone the night before, Erskine told me not to give him any more of that medicine because it had affected his breathing during the night. He said he was startled out of sleep several times because he had forgotten to breathe. So we stopped that medication and resumed the others. We came up with a dosing system where every four hours, I'd give him a different pain medicine. For example, I'd give him the Lortab and then four hours later the Tylenol 3, and I'd repeat the cycle every four hours. We continued this regimen all through the day and night. No matter how sleepy I was, I pushed myself to get up and give him his pain medicines and any other medicines he was required to take. And I kept a written record of every medication I administered to him and the times I gave it. I also recorded such things as his blood pressure readings and measurements of his urine output.

As I mentioned, it was Thanksgiving, and to my surprise, three of our daughters woke up that morning with flulike symptoms. Because I knew Erskine's immune system could not handle this, I quarantined them. Then the three well girls and I cleaned the house and prepared a portion of the Thanksgiving meal on which my mom, Mama Doll, and I had planned to collaborate.

That evening, Mama Doll and Nikki's girls, along with Mama, Papa Dewey and his uncle, Fred Johnson, who was the former lead singer for televangelist Jimmy Swaggart's Sunday morning television broadcast in the 1980s, all came together for Thanksgiving dinner. Because Erskine and our three sick girls could not join us in the dining room, and Erskine didn't have a desire to eat anything, made this a very awkward Thanksgiving, but nevertheless, we made the best of it.

Before everyone left for the evening, we all thought it would be a good idea to pray for Erskine, so we gathered in the bedroom around his recliner, and Uncle Fred prayed a moving prayer for my husband that greatly encouraged us to keep the faith.

Erskine was worried about the sick girls being contagious, as he had enough problems to deal with. So I promised him that as soon as morning came, I would take them to the doctor to be treated. However, by the time I got into bed that evening, I had an excruciating headache, which was not normal for me, and by morning, I too was exhibiting flulike symptoms. But I pressed my way to take the girls to the doctor, and I learned that our speculations were correct; they did have the flu. I also knew that if the girls had it, then that's exactly what I had. When we returned home, I called Dr. B to let him know that the flu was in our house and I was concerned about Erskine catching it. So, as a precaution, he decided to put Erskine on flu medication as well.

Impact 2012 would begin in a few days, and it felt very strange to us, having not been involved in its preparations. Usually by Thanksgiving, we would be heavily involved in preparing for the event, buying media supplies and equipment, cleaning the media room, creating disc labels, making a workers' schedule, and much more. But this year we could share no part in the excitement. That is until our friend Joyce Johnson got sick.

We were told that Sister Joyce, our friend and coworker in the media ministry, had been admitted into the hospital with pneumonia on Thanksgiving Day. Since she and her husband, Greg, had been holding down the ministry in our absence, we needed a replacement as soon as possible because Impact was in three days. My brother Dedrick, who used to direct the media ministry before he became director of the music ministry, decided to contact Cynthia Ward, another previous director of the media ministry, and she agreed to step in and help.

Because a lot had changed in the media department since Sister Ward's tenure, she, on a Saturday night, hours before the start of Impact, came to our house bearing soup and juice for Erskine and pen and paper to take down instructions from him about the equipment in the media room. That meeting helped my husband feel valued, needed, and appreciated, regardless of his sickness.

On Monday morning, Jasmine, who was still battling the flu, stayed out of school and went with me to take her dad to the doctor. Erskine had an appointment with Dr. D, the radiologist. This was the day the doctor would try the Cyberknife radiation procedure on Erskine's back in order to shrink the tumors found in his spine. When Dr. D's technician tried to lie him down for the procedure, Erskine could not lie flat, no matter how hard he tried. Nearly in tears, he said he wanted so much to cooperate, but he was extremely uncomfortable and he just couldn't do it. Dr. D had no choice but to give up, so we headed home, feeling defeated.

Out of the blue, about a half hour after returning home, my cousin, Esker Ware, stopped by our house and preached us a mini sermon. Esker didn't know what we had just experienced and how defeated we were feeling. He had no idea that our faith had been shaken and was slipping away. He simply felt urgency in his spirit to come by and give us a word from the Lord.

Everyone who knows my cousin Esker knows that he does not need a pulpit to preach. Esker can and will preach you a motivating sermon anytime and anywhere. When he was done preaching to us and encouraging us with the Word of the Lord, our faith was back as if it had never left! And once again, we were believing the report of the Lord and not the report of man.

Erskine was still not eating and had not eaten anything since before Thanksgiving. And though he was on oxygen, he seemed to be having difficulty breathing. It was evident that he needed to be hospitalized again, but as much as I begged and pleaded with him, he wouldn't comply because he was tired of being admitted. Also, because I wasn't feeling the best as I was dealing with the flu, he worried more about me than himself because I had not had a chance to go to the doctor yet since I was so busy taking care of him and the girls.

Because he wouldn't listen to me, I asked my dad to encourage Erskine to go to the hospital. When Daddy talked to him, Erskine told him that he didn't want to go until I had been taken care of first. And he promised me that as soon as I went to the doctor to be treated for the flu, he would then go to the emergency room. So Jessica stayed out of school to sit with her dad while I went to the doctor.

I was prescribed the same flu medication that Erskine and the girls were taking along with cough syrup and mucus relief pills that made me very drowsy. I knew with me caring for Erskine around the clock, I could not take those too often. Now that I had been treated, Erskine and I discussed his end of the bargain, and he agreed to allow me to take him to the hospital the next morning.

On Thursday morning, November 29, I called Dr. B's office and informed them of what was going on with Erskine and that I felt he needed to be seen. They agreed and encouraged me to take him to the emergency room where Dr. B would meet us. Knowing that they would be admitting him, I packed a bag for Erskine and myself and got us both dressed and ready to go.

After spending an hour or more going back and forth with him about when we should leave, Erskine finally explained to me that he felt too weak to walk from the house to the car and that he just didn't feel strong enough to make this trip to the hospital. That's when I realized my husband needed an ambulance.

I dreaded having to call an ambulance to our house because I didn't want to alarm the neighbors or draw attention. So when I called the ambulance service, I requested that they come quietly without sirens or lights, and they complied.

The spilt foyer entrance to our home posed a problem for the paramedics, as they felt it would not be such a wise decision to bring in the stretcher because it would be difficult getting it out with Erskine on it.

So they asked him if he could at least walk out to the sidewalk, and from there they would put him on the stretcher. He agreed to try.

I stayed very close to my husband as he, like an old feeble man, in pajama pants and a t-shirt, with his head bowed low and his oxygen tubing trailing him, shuffled slowly down the hallway from our bedroom to the living room. Then, down the steps and out to the sidewalk where the paramedics were waiting with the stretcher and a portable oxygen cylinder. Unbeknownst to us, that walk would be Erskine's last.

As they loaded him into the ambulance, I told my husband that I would be on my way, and without delay, I grabbed our bags, locked up the house, and headed for to the hospital.

They admitted him into the hospital as I suspected, and after he was settled in his room, he told me he had to use the restroom. So, per our routine at home, I helped him sit up on the edge of the bed, and then I stood in front of him with my back to him, this allowed him to use my shoulders to pull himself up to a standing position. Then, as he held on to me, we walked slowly toward the restroom. But this time was difficult, as he was having a hard time walking. And when we finally reached the toilet, he nearly fell down trying to sit on it. When I asked him what was wrong, he said that he could no longer feel his right leg.

When he was done, I allowed him to hold on to me again, and I literally had to drag him back to the bed. After that bit of drama, he told me that he wanted to be catheterized so that he wouldn't have to walk to the restroom again, as doing so had taken so much out of him. At first, I assumed that his leg was just asleep, but for him to suggest catheterization, I knew then that this leg issue had to be something serious.

December 2012

We were told that the tumor in Erskine's spine was pressing on a nerve, which is why his leg had stopped working. Funny thing is he could feel me touch it, but he couldn't move it. This is why Dr. D had tried so hard to do the Cyberknife radiation procedure, to prevent this from happening.

Dr. B consulted the neurosurgeon who had discovered those tumors in Erskine's spine because we wanted to know whether surgery was possible, and if so, could it reverse what was happening with his leg.

When the neurosurgeon came by Erskine's room to speak with us, his bedside manner was very poor as he displayed such a repulsive attitude while telling us frankly that he would not even consider doing surgery on Erskine because he knew he wouldn't survive it. That devastated us. This man's attitude had basically said to us, "You're dying! I can't fix you! Get over it!" I do understand that he wanted to be as open and honest with us as possible, but the way he did it was very hurtful. It was as if there was not one compassionate bone in his body. I'm sure he could have given us the same news in a more sympathetic way, which we would have received so much better.

Erskine was heartbroken to the point of tears, but I had actually closed a deaf ear to the surgeon's words because I was determined to continue believing God for my husband's healing until the end.

I assumed Dr. D had given up on Erskine also, but he hadn't. After I told him that Erskine had been admitted, he decided to do normal radiation on him from his hospital bed since the Cyberknife procedure didn't work out. Every day he sent a patient care tech to Erskine's room to wheel his whole bed down to the cancer center, which was on the ground level of the hospital, and once there, they would give him a dose of radiation.

This regimen was torture for Erskine, as his feeble body just couldn't handle the exertion or the pain. One day he declared to me that he had had enough and that he was ready to give up and die. He was tired of fighting to live, because he felt he had no more fight left in him. He told me to tell Dr. D that he wanted all radiation treatments to stop. Then he cried out in frustration, saying, "If God is going to take me, then I wish He would go on and take me now! I never wanted to suffer through death. I just wanted to die peacefully. I just don't believe I should have to suffer like this. I'm a child of God." Not knowing what to say, I just listened. And then, after telling him that I was willing to do whatever he needed me to do, I called Dr. D's office per his request and cancelled his radiation appointment.

After canceling the radiation appointment, I called Mama Doll and told her how Erskine was trying to give up. About an hour later, she and Aunt Gale were at the hospital. When they arrived, I asked them both if God had given them any sign, dream, or vision of Erskine dying. They both said no. They were absolutely positive that he would not die but live. Nevertheless, Erskine waited all day to die, refusing not only radiation but food, medications, and intravenous fluids.

Ever since we married, I had been Erskine's personal barber. Not that I had taken any barbering classes, rather I just knew how to cut all of his hair down low and give him a neat trim. Well, seeing as he didn't lose his hair during the chemotherapy treatments and I had not had an opportunity to cut it in a while with all that we were going through, he was now in desperate need of a haircut. And, as weird as it may seem, since he had decided to give up and die, the only thing I could think of was his hair, as I didn't want him to die without having that final haircut.

I asked Erskine for permission to call Shannon Edwards, our friend at church who is a barber. Then I asked Shannon if he would be willing to come to the hospital and cut Erskine's hair. Shannon came immediately after work that evening and blessed us with his services. His wife, Kiki, and our friend Erika King, who are beauticians, took the blessings a step further a few days later when they went to our house and did our girls' hair as well as mine. Their awesome act of love truly touched my heart.

The next morning, after having waited all day the previous day for God to take his life, Erskine woke up and realized he was still alive. So he began questioning me about whether he should really give up or continue to fight. I told him that as long as there was breath in his body, he should continue fighting to live. So, with those words, he told me to let his nurse know that he wanted to resume all of the things he had told them to stop, even the radiation treatments.

With so many children, Christmas had always been a big deal in our house. Erskine and I enjoyed shopping for gifts for the girls just as much as they enjoyed receiving them. And I loved decorating and setting the Christmas atmosphere in the house for them while they were at school and seeing their faces light up when they arrived home.

Before Erskine was admitted into the hospital, I had already ordered many of the girls' presents online and had been hiding them in our closet whenever they were delivered. One of those presents was a laptop for Jessica. It arrived while they were at school one day, and so I took the opportunity to get Erskine to set it up before I hid it. That turned out to be a good idea because it gave him something to do to get his mind off his pain.

But now, while stuck in the hospital, I worried about the presents being delivered while I was away, and I hoped that nothing came in packaging that would reveal its contents, as I didn't want the girls to see their gifts. I also worried about there being no Christmas decorations or atmosphere set for the girls at home. They told me that they had recently put the tree up by themselves but they had not yet decorated it. I hated that they had to do all of this without their parents.

One day when my dad came to the hospital to see Erskine and me, I asked him if he would sit with Erskine a little while so that I could run home to take care of some things. As I drove, I mentally planned all of the things I needed to do in that small window of time. I stopped by the store and purchased Christmas candy, candy dishes, a Christmas tablecloth, placemats and centerpiece, and a door wreath. Then I ran home and decorated the dining room table, filled the candy dishes with candy, hung the wreath on the front door, and wrote love notes to each of the girls. I attached each note to a piece of candy and left them lying on the sofa for the girls to notice as soon as they got home. After that, I grabbed my extra clothing and toiletries and hurried back to the hospital where my dad and Erskine had both begun to wonder what was taking me so long.

Erskine was starting to hold on to me tighter than normal, so much so that he would not take his eyes off me whenever I was in the room unless he was asleep. One day, as his mom watched him follow my every move with his eyes, she asked him, "Baby, what are you looking at?" and he responded in his usual southern drawl, "My wife."

I always knew my husband loved me, but now at this most desperate moment of his life, he seemed to be showing it the most. He not only kept his eyes on me, but many times when my dad would visit, Erskine's main topic of discussion would be his wife. He was still stuck on his desire to live just so he could spend the rest of his life making me happy and showing me how much he loved and appreciated me for taking care of him during his sickness. I actually didn't think I had done anything so great. I was just doing my job as a wife. And taking care of him was the least I could do because he had worked very hard for many years, even in sickness, providing for our girls and me, so for that, I was tremendously grateful.

Erskine seemed very torn because he wanted to live, but at the same time, he had grown tired and was ready to die. This left me somewhat confused because I no longer knew how to pray for him. So I started praying, "Lord, let Your will be done," but secretly I hoped that God's will would be for him to live and not die. I hoped this was only a faith test and that once God felt we had passed, He would began to heal my husband.

However, each day, rather than grow better, Erskine seemed to grow worse. He not only lost the use of his right leg, but a week later, he could not use his left leg. He would wake me up at all hours of the night asking me to bend his legs for him, and he would beg me to shift his pillows repeatedly in an effort to help him get more comfortable. There was so little I could do to help him, but I tried my best.

To help him with his pain and anxiety, a nurse suggested giving him a dose of morphine, as she said it could help him relax and get some sleep. We agreed to try it. About three to four minutes after receiving the morphine through his IV, I thought my husband was dying. I literally began to freak out because he suddenly became unresponsive, and when I did get him to respond, his speech was slurred. I panicked even more when I raised my voice and shook him and he didn't answer me, so I ran outside to the nurse's station and told them what was going on. The nurse came in to see what I was so worried about, and she pretended to be unalarmed for my sake, but I could tell she sensed there was a problem when she tried to wake him.

As time ticked away, the medicine began wearing off through the night, but it had him feeling very confused. He started talking nonsense, and he knew it was nonsense, but he just couldn't seem to fix his words. This frustrated him to no end.

I explained to him what had happened concerning the morphine and how it was the reason that he was feeling so weird. This really upset him, and together we asked the next nurse on shift to make sure he was not given any more of that medicine. Surprisingly, she told us that it had already been written in his records to discontinue use of that drug.

Erskine told me he wanted to see my dad, so he asked me to call him. Because it was a Sunday morning, Daddy was at church for 8:00 a.m. worship service. I left a message with one of his armor bearers, requesting that Daddy come to the hospital after service to speak with Erskine. While waiting for Daddy, Erskine began sharing with me how he felt about dying, and as he spoke, I began recording him with my tablet just in case he said something that the rest of the family needed to hear.

Erskine: "I don't want to suffer. Okay?"

Tracy: "Uhm hum."

Erskine: "I said early on that I didn't want to suffer through a sickness to leave here."

Tracy: "That's right."

Erskine: "I want to die in peace. You know. I don't like talking about this."

Tracy: "I know."

Erskine: "But I want to die in peace. I want God to give me peace. I see so many people like my sister suffer through sickness. My daddy suffered sickness. I don't want to go out like that." (He began to cry.) "I'm a child of God, and I should be able to just go out peacefully."

Tracy: "That's right."

Erskine: "I should not have to suffer, I don't think. I don't want to suffer, you know. God is my God. And I should just sleep away. You know? I don't want to suffer. Lord God, I don't want to suffer. You know what I'm saying?"

Tracy: "I know. And that's why I asked you if you wanted to keep going through the radiation. Do you really want to keep doing that?"

Erskine: "It's hard for me to decide. Because I don't want to go (die). You know? I wanted to fight. I wanted to be that testimony God raised back up. You know?"

Immediately after the 8:00 a.m. service, Daddy, along with two of his armor bearers, Robert Mauldin and Barry Melton, came to the hospital to see about my husband.

When they got there, Erskine began to cry and pour his heart out as he was still fighting terrible mental battles. He was confused because he no longer knew how to pray, as he had no idea if God wanted him to live or die. And should he die, he wanted to be very sure of his spiritual preparedness to exit earth, as he didn't want there to be anything that would keep him from going to heaven.

To be honest, I really couldn't understand why Erskine worried so much about whether he would make it into heaven. I knew him to be a man who was saved, sanctified, and filled with the Holy Spirit, and he definitely had a personal relationship with God. In addition, he was a man of integrity and great character who instilled the same in his children. He was a great husband, father, and provider, and he spent much of his life doing kingdom work. Seeing how worried he was made me feel very sorry for him, and I prayed that God would give him peace concerning this.

My dad so compassionately did as he had always done; he prayed for Erskine. Then he and his armor bearers laid hands on him and encouraged him. While this was going on, I began filming and taking photos, hoping that this day would be a significant part of Erskine's testimony in the future when God miraculously raised him from his sickbed. I was patiently waiting for this somber trial to transform into our supernatural triumph as God had so faithfully done for us through the years.

I don't know what the doctors and nurses had been discussing amongst themselves concerning Erskine, but I could tell some decisions were being made in private because things started to get a little strange.

A tech came to take Erskine down to the cancer center for radiation on Monday. While he was gone, I sat on my makeshift bed in his hospital room balancing my checkbook and paying our monthly bills online. As I worked, one of the doctors and a nurse entered the room to talk to me. They looked concerned as they made suggestions about me getting out for a while to maybe get some fresh air and take care of any business I needed to take care of. I told them that I was okay and that Erskine didn't want me to leave anyway.

About an hour or so later, I decided to take their advice. And after getting dressed, I asked a kind nurse to look after Erskine for me and I promised not to be gone too long. When I arrived back at the hospital, I was told by the nurse that she had to give Erskine an extra dose of pain medication not only because of his pain but also to calm him down, as he had been very agitated. She said much of his frustration had been because he was looking for me. I panicked when she mentioned the medicine because I assumed she had given him morphine again, but she assured me she had not.

The nurse also informed me that Erskine had completed his radiation treatments. That really confused me because Dr. D had said the treatments would last two weeks, so I wondered why he had decided to end them early. The nurse had no answers for me, and I could tell that she thought I should be happy about him being done with the treatments rather than drilling her as to why they had ended. But I had already been sensing that something wasn't right, and her news only increased those feelings.

I needed answers, and I needed them immediately, so I tried to call Dr. D's office, but he was already gone for the day, so my question would have to wait until the next morning, but I wondered about it all night long. I even questioned Erskine as to why Dr. D had ended his radiation treatments so soon, but he had no clue and really didn't care because he was tired of them anyway.

The next morning, I explained to Erskine that I was going to the cancer center to talk to Dr. D, and I assured him that I would be back soon. As I took the elevator down to the ground floor where the cancer center was located, I was determined that I would not leave that place without an answer. When I went in and asked to see Dr. D, I was told that he was with a patient, so I asked if I could wait for him. They allowed me to wait in one of the exam rooms.

When Dr. D was done with his patient, he came into the exam room to speak with me, and I questioned him about why he had ended Erskine's radiation treatments so soon. A look of compassion came over his face as he led me to his office where he pulled up Erskine's most recent CAT scans on his computer. He explained that although the chemo had begun to shrink the tumor back in May, because Mesothelioma was such a powerful disease, it had begun to fight back with a vengeance. According to the scans, it was no longer contained in its original spot but had spread throughout his body dramatically, including his bones. Therefore, the doctors had conversed and decided that they should cease radiation. Basically, they had given up. And with it being so close to Christmas, they didn't want Erskine to spend his last days in the hospital. They wanted him at home with his family.

I left Dr. D's office in a daze. And I didn't really have time to process his words before I arrived back to Erskine's room. Because I wanted to keep a positive attitude for my husband, I pushed Dr. D's words to the back of my mind, purposely not telling Erskine what the doctor and I had discussed. And he never asked.

Though the doctors may have been giving up on my husband, I was still not ready to give up. I was determined to believe God until the end for some type of miracle. Since there was still breath in his body, I knew it wasn't the end, so I couldn't give up. I had to keep the faith, not only for myself but also for him and the girls. I felt that some way or another, God was going to step in supernaturally, even if it was at the final hour, and save my husband's life.

The next day a thought hit me like a ton of bricks. *Erskine doesn't have a will.* Because I knew I'd rather be better safe than sorry, I quickly phoned the lawyers that were helping us with our Mesothelioma case and asked them if they would prepare him a will. They immediately went to work on my request, promising to be at the hospital the next day in order for him to sign it.

After the call to the lawyers, I decided to talk to Erskine about some things that were running through my head. Death was a subject neither of us ever liked discussing, especially Erskine. In fact, he always declared that he was not going to die but that he would be caught up in the rapture when Jesus comes back. However, at this moment in our lives, we needed to put aside how we felt about the topic of death and discuss some issues concerning it.

I asked him, in the calmest way possible, how he felt about me remarrying if God allowed him to pass. He answered, "Baby, do whatever God tells you to do." Then I asked him about a house.

On several occasions, Erskine and I discussed purchasing a new home because, with our six girls being older now, we felt the need for more space. Other things we needed were a third bathroom, a fifth bedroom, and a larger kitchen. At one point, we were even thinking about building a new home and had even scouted out some land that we were considering purchasing. But life kept getting in the way, pulling that dream further and further from our reach. And now that it appeared Erskine might be dying, I wanted clarity on our dream. Should I continue to pursue it or should I let it go? He had no answers for me. So then I decided to ask, "Well, if I were to buy a new house, could I look at it as a gift from you?" and he answered, "Yes."

Next, I tried to discuss funeral arrangements because I wanted to know if he had any last wishes or special request that I should be aware of, and that's when he began to lose interest in the conversation. A funeral was nothing he wanted to think about, especially his own funeral. So after answering a couple of questions, he told me that he trusted me to handle everything and that he had no specific request.

After so much talk about his possible death, I shared with Erskine that if God did allow him to die, as soon as the funeral was over, the girls and I were going to run to Atlanta, Georgia, to my brother William and his family just to get away. I felt that I would be a lost, devastated, pathetic bundle of nerves on the verge of a mental breakdown if I remained anywhere near home after losing my best friend. Therefore, I would need to get away for a while in order to regroup. Though Erskine agreed, we both hoped it wouldn't have to come to that.

The following day, the lawyers showed up as they had promised, and Erskine felt well enough to sit up and sign his will. When the lawyers left, I decided to leave also. I explained to Erskine that I had some important things to take care of at home and that I'd be returning as soon as I could.

One of the reasons I wanted to go home was to talk to the girls about their dad. At the hospital, the possibility of sending Erskine home on hospice was being discussed and I didn't think it was fair to withhold this important information from the girls. And God forbid if he were to suddenly die and I failed to prepare the girls beforehand. So I explained to them as calmly as I could that there was a possibility their dad would not make it. Then Joycelyn, our twelve-year-old, asked, "Mama, what do you mean?" And I replied, "He's not doing very well. He may die."

Joycelyn was confused because all year I'd been adamantly declaring that their dad would be healed, and now I was telling them that he might die. So she boldly shared with me how every night she had been hearing the words in her spirit, "You can't have a testimony without a test," and she was positive that God was telling her that all of this was just a test for her dad and that he would be healed and have a great testimony. I told Joycelyn and her sisters that although things looked bad for their dad, we would continue to believe God for his healing until the end. Suddenly, Jasmine burst into tears, crying uncontrollably. Then some of the other girls started to cry. I didn't know what to do at that moment because though I wanted to comfort them, I also wanted to cry with them.

Zambia and Andrea had not arrived yet, however I really needed someone to help me console my children. So I phoned my neighbor Yolanda Blevins and asked her to come over and help me. Yolanda came to our rescue immediately and she was a loving comfort to my children and a dose of strength for me.

After we dried our tears and Yolanda left, I went into my bedroom and shut the door to wrap some of the girls' Christmas gifts that were delivered by UPS a few days earlier. I was fighting so hard to give them a sense of normalcy in their abnormal world. As soon as I finished wrapping the gifts, I had Jessica and Jasmine to come in and help me change the comforter on my bed to a more teen-friendly one that I picked up from the store on the way home because I was about to turn my and Erskine's bedroom into theirs.

Since the den downstairs was the largest area that could accommodate a hospital bed, I planned to make that Erskine's room if they actually did send him home on hospice. Therefore, I needed to create a new den where the children could watch television and do homework, so I decided to turn Jessica and Jasmine's tiny bedroom under the stairs into the new den and allow them to have our bedroom upstairs.

Because I didn't know when Erskine would be coming home, I decided I'd better get started making my changes as soon as possible. I frantically cleaned out our drawers, putting everything in garbage bags, and I told Jessica and Jasmine to finish the job after I had gone back to the hospital because it was getting late and I knew Erskine would be looking for me. Sure enough, before I could finish, he called. Actually, his mom called. Mama Doll was there at the hospital visiting him, and she said that he was so worried about where I was that he insisted she call me for him.

Erskine pitifully told me how he had been asleep, and when he awoke and didn't see me for a long time, he assumed I'd left him, for good. He said while he was asleep, he dreamed that a doctor had told me that he was dying and that I should probably just leave, so he thought that's what I had done, left him. Those words broke my heart, and I immediately stopped what I was doing and made my way back to that hospital.

When I reached the hospital, I discovered what might have given Erskine that troubling dream. I ran into Dr. B in the hallway on my way to Erskine's room, and he shared with me that while I was away, Erskine had given his consent to hospice care and that he would be going home in two days. This had to be the conversation Erskine was having before he fell asleep. I also figured this to be the reason for that weird visit from that doctor and nurse who had come to me the day before, suggesting that I leave the hospital for a while. They probably wanted to talk to Erskine alone, assuming I would have hindered him from consenting.

Because I didn't understand the way hospice worked, I asked Dr. B if I could bring Erskine back to him if things didn't improve while he was at home on hospice. The sorrow that I saw in that man's eyes when I asked him that question made me feel very uncomfortable.

In answering my question, he explained that once a patient consents to hospice care, they are no longer under their doctor's care. So in essence, Erskine's health was out of his hands. He also explained that I would not be able to call him or 911 in case of an emergency. I could only call the hospice service. Right away, my heart sank because this was terribly shocking to me, and as I walked away from Dr. B, I couldn't help but feel that we were trapped in a bad decision.

After explaining to Erskine what I had just discovered about hospice, I asked him if he knew all of that when he consented. He said he didn't. So then I felt a really big mistake had been made. I ran back to the nurse's station, hoping Dr. B would still be there, and he was. I told him we had decided to change our minds concerning the hospice care, and he explained to me that there was no other option. My heart sank again, and immediately I imagined myself grabbing this man by both arms, shaking him, and screaming to the top of my lungs, "Dr. B! You can't give up on my husband! You've got to help him like you did back in 2000!" But realizing there was nothing he could do this time, I kept my hands to myself and just walked away, once again feeling defeated.

I had no other choice but to leave Erskine at the hospital alone the next day, which was a Friday, because I was on a mission to get the den rearranged for his return, as he would be coming home on Saturday.

The first stop I made was at the high school to check out my oldest three daughters. I had not warned them that I was coming, so when they came to the office, they looked very worried. When we got in the car, they began asking me what was going on, and that's when I got very real with them. I said, "I need ya'll. I have to prepare the house for your daddy to come home tomorrow, and I can't do this by myself. And I'm not just saying I need your help today, because if he does die, I am going to need the three of you to help me raise your younger sisters." Then I spoke directly to Jasmine, who was looking as if she wished not to be having this conversation. I said, "Jasmine, I know you don't like talking about this, but Mama needs you to put on your big-girl pants now and help me!" I worried a lot about that girl during her dad's sickness, as she was the one who seemed to take it the hardest. I just knew that if he ever passed, Jasmine would have the worst time getting over it.

After our talk, the girls agreed to do whatever I needed them to do, so we headed home, where Mama and Papa Dewey were waiting with boxes ready to help us.

We emptied the entertainment center, bookshelves, and dresser drawers that were in the den and packed the items in boxes. Then my uncle Michael Newell and his friend hauled away the furniture, electronics, and other items that I was forced to give away. Afterward, we lined our many boxes of belongings around the walls of the den. Before long, Daddy was there with my uncle Lonzo Arrington, who was installing a new hot water tank as our old one had recently crashed. And my brother Dedrick, my cousin Corey Bodley, and our neighbor Robert Blevins showed up to help us move all of the furniture.

When it was all over and nearly everyone was gone, I headed back to the hospital to be with Erskine. After I left, Zambia arrived, and she helped the girls and my mom, who was giving orders like a drill sergeant: sweep, mop, dust, wash walls, and clean baseboards. Mama even took it a step further and had the girls hang Christmas lights in the den, hoping to bring the Christmas spirit downstairs to Erskine since he wouldn't be able to see the decorations or the tree that were upstairs.

God's Girl

On Saturday morning, Mama and Papa Dewey were at our house to receive the hospital bed and other medical equipment that were delivered that afternoon. And later, upon realizing that the hospital bed had come without linen, they ran off in search of white bed linen, which they put on the bed just moments before Erskine's arrival.

After a total of sixteen days in the hospital, Erskine finally returned home to his family on a cold Saturday evening in mid-December.

The ambulance in which Erskine was transported followed me from the hospital to our house. When we arrived, I called inside and told the girls to open the double doors of the playroom, which was once a garage years before we bought the house.

It was a bit of a struggle getting Erskine from the playroom to the den because of the oddly shaped entryway. I was sure that at any moment he was going to beg them to leave him alone, as they were pushing and pulling and taking him through such turmoil trying to get him through that doorway. But to my surprise, Erskine continued to smile, letting me know that he was just happy to be home.

About thirty to forty-five minutes after the paramedics left, the hospice nurse arrived. She introduced herself to us, assessed Erskine's vital signs, and explained to us how hospice works. She also informed us that she was not his assigned nurse, as she was only filling in for her. She said the assigned nurse would be by the following day.

Later, after the nurse had gone, I realized that during all of my preparing for Erskine's arrival, I never once thought about preparing a place for me to sleep. So I ended up making a pallet on the cold, hard linoleum floor next to his bed, which wasn't very comfortable. But comfort for me didn't matter at the time because I was up all night seeing about his comfort.

Early Sunday morning, while Erskine was sleeping, I ran to the local Walmart and purchased a camping cot, which I placed alongside his bed as a makeshift bed for me. Later that day, his actual hospice nurse arrived.

She was an elderly lady who asked me question after question concerning Erskine's abilities, disabilities, and other medical issues as she filled out a checklist. And according to her checklist, Erskine was displaying the symptoms of someone who was near death. I didn't want to hear that, nor did I want to believe it. I was sure she had no idea what she was talking about, even with the many years of experience she claimed to have had.

One of the things she added to her checklist was how I had mentioned that Erskine would occasionally talk out of his head. He would blurt out things that just didn't make sense to us. But rather than believe it was one of the symptoms of his demise, as she claimed, I felt sure that it was just a side effect of some of the medicines he'd been prescribed. However, she was adamant about what she knew. And her sternness made my girls and me dislike her very much. I wondered why the hospice service had sent this negative old woman to us. But in hindsight, I realize she wasn't being negative; she was just being real.

About an hour after the hospice nurse had gone, Erskine had a bowel movement that I assumed I could handle by myself. I was sadly mistaken, as I discovered that changing a baby's diaper was nothing like changing an adult's, especially a paralyzed adult. I felt so helpless. After cleaning him as best I could, I took a few moments to brainstorm. *Who could I call to help me?* I was not about to ask my young daughters for help, and I was not about to call that negative hospice nurse back. As I continued to think, I heard in my spirit, "Sister Shelia."

Shelia Porter was a retired dialysis nurse and a member of our church. When I called her, she was at the church's Christmas program singing in the choir. She promised me that as soon as the program was over, she would be by to help me.

Sister Shelia was a lifesaver! Not only did she help me clean and change my husband, but her presence, her sweet spirit, and her friendly advice were so calming to Erskine and me both. She even returned on Monday morning and stayed with me a good while, helping me to care for Erskine.

God's Girl

A while later, Erskine's cousin Daphne Stout Jones came to assist me and before long, the hospice nurse returned.

The hospice nurse, whom I'd venture to say was about five feet and six inches in height, about 165 pounds, and about seventy-plus years of age, decided to change Erskine's bed sheets. Knowing Erskine could not move his bottom half, I wondered how in the world she was going to perform that task. And when I questioned her about it, she was dead-set on showing me.

With my and Daphne's assistance, as Sister Shelia was gone by this point, the nurse did some rigorous maneuvering trying to change the linen while Erskine was still lying in the bed. Because of the tumor in his back, he groaned in pain and begged us to stop. Daphne and I both stopped, but the nurse encouraged me to continue, saying it wouldn't take long at all.

Daphne, who was once a nurse herself, was so distraught watching her cousin go through such agony that she sat on my cot and fell over crying. Finally, I told the nurse that this was not working and we needed to stop; however, she was very adamant about finishing the job.

To make the job easier, the nurse decided that she and I should put Erskine in his recliner. But I wondered how in the world we were going to do that. After pushing the recliner close to the bed, she had me hold one side of the sheet that was under him, and she held the other side. Then together we tried dragging him to the edge of the bed where we would do a quick lift from the bed's edge to the recliner. But the whole time we worked, Erskine was begging us to stop. I'm sure he was worried because he knew I was too short for the job and she was too old. By the time we got him halfway into the recliner, he looked me square in the eye and said, very breathlessly, "Tracy, listen to me." His words and tone grieved me, and I became quite confused because I didn't know whether, by obeying the nurse, I was helping or hurting my husband.

This sheet-changing job had not been as simple as the nurse promised it would be. And rather than lift Erskine into the chair, it was more as if we dragged him into that chair. And when it was all over, I didn't feel a sense of accomplishment, rather I felt crushed because I had played a hand in torturing my sick husband.

When she finished making his bed, I told the nurse I wanted Erskine to remain in his recliner. I just couldn't allow her to cause him any more unnecessary pain.

A few hours later after the nurse and Daphne had gone, the girls arrived home from school, and they were very surprised to see their dad sitting in his recliner watching television. That was the most normal thing they had seen him do in a long time.

Erskine later began to get irritable because he was tired of sitting in that position; he wanted to lie down again. So our friend David Davis came over to help me get him back in bed.

Unaware that Erskine was paralyzed from the waist down, David attempted to pull him up to a standing position when I suddenly yelled, "No! He can't walk!" I'm sure I frightened David, but thinking of the potential danger that my husband was in actually frightened me. And Erskine's afternoon had already included enough pain and agony for the both of us.

It had been close to two weeks since Erskine's last haircut, so I called Shannon earlier in the day and asked if he would come by our house and give him another cut. He kindly obliged saying he would be by later that evening. So, not long after David had settled Erskine back into his bed, Shannon arrived.

I could tell that it bothered Shannon and David to see Erskine's condition had grown worse since they saw him last. I could tell because the sadness showed on their faces, especially Shannon's. However, I understood their sadness because their friend didn't quite look or act like himself anymore. Nor did he talk as much as he used to; he just smiled at them and repeated whatever I told him to say.

For some reason, rather than give Erskine the same type haircut he had given him in the hospital, this time Shannon cut it off very low, only leaving him with stubble. To be honest, I was a little disappointed as I watched him do this, wondering why he had made him so bald. I later learned that Shannon had sensed this haircut would be Erskine's last, as he saw how fast he was deteriorating. I assume he felt that Erskine would not be able to withstand another haircut even if he lived another two weeks, so he wanted to make this one last longer. When Shannon was done, I told Erskine to say "Thank you," and he gave Shannon a big smile and then repeated my words.

That night, after everyone left, the girls and I noticed that Erskine's condition was growing worse because he was blurting out things that didn't make sense and trying over and over to snatch off his covers, his clothing, and his oxygen tubing. It felt as if he were reverting to a child. But the next morning, he was surprisingly much calmer. And as the hours passed, he actually said less and less; he just lay there sleeping. I figured he was just tired from being up so late. But the further into the afternoon it became, I noticed he was still not saying much, and whenever I tried talking to him, sometimes he'd respond, and sometimes he wouldn't. Finally, when he wouldn't say anything at all, I called his mom and told her that something was going on because he had become unresponsive. It seemed he was slipping away. Mama Doll and Aunt Gale and their older sister, Aunt Rachel Hinton, who was in town visiting that week, were at our house in a heartbeat.

After calling the hospice nurse, I called my parents and told them that I felt we needed to administer communion to Erskine immediately because he was trying to leave us. In minutes, there were family members, church members, and neighbors at our house. And my brother William and his family, who had just arrived minutes earlier from Atlanta, Georgia, to see Erskine, did not expect the drama they walked into.

During all of the commotion, our girls were coming in from school looking confused because of all the people in our house. It hurt my heart to have to tell them that their dad had become unresponsive. I tried with everything in me not to say he was dying because I didn't want to break their hearts.

As everyone came in, they each went to Erskine's bedside to speak to him. Our daughter Jasmine, who was watching from across the room, was disturbed by the fact that her dad was not responding to anyone. She watched as her Grandma Trish and her cousin Daphne both stood over him calling his name and lightly tapping him with no response. Finally, she went over to his bedside, shook him, and called out, "Daddy!" and he opened his eyes. Then she heard Mama Trish say, "He knows his baby's voice." At that moment, Jasmine said she could feel the tears that she had been holding back trying to force their way out, so she hurried away from her dad's bedside and went into the playroom where her Grandma Doll and several others happened to be gathered. Jasmine threw her arms around her grandma's neck and sobbed uncontrollably.

Through her tears, she questioned Mama Doll, saying, "I don't understand. I thought God said that He would heal my daddy. I don't understand." Sadly, her grandma had no answers, but she hugged her, cried with her, and let her know that her daddy loved her very much. Then Mama Doll took the opportunity to give Jasmine a big-girl talk, as she explained to her the mistakes her own daughter Karilyn had made in life, and she encouraged Jasmine not to make those same mistakes, such as using sex, drugs, or alcohol as comfort tools. She encouraged Jasmine to always find her comfort in God.

After crying on her grandma's shoulder, Jasmine left the room to find Zambia, whom she and her sisters had nicknamed "T-Nanny Z" because she was like an aunt and a nanny all in one. God used Zambia during that season to be an awesome source of strength and comfort for my girls.

When we all gathered in the den around Erskine's bed for communion, amazingly he woke up for this sacred ceremony, smiling, waving, and looking around at everyone. And to my surprise, he even swallowed the juice and the wafer with no problems at all.

After all of our company had gone, everyone except for my brother William and his family who were staying the night with us, we began to settle down for the evening because the girls had school the next day. As I mentioned a few chapters back, during Erskine's sickness, the girls and I recited healing scriptures and prayed over him almost every night. So on this particular night, we all gathered around his bed and did that, with William, his wife Bridgette and their son and daughter joining us in prayer.

As weird as it may sound, as each of the girls and I recited our scriptures, I was hoping Erskine didn't want to recite his scripture. You see, by this point, I had started to become very disheartened because I was trying so hard to keep the faith, but at the same time, I was witnessing the rapid decline of my husband's health. Therefore, I felt his scripture, which was Psalms 118:17, "I shall not die, but live, and declare the works of the Lord," no longer pertained to him because clearly he was dying. I didn't want to keep tormenting him or myself by allowing those words to continue hanging on the wall near his bed. Therefore, earlier that day, I removed the scripture from the wall and placed it in a drawer while he was sleeping.

However, as soon as the last scripture was recited by the girls and me, Erskine, the same man who was unresponsive just a few short hours earlier, decided he wanted to say his scripture too. So he began looking around the wall for it, and when he didn't see it, he asked, "Where's my scripture?" Then everyone started questioning me saying, "Where is his scripture?" I reluctantly went over to the drawer, pulled it out, and taped it back to the wall. Then we all helped him recite it, as he was having difficulty with his words. When he was done, he had the biggest grin on his face. But there was a bit of sadness in my heart because I couldn't understand why God was allowing him to put his trust in words that were turning out to be so untrue for him.

After everyone went to bed, I stayed up for a while dealing with Erskine because, out of frustration, he kept pulling off his oxygen and his hospital gown. I was trying to stop him because I didn't want him to deprive himself of oxygen, and I didn't want him to be exposed if the girls happened to walk in. We had no real privacy in the den because there was not a real door to the den, only a makeshift door that my mom and pop had fashioned with a freestanding room divider. But Erskine was frustrated because he wanted to get out of that bed. He wanted to walk. And he wanted to go upstairs. I had to tell him repeatedly that he couldn't go up there. I finally called the hospice service and they had his nurse to return my call. Because Erskine wasn't swallowing food or pills anymore, the nurse instructed me to crush two of his pain pills and mix them with a few drops of water. Then, using a syringe, I was to put the mixture in the back of his mouth so that he would swallow it. I did just as I was instructed, and it wasn't long before he drifted off to sleep.

The next morning, Erskine was just as restless as he was during the night, and I felt so sorry for him because I couldn't help him. I called the hospice service again, and because his normal nurse was unavailable, they sent out two other nurses in her place. After observing Erskine, the nurses decided he needed morphine, and they gave me a prescription to go out and have filled immediately. They said they would sit with Erskine while I went to the drugstore, but I was a bit nervous in leaving him because I knew how attached to me he was. I was afraid he would assume I'd left him again.

With their urging, I went on to the drugstore and tried to come back as quickly as I could. When I returned, they told me that Erskine looked around the room frantically the entire time I was away, searching for me. After explaining how to administer the morphine to him, the nurses watched me do it and then left. And when the medicine hit his bloodstream, he fell fast asleep.

That night, as the girls hung out upstairs with T'NannyZ, I stayed downstairs catering to Erskine. After having to give him more morphine for restlessness, he was finally settling down again. While he lay there drifting off to sleep, I decided to lie on my cot and get a few minutes of sleep as well. I don't know how long I slept, whether it was a few minutes or more; all I know is something within me made me jump straight up and look at my husband. When I looked at him, I was a bit startled because he looked dead. But I noticed he was still breathing, so I calmed down. But immediately the Holy Spirit spoke to me, telling me it was time. I knew exactly what that meant. It was time to let go.

I marched straight upstairs to the living room where the girls were still spending time with Zambia. I then shared with them what the Holy Spirit had just revealed to me, and I told them that it was time to release their dad because he was ready to go. I told them he was about to be leaving us soon, whether we liked it or not, so it would be best if they released him. Then I went back downstairs and did exactly what I had told them to do. I released my husband. In tears, I kissed him and whispered in his ear that it was okay, he could let go now. And I assured him again that the girls and I would be just fine.

I learned later that after I left the living room, there was total silence as my girls were in complete shock and their faces were dripping with silent tears. Hearing me, the woman who had been so full of faith, now saying, "Release your dad," was just too much for them to absorb. Jasmine remembers sitting at the top of the stairs with her arms around Janay as they both cried. And Zambia, who tried her best to be a comfort to my girls and who had lost her own dad during a Christmas season when she was very young, remembers holding back tears as she got in her car to leave that night. But when Deitrick Haddon's song "Well Done" started to play on her radio, she said a dam broke inside of her, forcing out a flood of painful tears.

The next day, the girls released their dad at different times during the day. Then when evening came, a flood of visitors came with it, which was strange because I had not shared with anyone besides my immediate family what the Holy Spirit had revealed to me. But it was as if the Holy Spirit had told these people, "Go see him before it's too late," as nearly every thirty minutes our doorbell was ringing.

LaTanya Tarver Lee, my friend from childhood, and her husband, Vincent Lee, were some of those who came by to see Erskine that night. Vincent remembered visiting Erskine in the hospital the week before and promising him that he would return on another day. He said he didn't want Erskine to pass before he had the opportunity to keep his promise, so he and LaTanya came by with a CD of healing verses read by one of my dad's friends, Dr. Michael Moore of Faith Chapel Christian Center in Birmingham, Alabama.

During the visits, Erskine, who by now seemed to have lost his ability to talk, was trying to remove his oxygen tubing and undress himself while people were in the room. I was struggling to stop him. It felt as if he was acting out of frustration because he wanted to say something to me but couldn't. It reminded of a dream he told me he had a month or so earlier.

One morning he woke up telling me he had dreamed that there were motorcycles all over our lawn and several people in our house. He said that he was getting frustrated in the dream because he kept trying to talk to me, but I couldn't hear him for all of the people and the noise. Well, because of all of the people that were coming by to see him now and the fact that he couldn't talk anymore, resulting in his acting out by tearing at his clothes and oxygen tubing, makes me wonder if this was actually the manifestation of his dream.

Because of Erskine's aggravation and my frustration, our guests kindly cut their visits short. And when Erskine and I were finally alone again, I put on the healing scriptures CD that LaTanya and Vincent had given us. As Dr. Moore read the scriptures aloud, I repeated each word to Erskine while anointing him with oil from head to toe. Then, with tears flowing from my heavy heart, I prayed passionately for my husband while massaging his paralyzed legs.

Though I saw Erskine swiftly fading before me, I secretly wondered if God still had some type of miraculous healing plan up His sleeve. Was He going to raise him up from his sick bed minutes before he took his last breath? Or was He actually going to allow him to die then raise him as He did Lazarus? Whatever His plan, I was desperately awaiting it.

As I prayed for my husband, anointed him, and massaged him, he watched me intently. This kept him incredibly calm and relaxed. But when I was done and attempted to lie down to get some sleep, his agitation returned, as either he wanted me to continue or he still wanted to say something to me. I just didn't know. But to calm him down, I gave him a dose of morphine. And a few minutes later, he was asleep.

20

My Apocalypse

> Then I heard a voice from heaven say, "Write this: Blessed are the dead who die in the Lord from now on." "Yes," says the Spirit, "they will rest from their labor, for their deeds will follow them."
>
> —Revelation 14:13 (NIV)

The continuation of my story begins on Friday, December 21, 2012, and in my research of that day in history, I made two very surprising discoveries that I'd like to share with you before continuing my story.

First of all, though it had been rainy and bitterly cold for several days prior, the calendar marked December 21, 2012, as its first official day of winter. I found this quite interesting because in my literature classes in grade school and college, I remember learning that a reference to winter symbolized the end of something or, more commonly, death.

Lastly, as it relates to calendars, on November 13, 2009, Sony Pictures released the disaster movie *2012* regarding the near-total destruction of planet Earth. I'm sure many of you remember that movie, but what many of you may not remember is that movie was actually based on predictions made by ancient Mayans thousands of years ago. According to the Mayan calendar, it was predicted that the world would end in the year 2012, as they feared an apocalypse would occur on earth during that year.

If you can recall, when the year 2012 drew closer, rumors of the coming doom began spreading like wildfire. There were many who believed the rumors and had actually begun making doom day preparations, and then there were those who didn't take the predictions very seriously. Nevertheless, in my recent research, I was stunned to discover an important piece of information that I did not remember hearing during all of that talk of impending doom. Ancient Mayans had not only predicted the year of the doom, but they had also calculated a specific date in which the world was due to end. December 21, 2012.

Although the world may not have ended on that day as had been predicted, that was the day my world ended. That was the day my girls and I had our own apocalypse. That was the day our strongman, our godly covering, our spiritual covering, our beloved husband and father, Erskine Daniel Jr., went home to be with the Lord.

During the night of December 20, after I had given him the morphine and he fell asleep, I went to sleep also. In the middle of the night, I remember checking on him as I got up to use the bathroom, and he was still asleep. I was actually surprised that he was still sleeping so soundly, but I figured the medicine was still working, so there was no cause for alarm. When I went to the bathroom again, somewhere around 5:00 a.m., I looked at him and thought for a second that he had died, but I saw his chest move, so I calmed down. About two hours later, 7:00 a.m. to be exact, the Holy Spirit shook me, just as it did the night before when I woke up and went upstairs to talk to the girls about releasing their dad.

This time when I looked at my husband, he looked the same as he did the first two times. He was lying in the same reclined position with his mouth open. I looked at his chest as I had done when I checked on him earlier, but this time I didn't see it move. Then, to make sure I wasn't hallucinating, I tore up my cot in a desperate search for my eyeglasses and frantically threw them on my face. Then I stared at his chest again. It still wasn't moving. Instantly, I felt as if I'd stepped into a wildly surreal ambiance as everything that transpired from that moment forward felt like a dream. That's because as soon as I discovered my husband had died,

God's Girl

God scooped me up, placed me away in a safe place, and allowed the Holy Spirit in me to take control.

I ran to the phone and called the hospice service as I had been instructed to do in such an event, but surprisingly the line was busy. I hung up and tried again. Still busy. Not knowing what to do next, I called Daddy and Mama Trish. When Mama Trish answered, I said, "Mama, he's gone." Then she woke Daddy and said, "Baby, Tracy said he's gone." Daddy told her to tell me that he was on the way, and I told her to tell him to hurry, as I had not yet told my girls, who were still sleeping, because I wanted him to break it to them.

I called the hospice service again, and this time I got an answer. I told them my husband had died, and they said they would be sending the nurse out immediately. Then I called Mama Doll, Mama and Papa Dewey, Sister Shelia, Zambia, and David.

Word of Erskine's death began to spread rapidly, as a few minutes after making those phone calls, I received a call from my friend Kiki who wanted to give her condolences and check on me. During our conversation, I asked her if she would please refrain from posting anything concerning Erskine on Facebook because I had not yet broke the news to my kids. I knew that sometimes my girls would lie in bed and scroll social media before getting up, and I did not want that to be the way they found out their dad had died. I then asked Kiki if she would be so kind as to keep a watch on social media for a couple of hours to make sure no one posted it before my girls found out.

Arriving simultaneously was Zambia and Sister Shelia. When I called them, I had asked that they not ring the doorbell as not to wake the girls. Therefore, I had to listen for their light knocks at the door. When they arrived, we all spoke in hushed tones, still trying to let the girls sleep until my dad arrived.

Sister Shelia went straight to the den to see Erskine's body. When she felt him, she stated that he was still warm, which confirmed to me that he had just died around 7:00 am as I suspected.

A few minutes later, David arrived at the back door, and shortly afterward, I was surprised to see Sister Ward show up. It seemed like forever before Daddy arrived, but that was because I was so anxious to get past the hard part of telling my children. David and I kept an eye out for Daddy at the back door, and as soon as he got there, we whisked him upstairs into the living room where he sat and waited on Zambia and me to wake the girls.

Zambia and I went into different bedrooms to wake the girls, explaining that they needed to come into the living room because their granddad wanted to talk to them. A few of the girls did not cooperate immediately because they were concerned about their morning appearance. But after much coercing, they came. Later they all said they had a feeling the conversation would involve bad news about their dad, especially after seeing other people in the house so early in the morning.

As soon as the girls were in the living room with Daddy, the doorbell rang. It was the hospice nurse. I was so glad we had the opportunity to wake the girls before that doorbell woke them up. While Daddy talked to the girls, Zambia, David, and Cynthia stayed near to comfort them. Meanwhile, Sister Shelia and I went downstairs to talk to the nurse.

I told the nurse that Erskine died around 7:00 a.m. But she listed the time of death as 7:45 a.m. because she said it was protocol to report the time she found him deceased. She did her paperwork and made the necessary phone calls, which included calling the funeral home to come and pick up his body. Sister Shelia helped her clean his body and prepare him for his departure to the funeral home.

My girls, who remember many of the things their granddad said to them that day, has mentioned that having him break the news to them was a good idea, as it actually helped to ease their hurt. They remember him calmly saying, "Girls, your daddy is not suffering anymore. He has gone on to be with the Lord. And he's doing much better up there with Him." He also told them, "It's okay to cry, but when you are done, wipe those tears away and continue to live." Realizing that they would be going downstairs to see their dad's body, he added, "When you go see him, just remember that body you're looking at is not your daddy. It's just a house that his spirit used while living here on earth. Erskine's spirit is now with the Lord."

By this time, Mama Doll and my nieces, Mama and Papa Dewey, and

God's Girl

Mama Trish were there along with several other people and many more on the way. Everyone stood around with tears in their eyes as they watched the girls say goodbye to their dad. I remember being so worried about how Jasmine was going to handle it since she had been the one that took his sickness the hardest. But to my surprise, she was the one comforting her sisters. She says hearing her granddaddy say repeatedly, "That body you're looking at is not your daddy. He is with the Lord," is what helped her hold herself together.

Sadly, the longer the girls looked upon their dad's deceased body, they began breaking down left and right. I thank God that we had family and friends there to offer comfort. It grieved everyone to hear Jessica, our twelfth grader, sobbing and saying, "He won't be able to see me graduate." That actually broke my heart into a million pieces because all I ever wanted when I married their dad, besides living happily ever after, was for us to never divorce, as I wanted to save my children the mental anguish I suffered as a child. And in my efforts to protect them from the negative effects of divorce, I never considered that they could experience something far worse than the divorce of their parents, which was the death of a parent.

Also, I fought hard to protect my children's hearts and faith during their dad's sickness, and now that he was gone and I saw them grieving uncontrollably, I felt as if I had let them down. At this moment, I realized there was nothing more I could do to help them. Their dad was gone, and no amount of praying, singing, or scripture reading was going to change that.

My heart even ached for Erskine's mom, who had lost her husband in 2004, her only daughter in 2011, and now her only son in 2012. I can't even imagine what that must have felt like, to have your whole family disappear, one by one before your eyes. Her situation reminded me of Naomi in the book of Ruth who also lost her husband and only two children. I must say though, I was truly amazed at the supernatural strength God gave my mother-in-law to make it through such a terrible misfortune with her faith in God still intact.

Not long after we said our goodbyes, the people from the funeral home arrived to take Erskine away. Shortly afterward, the medical supply company showed up to get the bed, the oxygen, and all other medical equipment we had been leasing. During all of this activity, my brain had already leaped to the next phase, funeral planning. I asked Mama Trish to help me find matching fuchsia dresses for the girls to wear to the funeral, and she got on it immediately. And though the color I had chosen was out of season, she pulled her tablet from her purse and, with the help of her best friend, Anita Carlisle, whom my siblings and I nicknamed "Auntie Nita," they began searching several websites and didn't stop until they had found the perfect dresses.

In an effort to lift the girls' spirits, Zambia decided she wanted to take them to a Christmas party that the church youth ministry was having that night. So, in the midst of the many people coming in and out of my house to give their condolences, I told the girls to wash their hair, and my sister Fran and my cousin Andrea helped me style each of the girls' hair for the party.

When the house finally thinned of its visitors, I remember trying to fit in a quick bath, but as soon as I sat down in the tub, the visitations started up again, forcing me to make my bath even quicker than I had planned. All day as word spread of Erskine's death, people were stopping by nearly every hour to bring food, drinks, monetary gifts, and love.

When it was time for bed, Jessica and Jasmine assumed I would return to my old bedroom to sleep with them, but I didn't. I didn't want to return to the bed that their dad and I once shared, and I for sure didn't want to return to the cot in the den where he passed away. So I chose to make my bed on the sofa in the living room.

The constant activity that had transpired in my house all that day never gave me the opportunity to absorb the real reason behind it all. I mean, it really had not soaked in my brain that all of this commotion was because my husband was gone. I was a widow. My children were fatherless. But as I lay thinking about all of this, God intervened just before I could start enjoying my pity party as He instantly rocked me to sleep. A good sleep. The kind I had not enjoyed in a very long time.

Our weekend was filled with even more visitors, and we barely had time to get out of bed and get dressed before they started arriving. On Sunday, the girls and I went to church because that was all we knew to do. It felt weird though, being there without Erskine. It also felt weird because I sat in the pew on the main floor, alone. The girls didn't want to sit on the main floor, as they wanted to sit in their usual place, which was in the balcony. But my and Erskine's usual place was in the media room, which was located in the balcony also. That's where you could find us every Sunday, working like busy bees. Now that he was gone, I had no desire to be anywhere near the media room, so I sat on the main floor in the pew with the other church members, feeling awkward.

After church, we went home where there was plenty of food to eat from all of the loving condolences. And later, our support team, which consisted of Mama and Papa Dewey, Zambia and her son, Iain, my cousin Andrea and her girls, Deandrea and Ava, and later Daddy. They all gathered to check on us and to just spend time with us. As we sat around eating, laughing, and talking, Donald Lawrence's song "I'm Healed" began to play on the radio. Before long, we were all standing up, singing loud, swaying and clapping our hands as Donald Lawrence and his choir ministered to our souls. As I think about it today, that song was actually prophesy for the girls and me, as it was telling us that no matter how we felt at the time, God had already started the process of healing us.

On Monday, my parents, Erskine's mom, and I went to the funeral home to make the final arrangements. We scheduled the funeral for five days later, which would be Saturday, December 29, at 11:00 a.m. As I sat in the funeral home office making the arrangements, I could hardly believe I was doing this all over again. Nineteen years prior, during the exact same month, I sat in the same office of the same funeral home making final arrangements for our son, Brian's, funeral. I desperately wished that it were all just a bad dream. But it wasn't.

The following day was Christmas, and as soon as the girls and I opened our gifts, my mind shifted gears to funeral planning. My friend from church, Chrys McDaniel came over, and together she and I spent the rest of the day putting together Erskine's funeral program and obituary while Mama and Papa Dewey supplied dinner and the girls enjoyed their Christmas gifts.

I phoned several people that day asking them to take part in the service. I also spoke to Cledis Ward, Erskine's coworker and friend, several times that day as he worked hard on getting a proclamation made from the county board of education concerning Erskine's faithful fifteen-year tenure there.

The next day, my dad and I went shopping for a suit and shoes for Erskine and a matching outfit for me. I would wear a gray jacket and skirt to match his gray suit. And I would accent my outfit with a fuchsia blouse and Erskine's suit with a fuchsia tie to match the girls' dresses.

When we took his clothing to the funeral home that evening, they had been anticipating our arrival in order to give us a bit of bad news and some not-so-bad news. Because of bad traveling conditions due to snow and ice, the casket I'd chosen for Erskine was delayed in the state from which it was being shipped. So the funeral home owner came up with a plan to save the day by allowing me to have a more expensive casket at no extra charge, which she already had on hand. This casket was a beautiful smoke gray trimmed in gold, and it was a full body casket, exposing Erskine from head to toe. The inside of the casket was lined in a deep purple velvet material, which gave it a look of royalty. As the directress stood there hoping I would agree to her plan, I expressed to her that I loved it, but there was one concern, his tie.

I thought the fuchsia tie that Dad and I had just purchased would be a bit tacky with all of the purple surrounding him. And I didn't have time to go shopping for another tie because I had a thousand other things to do before Saturday. In addition, I wanted him to have the fuchsia to match his daughters. Then, the directress briefly left the room and came back with a new gorgeous tie and handkerchief set from a collection, which she said she normally kept on hand. Amazingly, the primary colors in this set were purple and fuchsia, which effortlessly tied together the girls' dresses and the casket lining. In that brief dilemma, God proved to me that He was concerned about every little thing that concerned me.

After the casket issue was taken care of, we headed back to my house where people were still gathering to pay their respects.

On the next evening, Pastor George Keys from Omaha, Nebraska, flew in to be with us. It touched my heart and brings tears to my eyes even now to think that after twenty years this man and his family still loved and cared enough about us that he was willing to fly in freezing temperatures, from the Midwest to the South just to give us his support. He could have easily given us his condolences over the phone or via mail, but he wanted to do it in person.

Pastor Keys came at a perfect time because the next day, which was Friday, my dad was going to take the girls and me to view Erskine's body. We were to look it over and approve it before they made it available for public viewing. Since Pastor Keys had been like a godfather to Erskine and me when we lived in Nebraska, I thought it only befitting that he accompany us to inspect the body.

It had been a week since the girls and I saw their dad last, so, for me, viewing his body at the funeral home that Friday afternoon was bittersweet, as I was glad to see him but not in this condition. When I saw Pastor Keys crying, I realized I had not shed a tear since Erskine passed, and even at that moment while viewing his body, there were no tears. I guess I just didn't have time to cry.

Most of my time was spent in the business of Erskine's funeral and burial, so my emotions were on lockdown. And not only that but I was still nestled in that safe place where the Lord had placed me a week ago; therefore, the pain of my loss had not touched me yet.

As I continued to take care of business, I inspected Erskine from head to toe and informed the directress of the changes I needed her to make.

First, I decided I wanted him to have on his eyeglasses in order that he would look like the Erskine we were familiar with. Then I told her that I wanted gloves to be placed on his hands because his fingers had turned dark. She obliged me by placing his glasses on his face and putting white gloves on his hands. When I looked at his head, I was a little disappointed that his hair had not grown back enough to cover the dry patches on his scalp, but there was nothing that could be done about it, so I had to let that go.

After those minor changes, I stood back, took one last look at my husband, and realized he looked more at peace at that moment than I had seen him look in a very long time. Actually, he looked free. Free from worry. Free from sickness. Free from pain. Free from the cares of this world. As God's Word says in John 8:36 (TLB), "If the Son sets you free, you will indeed be free," Erskine was indeed free!

The night before the funeral, my friends Kiki Edwards and Erika King came to our house that evening to do my and the girls' hair. Then Chrys showed up with accessories for the girls to wear with their dresses. Without my asking, Zambia, Erika, and Chrys then decided to spend the night in order to help the girls and I get ready for the funeral the next morning. They wanted to make sure our morning was flawless. As I write this, I'm moved to tears just thinking about how my friends sacrificed their time and talents for the support of my family.

I didn't rest well that night because I slept in the middle of my and Erskine's king-sized bed with Jessica and Jasmine on either side of me, as one of my guests had the living room sofa where I normally slept. It was very uncomfortable sleeping in the middle, but since each of them desired to sleep beside me, I had no choice. I also didn't rest well because my brain was on overload as I worried all night about us making it to the church on time. You see, my large family is always late … to everything. So all night I mentally prepared for our morning adventure, in hopes that we would not be late to Erskine's funeral.

I arose at daybreak to get a head start on the huge task of getting my kids dressed and ready to go by 10:00 a.m., the time the funeral directors

God's Girl

were due to arrive at our house. But with the help of my friends, our morning went very smoothly, and the huge task that I worried about all night was hardly a task at all.

Erika, who is also a makeup artist, made up my and my oldest two daughters' faces that morning. When I sat down for her to do my makeup, I gave her strict instructions to go light, as she is known for her remarkable ability to totally transform people. I told her, "Erika, I want Erskine to be able to recognize his wife." This broke the tension for us as we all burst into much needed laughter.

Before long, our extended family members began arriving with the funeral directors not far behind. Since my dad would be doing the eulogy, he and Mama Trish didn't come to our house but went on to the church. However, he instructed me to tell my brother William to lead us in a word of prayer before leaving my house. After calling everyone together, William, who had arrived early that morning from Georgia with his family, said a brief but powerful prayer for us, and then we all lined up for the automobile processional.

The funeral directors led my girls and me to the first of the two family limousines that were parked in front of our house. I requested that Zambia ride in it with us. In the second limo were Mama Doll, Erskine's three nieces, Joelle, Kadejah, and Jori, and Mama and Papa Dewey.

The ride to the church is a blur to me. However, I do not remember any shedding of tears or feelings of sadness among us, just the girls talking and being silly as usual. Maybe it was because everything was happening so fast. Or because we had Zambia, whom the girls called "T'Nanny-Z", with us, who has a knack for making us smile. Or maybe it was simply the fact that the Holy Spirit was riding with us and doing what He does best ... providing comfort.

When we entered the church foyer, the funeral directors tried to line us up two by two. My four oldest girls paired up, and I was paired with one of the female funeral directors. But Zambia made a threesome with the twins.

The ushers took our coats as we stood in line waiting to enter the sanctuary. Then one of the funeral directors standing in front of me turned around and asked me a question. She wanted to know if the girls and I would be willing to close the casket when it was time. She thought it would be a nice touch. I had never heard of such a thing. At all of the funerals I'd ever attended, the funeral directors always closed the casket. After turning to ask my two oldest daughters who were standing directly behind me, I told the director that we approved. Then as I thought about it, I felt it would only be befitting, seeing as we always gathered around their dad at bedtime to pray for him during his sickness. This would be our last gathering around him, and I was sure he would have wanted it this way.

For the media screen during the funeral, the girls and I settled on a simple collage of four pictures that would stay on the screen for the duration of the funeral. The two pictures at the top of the collage were a photo of him and me and, beside it, one of him and the girls. Then, the two pictures on the bottom were of me kissing him and the other of all six girls kissing him at once. That was the picture that we took back in March when he said we were acting as if he was going to die. I guess our spirits felt it coming.

As the sanctuary doors opened, one of the funeral directors looked at me and asked, "Are you ready?" After a deep sigh, I said, "Yes," and the processional began. Inside the sanctuary, I looked up to see my husband's smiling face on that screen, and it gave me such a pain in my gut. But I began talking to myself mentally, *Come on, Tracy, you can do this. Be strong for the girls.*

When we reached the casket, I looked at my husband lying there so peacefully. I was sure that even if he could, he would not come back to this place. I kissed my hand and placed it gently on his lips before going to my seat.

From my seat, I could see my girls as they approached the casket, and they seemed to be having a difficult time. I think I was hurting more for them than I was for myself. I held back the tears that tried to escape my eyes, and I did my best to remain strong for them because I knew if I were to become hysterical, they would too.

I'm sure crying fits and fainting spells were probably expected of us,

God's Girl

and it would have been completely understood by all, but I didn't want us to come there to have a big pity party. I wanted our gathering to be about celebrating the life of a great man of God. Any uncontrollable grieving could be done in the privacy of our own home, not in the public eye.

Before leaving home, I had taken my blood pressure medication as normal, but if I had been thinking clearly, I would have waited until after the funeral to take it, as it forced me to leave the sanctuary several times to use the restroom. I ran across the hall to my dad's office repeatedly, relieving myself and rushing back into the service. At one point, Daddy's armor bearer Rodreecas Brown came looking for me because it was time to close the casket and the funeral directors couldn't find me.

When I hurried back into the sanctuary, a funeral director directed me toward the casket and began encouraging my girls to get up and join me. I could see the confused look on the younger girls' faces as they were totally in the dark as to what was about to happen.

As we all stood at the casket, staring down at Erskine, my brother Dedrick, who was the church's musician at the time, began to play softly. Then my dad, who was sitting on the pulpit with the other ministers, could see my girls starting to break down, so he came down and stood behind us. We stood there for a few seconds looking at Erskine, touching him and shedding tears. Suddenly, Karen, the oldest of my twins, began crying uncontrollably, and my dad grabbed her and took her to sit with Zambia. But I immediately turned away from the casket and said to him, "Bring me my baby." So he got her and brought her to me, and I put my arm around her, pulling her close to me. My feelings at that moment were, "Baby, cry if you must, but we will stand here together as a family and say goodbye to Daddy."

Finally, with help from the funeral directors on each end, we began to lower the casket lid. As the lid was lowered, the instrumental piece Dedrick was playing became louder and more dramatic as his feelings were rendered through his music. At that moment, there was not a dry eye in the building as everyone in attendance watched us intently like a heartbreaking Lifetime movie.

On a lighter note, allow me to tell you about the choir that was up next to sing. Our church has a magnificent choir. On Sunday mornings, their performance is the highlight of the service for many, so I didn't imagine there'd be any problems with them singing at the funeral, as they always sang at funerals.

The song the girls and I had chosen for the choir to sing was "For Every Mountain," by Kurt Carr and the Kurt Carr Singers. We had heard them sing this song on several occasions, and we loved it because its lyrics always ministered to our spirit. A few of the song's moving lyrics were … "For every mountain You brought me over, For every trial You've seen me through, For every blessing, Hallelujah, for this I give You praise." Considering all that the girls and I had gone through in 2012 alone, it gave us a new appreciation for the words of that song.

Well, I'm not sure what the problem was, but clearly there was an issue because when the choir began to sing, the song just didn't sound quite right, so the choir director stopped them midway and had them start all over again. But surprisingly, nothing changed. Something still wasn't right. The musicians then decided to play musical chairs as they stopped the song three more times to change pianist. It felt like we were sitting in the midst of a Thursday night choir rehearsal. I tried to lighten the embarrassing mood by yelling, "Yall, get it right for Erskine now!" But that didn't help. I don't know if grief was hindering them or if a key choir member or musician was absent. Whatever the case, they continued to trudge on through that song as best they could, and though they did improve a little, I actually breathed a sigh of relief when they were done.

During the funeral, there were special words from different family members and friends who all spoke very highly of Erskine. However, there were words spoken by my brother William and our friend Robert Carlisle that I felt my girls would need to remember about their dad. William said, "Listen, it's been said that we shouldn't count the years or the number of days in our life but make the days count. This is a man that made the days count. Listen, we see this particular battle that he went through, but what we don't understand is he had more battles before this one. And he won. He won because it's been said that if you can get a child to the age of seven, you've pretty much laid the foundation for who they are going to be. See, the devil came in one time, but Erskine held on. Now these babies are well past seven. And he laid the foundation for who they will become."

Robert Carlisle, whom we affectionately called "Shug," said, "He (Erskine) wasn't the type of guy that hung out with the fellows. He enjoyed spending time with his wife and kids. His wife and kids were his life, the church was his church, and he took care of it like it was his own house."

Our neighbors, Robert and Yolanda Blevins, were on program to speak of Erskine as a neighbor, and they delivered some touching words as well. Yolanda said to me, "I remember the day that I saw you get out of your car. My husband and I were in our car, and we saw you get out of your car. And we sat and watched you for a minute, you got Erskine out of the car and you put him on your back. And you were walking toward your house, and all I could say was, you were leaning on God, and Erskine was leaning on you. And the same God that led you to the house is the same God that's going to take you through."

Her husband Robert then shared, "What I always liked about this family is every time you went down there, you were guaranteed to get eight hugs. They are a loving family. He (Erskine) was a man who loved his family, and he loved God. And it's proof by the way these young ladies carry themselves. And I thank God for the opportunity to have a neighbor that was more than a neighbor. He was a friend."

It was wonderful seeing family members and old friends who had traveled from near and far just to be with us. And it truly blessed me to see two special groups of people sitting in the balcony. The first group were Erskine's coworkers from the county board of education, and the other was a group of our classmates from Hueytown High School, class of 1987.

Tracy O'Neal Daniel Lee

It was touching to hear our old friends from school, Melissa Powell and Chester Porter, speak so highly of my husband.

As Daddy began his eulogy, he started by speaking directly to the girls and me. I felt the need to share those words with you, along with several other special words that were sprinkled throughout his eulogy, as he not only spoke memorable words but prophetic words, which I've had to refer to on several occasions since Erskine's death.

He began by saying, "I want you to know, Tracy, Daddy is proud of you. Let me put it like this, not only Daddy but also Teresa, Dewey, Marilyn, Patricia, and myself, we are proud of the way you handled your trial. You've been a woman. You've been a wife. You've set an example of what a real woman does when her man gets in trouble. You never left his bedside. You slept there at night. As long as he was in that hospital, you were in the hospital. And whatever they gave him, you wanted to know what it was. And I like that example Sister Blevins gave. She said that she saw you carrying your man. You didn't say, 'You're too heavy. Maybe I need to get somebody.' You said, 'Come on, baby, we can make it. With Jesus on our side, we can make it.' There are a lot of women and men who, when their spouse gets in trouble, they get caught up and they find other interests. But you stayed right there. You have nothing to be ashamed of. You did your part, and Daddy is proud of you.

"I am proud of these girls and how they handled their trial. These girls have been exemplary. They have been daughters that have set an example for other daughters. I'm proud of how they stood by their daddy. How they prayed for their daddy. How they learned scriptures that they didn't know before, but they learned them because they wanted their daddy healed. Girls, I want you to know today that your daddy *is* healed, and he's well. And he's leaning over the balconies of heaven and saying, 'Well done, my children, well done.'

"He (Erskine) had an opportunity to impact his children with truth. And there's something about truth; it will never die. It will go on from one generation to the next. They have been so emphatically blessed by their daddy's life.

"A mama. Six girls. No daddy. All their life their depending on the strong man of the house. God is about to give them a revelation. What they thought their daddy was doing, God said, 'Hey, I want you to know it's been Me all the time. It was Me all the time, and I'll never leave you or forsake you. I'm a very present help in the time of trouble! I'm here and I'm with you, and I'm going to see you through this thing!'

"In my talk with Erskine, Erskine in his flesh did not want to leave because he saw the need for his children and his wife. He said to me, 'Daddy, since I've been sick, I got a new appreciation for my wife. And I just want to live so I can show her how much I appreciate her. And, Daddy, there's so much in the media ministry I want to finish.' But I believe Jesus had a talk with Erskine, and in their conversation, He told him, 'Son, I know where you are because, son, I was in the Garden of Gethsemane, and I prayed all night until sweat like drops of blood fell from my brow. I just kept on praying until I prayed through. My prayer was, 'God, if it's your will, let this cup pass from Me. I don't want to die. It's so much work to be done. Nevertheless, not My will but Your will be done.' I believe Erskine (finally) accepted God's will for his life.

"Tracy, supernaturally you're going to be taken care of. Folks are not going to be able to understand. 'How is it that they're going to college? How is it that they're going to finish and their tuition is going to be paid?' And every time the barrel runs low, there's going to be a knock at the door. Supernaturally you're not going to have to go back to work 'cause God's got your back. It's too much work at home to finish. It would not be God to put you out to work when you've been at home all the time raising these girls. God's going to finish what he started. God's going to finish what he started in you."

While sitting through the burial ceremony at the gravesite, the most memorable thing for me was how dreadfully cold it was that day. Oh, my goodness it was so cold! There was a sharp, brittle breeze that whipped our faces endlessly as we listened to my dad speak his final words over Erskine's casket.

Two representatives of the air force were present to play "Taps" and to do the customary twenty-one-gun salute. After that, the two of them took the longest time folding the flag that had draped Erskine's casket. The girls and I watched them in frustration as our legs shook and our teeth chattered. When they were finally done, they presented the flag to me.

As we finally left the gravesite, I remember how horrible it felt having to leave my husband there at the cemetery. That was my best friend. It felt so wrong leaving him behind. While writing this book, I happened to do a search for "Taps" and learned from scoutsongs.com that there are actual words to accompany that piece of music, and the first verse took my mind back to that cold, somber day as we left the cemetery.

> Day is done, gone the sun,
> From the lake, from the hills, from the sky;
> All is well, safely rest, God is nigh.

I wished there were some way that I could let Erskine know, "Baby, we are about to leave now, but don't worry, all is well, you can rest safely now because God is watching over you," but I'm sure he knew that already.

When we arrived back at the church for the repast, it lifted our spirits to eat, laugh, and fellowship with our loved ones. But when it was over and time to go home, I felt a bit of dread inside.

I had spent a whole year caring for my sick husband and a week and a half planning his funeral, and now that it was all over, I didn't know what to do next. That's why I was looking so forward to hitting the road to Georgia, just to have a chance to release my grief and reassess my life. My brother William and his family headed back home to Georgia immediately after the repast, well aware that the girls and I would be joining them soon.

Pastor Keys and Erskine's friend Cledis were the last two guests to leave our house that evening after the funeral, as I spent time giving them as much of Erskine's clothing as they could fit. The way I saw it, there was no need for me to hold on to all of those things, as Erskine was no longer here to use them. I may be a sentimental person but not to that degree.

When our guests finally left, the girls and I wasted no time getting into bed, as we were extremely tired. And while settling into my sleeping quarters on the living room sofa, I thought about my husband who was settling into his new quarters under a cold, dark, and lonely ground. I thank God for the assurance that Erskine's spirit was not in that ground but rather it was with Him.

During the night, Erskine briefly visited me in a dream. There were no words spoken, only that big grin on his face that he's known for. I was in the master bedroom, and I could see him coming down the hall toward me while holding a bag. It was the bag that we've always kept in the basement closet, which contained the children's snow gear such as hats, gloves, scarves, and earmuffs. I had no idea why he was coming toward me with that bag because I suddenly woke up.

Pastor Keys, who was still in town, was scheduled to preach during our church's 11:00 a.m. service, and of course, he wanted the girls and me to go with him. But to be honest, I don't think we would have gone to church if it weren't for him because I could feel my body and my emotions giving me signs that it was time to rest and reflect. And though that time was indeed drawing close, God wasn't ready for me to do so just yet, which is why He had Pastor Keys encourage me to get up and go to church.

It was comforting being in the presence of our church family, as they showered us with so much love, but at the same time, it felt awkward being there yet another Sunday without Erskine. It was so hard accepting this as my new normal.

After church, we came home and ate dinner with Pastor Keys and several other family members who came by. Later in the evening, my friend Lisa and her daughter Kaitlyn stopped by to see us.

I told Lisa about the dream I had concerning Erskine and that bag, and she wondered if there was something in the bag that Erskine wanted me to find. Though I didn't go right away, days later I went to the basement closet and found that bag. When I searched it, I found nothing in it out of the ordinary. So I rested in the fact that if there was a significant meaning to the dream, God would reveal it in time because He always does.

On Monday morning, New Year's Eve, Pastor Keys left us. I kind of hated to see him go because that was a sign to me that life was about to go back to normal for everyone who had been comforting us, but it would never go back to normal for us. I think I was a bit afraid of facing our new normal alone.

The girls talked me into shopping for outfits for our New Year's Eve church service scheduled for that night. They were really looking forward to it because everyone would be dressing up in seventies attire. I was anxious to do anything that would keep my mind occupied, so I jumped into this costume game with two feet, visiting thrift shops for clothes and the beauty supply store for wigs, trying to help the girls find the seventies look they desired.

All seven of us dressed in costumes for the service, and the girls seemed to have a great time. But as for me, my body was present in the service, but my mind wasn't. I was busy trying to push back tears and hold on to the fake smile that I was using to hide the sharp pain that was waking up inside of me. As I looked around at all of my coupled friends who were bringing in the new year together, I was hurt. Here I was about to enter a new year without my other half. I was without the man whom I'd entered the last twenty new years with. I just didn't feel like I fit in at my church anymore. I really wanted to just go home, pack my bags, and wait for morning so I could run away. But I stayed there for the sake of my girls.

Early the next morning, the girls and I started packing. I felt the need to run away quickly because my heartbreak and pain were steadily surfacing, and I did not want to break down while alone with my children. As I packed for our run-away trip, I simultaneously packed the rest of Erskine's clothes in several large trash bags. I couldn't stand the thought of coming back home and seeing his clothes hanging in the closet, as I knew it would hurt me very much. I figured, what would be the point in running away and having to come back home to all of this? So I called my friend

God's Girl

Erika, who promised to come by my house and pick up the bags from my front porch. I asked her to give them to our friend Shannon.

During our years together, Erskine was the one who did most of the driving when it came to out-of-town trips, as I had developed a fear of driving in areas that were out of my comfort zone. If it wasn't near home, I would not drive. Therefore, my running-away plan involved my brother William. Because his wife, Bridgette, worked for an airline company and could get him a free trip, he was going to fly to Birmingham and drive us back to Atlanta. Well, things didn't quite work out as we had planned.

William sat in the Atlanta airport on standby for several hours awaiting a free seat on a plane to Birmingham, but there were none available. Finally, I told him to go back home. I was going to drive. He and my parents were very worried about my decision, but the adrenaline flowing inside of me gave me incredible courage. I needed to run away, and nothing was going to stop me. I figured, as long as I had a GPS, an address, and God on my side, the girls and I would be just fine.

We hit the road some time after 2:00 p.m. and, despite some slight issues such as rain and heavy traffic, we made it safely to my brother's house later that evening. My girls were so proud of their mama; actually, I was proud of myself. And if Erskine was watching from heaven, I know he was proud of me too.

After the girls and I fellowshipped with my brother and his family, I went to bed in my niece Kenadee's room while the girls stayed up enjoying Kenadee and her big brother, Will. Later I heard my brother clowning around with the girls, and that made me happy because I knew it was taking their mind off their dad and me, as my girls often worried about me. But I desperately needed this alone time as I was mentally, physically, and emotionally drained.

Though I tried, I couldn't go right to sleep because my brain kept wanting to review what I considered the worst year of my life. In my mind, I watched my own 2012 disaster movie, from the first day we discovered Erskine was sick up until the morning he took his last breath. As I continued lying there in the darkness, all of the pain that I'd been suppressing during that entire year came forth in an abundance of tears.

While I cried, my phone continuously alerted me of text messages that were coming in from friends saying, "Happy New Year!" And each message made me angrier and angrier as I thought, *How in the world do they expect this to be a happy new year for me?* I can't recall if I responded to their messages because I really didn't know how. And if I did respond, it was only by faith because I sure wasn't feeling it.

As I lay there crying in the darkness, my phone rang. It was my dad. I'm sure God put me in his spirit because I truly needed him at that moment. As I poured from my heart the hurt, anger, and mental anguish I was feeling, Daddy simply listened and encouraged me as best he could, as he had never lost a spouse to death; therefore, he couldn't truly identify with what I was going through. But after talking to him, I was able to calm down and drift off to sleep because he had prayed for me and encouraged me with the Word of God.

After staying about five days with my brother and his family, it was time for us to hit the road. We wanted to stay much longer because we really were enjoying ourselves with them, and that change of environment was exactly what we needed. But school was about to start soon, as the holidays were over and a new semester was about to begin. So we had no choice but to go home.

21

God, Why?

"For I know the plans I have for you," declares the Lord, "plans to prosper you and not to harm you, plans to give you hope and a future."

—Jeremiah 29:11 (NIV)

A few days after her dad's death, my daughter Joycelyn asked me why did she continuously hear in her spirit, "You can't have a testimony without a test," if God was not planning to heal her dad. Then God dropped the answer in my spirit as I told her that those words were never meant for her dad. They were meant for her, her sisters, and me. Twenty-twelve had been a year of testing for us, and one day in the future, we would be able to look back and view this test as an amazing testimony.

I know that answer had to come straight from God because I was so busy dealing with a thousand questions of my own that I couldn't really focus on giving my children answers for theirs.

I saved a few pieces of Erskine's clothing for the girls and myself for memory sake. And of those pieces, there were certain sweatshirts of his that I actually wore for many days after his death because I needed to feel him close to me.

The pain and agony of losing him hit me the hardest when I was home alone after the girls went back to school. During that time, I was a constant weeping widow. I know I could have easily gone back to work at the church to occupy my mind and my time, but I no longer had a desire to be there. It was even harder being at home, as I would sit around the house all day, crying, reminiscing, and counting the hours until the girls returned.

It hurt me to my core for our twenty-one-year marriage to end so prematurely, leaving me with a heart full of unfulfilled dreams. As a result, I questioned God daily, from morning to night.

"Lord, why would You make me a widow and my kids fatherless?"

"After all the prayers we prayed and scriptures we stood on, why did You still allow him to leave us?"

"Lord, where is the supernatural triumph in all of this?"

"Why did You allow a good man who has dedicated much of his life to You to die at such a young age?"

"Why do I have to raise all of these children alone?"

Whenever I wasn't crying on the outside, I was still crying on the inside. I remember telling a friend that it felt like I was always one teardrop away from a flood at any given moment. I didn't know how to handle the overwhelming feeling of emptiness that was inside of me. It was terribly painful. Many times, it gave me more than an urge to cry; it gave me the urge to moan and groan, the way a pregnant woman does when in labor. And those "labor pains" were in the pit of my stomach. Some days it hurt like a severed body part, as if my arm or leg had been chopped off. It was just that awful.

Growing up, I heard many renowned preachers and teachers proclaim that we must have faith, we must touch and agree, we must quote certain scriptures, and we must fast and pray when we are believing God for healing or other prayer requests. Well, the girls and I were confused because our family did all of that, yet Erskine still died. And it hurt me to think that I had encouraged my children to do all of this, explaining to them that it would help their dad receive his healing, but in the end it seemed our efforts had been in vain. And though others said, "Well, he *is* healed. He has his perfect healing." Our hopes were that he would be healed on this side of heaven, in the land of the living.

The girls and I were brokenhearted and confused, wondering where we went wrong and why God didn't come through for us. And I also worried if this situation would make them lose faith in the God that their dad and I had taught them to love and serve. Would they think their parents lied to them? Would they think praying is a joke or a waste of time?

The fact that I had no say in this drastic change of my life highly frustrated me. This was not the plan I had for myself, and I'm sure this was not the plan Erskine had for himself either. I wondered what in the world had we done to deserve such an early ending to our marriage. And what did Erskine do to deserve such an early ending to his life?

I was so focused on having unwavering faith when he was sick that I never allowed myself to entertain any thoughts of losing him. I just kept my focus on the mission of doing all I had to do to help him get well. But if I had it to do all over again, with what I know now, I would take the time to stare at him longer, talk to him longer, hold his hand longer, hug him longer, and kiss him longer.

I was still in love with that man. We shared a love that was growing stronger every day. So I couldn't understand why God would allow our story to end so soon. We never even had a chance to reach our happily ever after. We never had a chance to grow old together, to raise our grandkids together. I just needed to know why.

Another thing the girls and I couldn't understand was why God had allowed Erskine to believe, all the way up until the end, that he would be healed then allowed him to die. Why did He spontaneously send people our way during his sickness to encourage us to keep the faith? Whether it was at church, at home, at the hospital, or by phone, God always used someone to speak encouraging words of hope to us. And sometimes, it would be when we had received some discouraging news from the doctors. Erskine and the girls and I held on to the very end, just as we were instructed, believing that God had a supernatural plan to heal him. And because my husband was well loved by our church family, they were just as dumbfounded as we were when he died.

I pondered on this while sitting in church on the second Sunday in January 2013, which was my and the girls' first Sunday back at church since returning from Georgia. As I sat there thinking, God opened up my spiritual understanding and gave me His divine answer, which I had an opportunity to share with the congregation that morning. As my four oldest girls and I stood before the congregation to thank them for all they had done for us during their dad's sickness and death, I began to share with the church the revelation God had just given me concerning why He had allowed Erskine to keep believing until the end for his healing.

God said it was His desire for Erskine to die in faith. He said the way Erskine lived was just as important to Him as the way he died. Erskine lived as a man of faith, and he died a man of faith, believing until the end that God had the power to heal him completely. Though he never receive his earthly healing as we were expecting, he did receive his divine healing. And because of his faith, he was made worthy to be included among the faithful saints mentioned in Hebrews, chapter 11.

Hebrews 11:1, 2, 6, 7, 17, 22, 24, 31, 39 (KJV)

> Now faith is the substance of things hoped for, the evidence of things not seen.
>
> For by it the elders obtained a good report.
>
> But without faith it is impossible to please him: for he that cometh to God must believe that he is, and that he is a rewarder of them that diligently seek him.
>
> By faith Noah, being warned of God of things not seen as yet, moved with fear, prepared an ark to the saving of his house; by the which he condemned the world, and became heir of the righteousness which is by faith.
>
> Through faith also Sara herself received strength to conceive seed, and was delivered of a child when she was past age, because she judged him faithful who had promised.

> By faith Abraham, when he was tried, offered up Isaac: and he that had received the promises offered up his only begotten son,
>
> By faith Joseph, when he died, made mention of the departing of the children of Israel; and gave commandment concerning his bones.
>
> By faith Moses, when he was come to years, refused to be called the son of Pharaoh's daughter;
>
> By faith the harlot Rahab perished not with them that believed not, when she had received the spies with peace.
>
> And these all, having obtained a good report through faith, received not the promise:

As I read the testimonies of those saints who lived and died in faith, as mentioned in Hebrews, chapter 11, I imagine Erskine's testimony being written among theirs. "By faith, Erskine, provided for his large family and took great care of his church, while suffering through years of poor health."

Erskine's faith was evident even during childhood, as when he was in high school, God healed him of asthma during an Ernest Angley revival in Birmingham, Alabama. After his message, the preacher asked all those who were dealing with allergies to stand. To the surprise of his family, Erskine stood up. When he saw the confusion on his parents' faces, he said to them, "Asthma is an allergy." Then after the preacher prayed, Erskine said he felt a warm sensation in his chest, which was a sign of healing for him. And amazingly, from that day forward, he no longer dealt with asthma, as his faith had made him well.

James 1:12 (NIV) says, "Blessed is the one who perseveres under trial because, having stood the test, that person will receive the crown of life that the Lord has promised to those who love him." Erskine persevered under his trials and kept his faith in God until the day he died. And because he stood the test and kept the faith, he has received the crown of life.

The week that the girls returned to school was also the week the church's yearly Daniel fast started, and the girls and I decided to comply. I took the opportunity to get creative with meal planning, even coming up with a recipe for veggie nachos, which were the girls' favorite. I wholeheartedly welcomed this occasion as a way to get my mind on something other than my loss.

After Bible study the following week, my dad held his annual recipe contest where everyone who had discovered a new vegetable recipe could bring enough to share, and the best recipe would win a prize. The girls encouraged me to enter my veggie nachos, which I did. And although I didn't win a prize, the recipe seemed to be a big hit, especially among hungry men. One in particular was Brother Ryan, who asked if he could pay me to make him a bowl full. I agreed because I had nothing else to do other than sit around all day and grieve.

The writer in me decided to try keeping a diary to record my feelings. But after the painful entry below, I never wrote again until March.

January 17, 2013

> I was feeling pretty good this morning, but yesterday was miserable for me. Although I laughed with the kids as we worked together to straighten the house and put away laundry, inside I felt like I was dying. I felt even worse the day before that.
>
> After dropping the kids off at school this morning, I knew that I would spend my day in anxious anticipation of their return because for me right now, being alone hurts too bad. I can't control my constant thoughts of him. He is all over this house, and he is in me. He was my best friend, and I was his.
>
> Today I felt the urge to read all of his old letters to me, as I needed some kind of way to connect with him. The letters dated back to 1988 when we first started corresponding with one another. He was stationed in

God's Girl

Omaha, Nebraska, and I was still living at home in Hueytown, Alabama.

I don't know if reading those letters was a good idea or a bad one, but hearing his voice in my head as I read his words made a dam break inside of me that was uncontainable. I could hardly breathe for crying so hard. At one point I jumped up from the sofa and started walking around the house crying, "Why, Lord? Why? Why did you take him? Why?" I was hurting something awful, and it felt as if I was literally bleeding on the inside.

As I began to calm down and wipe the tears from my eyes, I looked out of my dining room window, and I saw snow falling. These were huge, fast-dropping snowflakes. Though the television weatherman had predicted there would be snow, he also said that it would not accumulate; therefore, no problems were expected. With that in mind, I put aside any worries about the speed and size of these snowflakes and simply enjoyed their beauty before going back to reading Erskine's letters.

Well, that was the end of my diary entry but not the end of that eventful day. While reading Erskine's letters, my dad called to check on me, and I poured my heart out to him yet again. Through the years, he always seemed to call me at the perfect time, just when I needed him the most. Anyway, awhile after we talked, I noticed how the snow was doing the opposite of what the weatherman had forecasted. Not only was it sticking, but it was also getting thick. Pretty soon, the school was calling, as they had decided to dismiss early due to the inclement weather.

I jumped up, threw on my coat, and scurried out of the house to get the girls before the roads got too bad. Because I had children in three different schools, my plan was to go to the elementary school to get the twins first. Then I would stop next door at the middle school to get Joycelyn, and afterward, head to the high school to get the oldest three. But I realized very quickly that this was not going to be a simple task. I had only made it about two blocks from my house before my SUV began sliding and spinning so badly on the icy road that I ended up facing the way from which I was coming. I took this as a sign that I needed to make my way back home. My kids had already lost one parent; I was not about to make them to lose another.

When I finally made it back home, which took awhile because of how slow I had to drive, I called Papa Dewey, who was very familiar with driving on snow and ice, as he was originally from Ohio. Pop was successful at making it to the high school to get the oldest three girls. And God blessed where he didn't have to go to the other two schools because our friend David Davis was already at the elementary school picking up his kids, and he offered to pick up the twins and even went next door to the middle school to get Joycelyn.

The snow had caught everyone off guard, even the weatherman. And there were many travel issues, car accidents, and utter confusion as people scrambled to leave their jobs and get their kids from school.

Throughout our marriage, Erskine was my and the girls' personal weatherman, as he was always the first one to leave the house every morning, so, if needed, he would call back home and prepare us for the day. If it was raining, he'd remind us to take umbrellas or wear raincoats. If it was cold, he'd remind us to bundle up, and if he heard on the radio that it was going to snow, he'd prepare us for that as well. So, at the end of the day, after Papa Dewey and David had brought my girls home to me safe and sound, God brought back to my remembrance the dream I'd had about Erskine the day after his funeral. It was the dream where I saw him coming down the hall holding the bag in which we kept the girls' winter gear, such as hats, scarves, gloves, and earmuffs. As unbelievable as it may sound, in my heart I truly believe that dream was Erskine's way of calling back home to prepare us for that surprising snowstorm that was on the way.

I started to notice that around a certain time each day, my pain and depression would become increasingly worse, so much that it felt like I would hyperventilate if I didn't run out of the house to get some air. This dark cloud hovered over me between the hours of 4:00 p.m. and 7:00 p.m. daily. I realized it had been during those hours when Erskine would come home from work, we'd eat dinner, talk about our day, watch the news, and help the kids with homework. This ritual was embedded in my mind, and although it had been broken during his yearlong sickness, for some reason my mind didn't choose to remember his sick days. It decided to reach back to our peaceful days.

Having to live in that house with all of my painful memories was pure torture for me because every room held a memory. For instance, the open space between the living room and dining room is where we gathered to pray every morning before the children went to school. The kitchen was where Erskine and I cooked breakfast together on Saturday mornings for the family. The master bedroom was where he and I spent most of our time together; it was also where he spent most of his sick days. Downstairs in the den hurt the most because it was where he spent his dying days. The kids' playroom held many of his work tools and equipment. And parking in our driveway even held a memory because facing us was the tool shed that the girls and I watched him build from the ground up. There was nowhere in or outside of our house that I could go and not have some kind of painful memory of my husband, so I considered having a new bedroom added on for myself, and I planned to spend a lot of time in it. But after finding out it wouldn't be possible to put it where I wanted it due to city regulations, I began making serious plans to move.

To realize that all the memories Erskine and I shared with one another were now only *my* memories was a bit depressing. How could so many memories of shared events be left up to one person to remember? That means when I'm gone, so are those memories. How sad. As I thought of the memories of our life in Nebraska, or the memories of our son, Brian, who was born and died there, it was hard to fathom that Erskine was no longer here to reminisce upon those times with me. Those memories now live in my head alone.

And just as the memories were now all mine, so were the kids, the house, the vehicles, the businesses, and everything else that we shared. It all belonged to me. Honestly, it felt better being shared.

Having to go on with life without my husband was tough, but God strengthened me daily to do it. I thought about him when I took Jasmine to the DMV to pick up her driver's license in mid January. If it hadn't been for him teaching her how to drive before he became very sick, she would not have been able to get her yellow card from her driver's education class, thereby allowing her to present it to the people at the DMV and get her licenses on the spot, without having to take their road test. I am still in awe at how God set that up. He knew I was going to need another driver in the house to help me on this new journey as a widow with six young children.

When my husband was alive, everything he envisioned for us was my job as his wife to help bring it to pass. Now that he was no longer with us, I felt a bit lost as to what my purpose in life would be and whose vision I should be working on. And until I had a chance to figure that out, I decided to recall the things my husband desired or would have desired for our home and our family.

While the girls and I were in Georgia, my brother's wife, Bridgette, and I made plans for our families to go on a Disney cruise together in November 2013. Not only did I feel the girls and I needed this getaway after everything we had gone through in 2012, but I also felt that Erskine would have wanted this for us. I felt he would have jumped at the opportunity to take his family on such a vacation had he been financially able to do so.

Then there was the mission of the trees. Erskine complained a lot about certain trees that were in our yard. One in particular was a tree that hung over our deck. Though it provided nice shade in the summer, it was a nuisance in the fall due to the pile of leaves that fell from it onto the deck. For some reason, those leaves highly annoyed him, and he said they were destroying the deck.

Another tree stood next to our driveway. Its roots had utterly destroyed the driveway by creating cracks across it and ultimately a large hump in the cement was formed. This irritated Erskine each time he drove over it. He constantly complained about the hump and the tree, saying he wished he had enough money to cut the tree down. Well, seeing as I had some money now, I had both trees cut down, for Erskine. And I planned to get the driveway fixed for him also. I was going to continue doing those things that I felt he would want me to do, as I hoped by staying busy this way, it would help heal me mentally.

I also decided to use my love for reading as a healing tool. I searched online for some interesting material and came across Dr. Joyce Brothers's book *Widowed*. Amazon's summary of her book caught my attention because Dr. Brothers's situation sounded a lot like mine. Her husband, whom she was married to for more than thirty years, died of cancer in 1989. And being a new widow, Dr. Brothers felt herself drowning in grief and self-pity because she felt lost and alone, exactly the way I was feeling. But remarkably, through time, her life came back together.

This gave me a glimmer of hope for my life because at the fresh state of grief that I was in, I had a hard time believing that I would ever stop grieving. I thought my pain would never end. I ordered Dr. Brothers's book and finished it in about a week. It was a great read, and it helped me a lot, but it wasn't the instant fix that I was hoping for. I had to realize that only God, through time, could heal my wounded heart. And no matter how much I desired it, there was nothing in the world that could heal me instantly. Or was there?

22

Mistakes of a Broken Heart

> The Lord is close to the brokenhearted and saves those who are crushed in spirit.
> —Psalm 34:18 (NIV)

Kelly Price's song, "Healing for My Soul," was the perfect theme song for this turbulent era in my life. As she sang, "Lord, I'm looking for a new life just for my soul. And I'm tired of crying all night just for my soul. Lord, I need thee, oh I need thee, to take away this pain and misery because God, I just can't do this by myself, I need help," every lyric touched my soul deeply because she was describing my situation perfectly.

After doing so much grieving, I was now at a point where I was yearning for something new, a fresh start. I was tired of the constant crying and sadness, and I desperately needed God to remove the terrible pain that was paralyzing me. I tried with everything in me to handle the feelings of loneliness but as I took care of my house, my kids, and everything else on my own, I realized more and more that I had no desire to keep living my life this way. I actually hated it. I was desperate for a new love.

Immediately after Erskine's funeral, I thought I was dead set on following the example of Dr. Martin Luther King Jr.'s widow, Coretta Scott King. I said I would never remarry. I would spend the rest of my days keeping my husband's legacy alive. I would make sure his words remained true, that he would live and not die and declare the works of the Lord by continuously sharing with others about his legacy of faith. I was even making plans to buy a cemetery plot next to his so that one day the girls could bury me beside him.

I ordered a photo blanket, which displayed a full body photo of him, from head to toe. I hung the blanket on the living room wall to give us the feeling that he was always present with us. And, in his honor, I ordered a large decal for my SUV, which my friend Robert Carlisle from church affixed to my back window. It read, "In Loving Memory of a Great Husband & Father, Erskine Nile Daniel, Jr. June 16, 1969 – December 21, 2012. You Will Forever Remain In Our Hearts."

Whatever I could think of to show my honor, respect, and love for that man, I tried to do it. But all of that homage only lasted a few weeks because as those weeks began turning into a month, I realized, "I can't live like this. I need a husband to help me."

I could no longer bear the thought of being by myself for the rest of my life. It just didn't feel right. Growing up, my biggest desire in life had always been to marry and have children, and for twenty-one years, God honored that. Now suddenly I was dealing with this big empty space in my life that I just couldn't ignore. And since I knew Erskine wasn't coming back, I prayed, "God, at least send me a replacement."

Losing Erskine made me feel so uncovered, unsafe, and helpless. And though I had watched my mom survive as a single parent for many years, I still wasn't comfortable with the idea of trying to live such a life. Time after time, I watched her call on her brothers, cousins, friends, and sometimes even the neighborhood strays to help her with cutting our grass, repairs around the house, fixing her car and other issues. But before Erskine took sick, I never had to call a fix-it man because I was married to the fix-it man. And if he couldn't fix it, it was his responsibility to find someone who could. Now, I was having to walk in my mom's old shoes, calling around to find someone to fix this and fix that. I was tired of having to call on someone else's husband for help. I needed God to give me my own.

The more I dwelled on it, the more discouraged I became as I asked myself, "What man in his right mind would want to marry me, a woman with six young children?" I even thought about several single women in our church who were much older than I was and who had never married. I was soon convinced, "If they can't get a husband and they have no children, I surely won't be able to get another one with six. Erskine made sure I would be his wife forever."

Then one day, God gave me a brief vision. I saw myself standing in the doorway of my kitchen as a tall, bald man walked past me down the hall toward the living room. As he passed me, I said, "Hey, Bae," in a very happy tone of voice. In the vision, I knew that man was my husband, and though I couldn't remember what he looked like, I do remember that he looked nothing like Erskine. In fact, he was much taller than Erskine was, which is why I'm sure it was someone other than him.

On another day while at the church, my cousin Linda Stallworth shared with me a dream she had concerning my future. She said in the dream she saw me having a wedding, and I was marrying a wealthy man that adored my children and me. I realized her dream and my vision were God's way of encouraging my heart, letting me know that He was working on something. But in my impatience, I decided He needed my help.

Near the end of January 2013, as I lay grieving on the living room sofa in the middle of the night, I began thinking about Brother Ryan. He was the man at our church for whom I had made the veggie nachos during the Daniel fast. Brother Ryan was a handsome, divorced, middle-aged man who was six or seven years older than I was. He had been divorced for about thirteen years and had four grown children. He was a good friend to Erskine and me and had been a member of our church for many years. As I lay there thinking about him, I decided that since we were such good friends and single adults, there should be no harm in us coming together as a couple.

Also, considering the vision God had given me of the tall, bald man, I assumed Ryan was the man I saw in the vision because I have had dreams in the past that turned out the opposite of what I saw in the dream. Therefore, I assumed this was one of those situations. For instance, I once had a dream about one of my brothers and his wife. But when the dream later unfolded, it turned out to be another one of my brothers and *his* wife.

God's Girl

So with that thought in mind, I felt Ryan could possibly be the man from my vision because his features were the opposite of what I saw, as he was not tall and he had a head full of hair.

With that glimmer of hope, I decided I would contact Ryan the next day, hoping that maybe, just maybe, he would agree to us building a relationship that would possibly result in a future marriage. I guess you can see I was very determined to help God fix me.

After contacting Ryan the next morning, to my surprise, he burst my bubble. He was very skeptical about my idea because he said he had never looked at me in any way other than as a little sister. So with that reason, plus several other issues that he addressed, he declined my idea. That disappointment pushed me even further into my depressed state of mind, and I soon felt as if I was grieving the death of two husbands.

I had deemed Ryan as the perfect man for me because we had known each other for many years. Also, he was saved, we attended the same church, he was a loving father to his kids, he was always loving to my kids, and I knew from past conversations that he wanted to remarry one day. But his rejection of my idea gave me even more reason to believe that there was not a man that would want me because of my six kids. Subsequently, my faith in God was slowly diminishing. And I began to get so desperate that I lowered my standards, thinking that's what I had to do to get this man to want me. I flirted and begged, trying to pry my way into his life. I even sent him heartfelt text messages explaining that I was no doubt the woman for him. And when those messages didn't do the trick, I sent him some of the lyrics to Jennifer Hudson's song from the movie *Dreamgirls*, *And I Am Telling You I'm Not Going*.

Though Ryan continued to say no to my suggestion of advancing our friendship, he didn't stop calling me. He called me every day, nearly five to six times during a day, and talked to me as he worked. This benefited both of us because it took my mind off my grief and it helped him get through his frustrating workday. Our conversations would be all over the place subject wise, but whenever I brought up the subject of a relationship between us, he'd always shoot it down.

One night, in a moment of desperation, I found myself at Ryan's house. When I noticed he wasn't home, I parked in his driveway and waited. When he arrived, rather than let me in his house, he sat in my truck with me and we talked. I shared with him my intentions for coming over; I needed him to sleep with me. Yes, I know, I was the pastor's daughter, a woman of God, a published author, a prayer warrior, and a devout virgin until I married. But that night I dropped all of those titles. I was simply a lonely woman desiring to be touched, held, and caressed by a man. A desperate widow yearning to be loved again.

But Ryan was not moved by my passionate plea for love and affection. He stood his ground, confidently telling me that he was not going to touch me in that way. Surprisingly, this man could see who I was better than I could. Actually, I really didn't care who I was. Nevertheless, Ryan remembered my relationship with God, and he knew there was a great anointing upon my life. That's why he wouldn't do what I wanted him to do, no matter how much I pressured him. I now realize that the Holy Spirit was sitting in the backseat of that truck, and even though He knew I didn't want to be kept from this sin, He kept me regardless.

Thanks to Mama, Papa Dewey, and the girls, I finally left the living room sofa and moved into my own bedroom. It was the tiny bedroom in the basement under the stairs, which used to belong to Jessica and Jasmine. As I mentioned earlier, I had given them my and Erskine's bedroom when he was sick, and I didn't want it back after he had died. The girls helped me clean up my new room, and my mom and pop went out and purchased me a twin mattress set with a frame and set it up for me. I guess they were eager to help me get a sense of normalcy back into my life. In fact, that's exactly what I wanted for myself, a normal life. That's why I was working so hard to get Ryan to see that my idea of he and I becoming a couple was actually a good one, as I thought remarrying right away would help me be normal again.

One day, not long after I had moved into my new room, I had a dream that felt so real. Erskine was standing in the hallway outside of my bedroom. It seemed he had just arrived home from work because he had on his uniform and was standing by the steps reading the mail. Then the

God's Girl

scene changed, and he was reclining in my small twin-sized bed, and I was lying next to him with my head on his chest. I was sharing with him how confused I was about my desire to marry again. And he said, "If I were you, I'd probably wait until all of the girls have graduated high school." After that, I woke up and realized his words made sense and they had even calmed me. Then I calculated the number of years it would take for all of my girls to graduate high school. Seven. And I figured, "Well, seven is God's perfect number, so I guess I can accept that."

Because of Erskine's words to me in the dream, I told myself that this friendship with Ryan would be just that, a friendship and nothing more. Nevertheless, the more he and I talked, the more my mind started changing because I was gradually pouring my heart into this man in our daily phone conversations. We then started going out on "friendship" dates. And he would even come over to the house, eat dinner, and spend time with the girls and me. But still, whenever I questioned him about us becoming a couple, he continued to give me excuses as to why we should not.

Tired of playing the cat and mouse game with Ryan, I tried pulling away from him by insisting that he stop calling me, and when he didn't stop, I sent his calls to voicemail. I did these things because I felt myself growing attached to him, but I no longer felt comfortable pouring my heart into a man who didn't desire me the way I desired him. So I tried to end our *situationship*.

Since things were not working out the way I wanted them to between Ryan and me, I started trying to catch other fish. And I did catch a few that I desperately tried to throw back, but it wasn't always so easy to do so. For instance, there was a guy that I met at my mailbox who happened to be on my street passing out flyers for his business. After talking to him in a flirtatious way, he asked for my number, and I gave it to him. But after a few days of hearing his annoying phone conversation, I soon realized he wasn't the man I was looking for, and I didn't trust him to ever come around my girls. I tried hard to shake him off, but this man wasn't letting go that easily, no matter how much I dodged his calls. I dreaded that he knew where I lived, as I hoped he never decided to show up unexpectedly. God made sure he never came back.

My parents were very worried about my desperate longing for a man; as a result, they kept giving me unsolicited advice. But I kept reminding them that I was almost forty-four years old, old enough to make my own decisions, and therefore they should just pray for me and let me handle my own business. I felt myself growing cold toward them and toward God. I knew my parents couldn't identify with me, as neither of them had ever lost a spouse to death, and I didn't understand why God had allowed me, His faithful and obedient daughter, to go through such a disruption in life. My life was just fine before He allowed sickness and death to enter it. In fact, I had done nothing but live a life sold out to Him. Why then did He allow my husband to be taken from me? Wasn't it enough that I had endured the sickness and death of my firstborn child? Why pile on more pain?

The urge to go against everything I knew that was right had come over me. Those things I had worried would happen to my girls as a result of God not answering their prayers to heal their dad began to happen to me. Nothing my parents had taught me about having faith in the Lord and His Word while growing up seemed to make sense anymore. What was it benefiting me to go to church and live holy? If this deep pain and loneliness was my reward for living my life solely for the Lord, then I was done. I no longer wanted any parts of this lifestyle. Don't get me wrong, I wasn't going to stop going to church; I just wasn't going to be as dedicated as I had been.

I tried not to care anymore about being a godly example for my girls. If they needed an example, they could follow my first example, the girl I was over thirty years ago before all of this pain. The girl who was very obedient to her parents. The girl that served God with all of her heart and wrote songs, poetry, and plays in expression of her love for Him. The girl who made it her goal to marry as a virgin in hopes of pleasing her natural father as well as her heavenly Father. That's the girl whose example my daughters should follow. But this new girl would not be such a good example, as she was tired of reaping hell in her life that she did not sow. She just wanted people to leave her alone and let her live her life her way. The most anyone could do for her was pray.

During my mental tantrum, I decided to throw away everything Erskine and I had built together. I no longer wanted to write, so I dissolved O'Neal-Daniel Productions and Good Morning Saints. I also dissolved We'll Fix It, which was our air-conditioning, heating, and computer repair business because I knew I could no longer maintain it without my husband. I felt that since the visions and plans we had for our businesses and personal life had basically died with him, there was no point in me holding on to the past, so I was willing to let it all go and start over fresh. That even included our house.

When Erskine and I first purchased our home, we also purchased homeowner's insurance, but we didn't see the importance of paying the extra to make sure the house would be paid off in the event of his death. I guess we just didn't think that would ever happen. Now, here I was wishing someone had forced us to pay that extra because I was stuck with a note after his death. Therefore, I had a portion of the house remodeled in order to help it sell because living in it was causing me pain. So for about six weeks, the main level of our home was all tore up, much like our life, due to the remodeling. Our lives felt very depressing and chaotic during that time.

Grieving had caused me to lose a considerable amount of weight, which resulted in my purchasing a brand-new wardrobe. And it wasn't the thrift store attire as I normally wore, but it was all brand-new items, which I could now afford.

I eagerly changed my style of dressing and experimented with different hairstyles and hair colors. I even began wearing more makeup than normal. And I adopted the YOLO slogan (you only live once) for my life because, after watching my husband die so young, I decided I was going to stop waiting to live and try my best to live life to the fullest.

I desired to get to know the long-lost side of Tracy. The side of me that disappeared when I married young and started having children. The side of me that stayed hidden as I took care of my large family and the business of the Lord. The side of me that totally disappeared when I became my sick husband's caregiver. I was very familiar with "Wife Tracy," "Mama Tracy," "Daughter Tracy," and "Sister Tracy," but who in the world was just "Tracy"? And what were her likes, dislikes, goals, and desires in life? Yes, who was that girl? I was eager to discover her.

After church one Sunday in March, my cousin Jonita Steele gave me an unexpected gift. It was a lovely black journal with a beautiful quote on the cover written in pink. The anonymous quote said, "Faith is about believing in something and knowing in your heart that it is true, even when your mind can't find the answers." I was surprised that my cousin had given me this gift for no certain reason, but I was even more surprised as to how God used the gift to speak to me.

Unaware that I had considered walking away from God and everything that Erskine and I had created together, Jonita's obedience in giving me that gift allowed me to receive an important message from God. Through that journal, God was telling me that because neither Erskine nor I had created my gift of writing, He was not going to allow me to throw it away. He had placed that gift inside of me at my conception and for a good reason, as it was my ministry.

I couldn't deny it. I knew God had given me my gift of writing, which was confirmed somewhere between 1979 and 1980 when I was in the fifth grade. Without trying, I won first place in an essay contest given to my elementary school by the local chapter of the Elks Club. The title of the essay they asked us to write was, "What It Means to Me to Be an American," and my social studies teacher, Mrs. Walker, encouraged every student in her class to write one. However, she made the mistake of telling us that it was optional. That was good news to me because I really didn't want to do it, so I didn't.

Well, on the essay due date, Mrs. Walker stunned us when after she asked who all had written their essay and only a few hands were raised, she made it mandatory for the rest of us to write one. So on the spot, we had to take out pencil and paper, write the essay, and turn in by the end of class.

For some reason, I've always worked better under pressure, which is why a week later, when the essays were judged, my teacher called my mom to give her the wonderful news that I had won first place in the essay contest. My mom didn't even know I had entered an essay contest, as I didn't think to tell her. I was just trying to stay out of trouble and turn in a last-minute assignment.

The Elks Club held a special ceremony at their lodge for the two runner-ups and me to read our essays and receive our prizes. I remember my mom and dad sitting there proudly as I stood at the podium reading

God's Girl

my essay. However, to this day, I have no idea what kind of prize I won, nor do I know where it went. I don't even know where my essay went, whether the Elks Club or my teacher kept it. But I do remember a note. There was a note given to my teacher by the essay judge, which my teacher made copies of and shared with my parents. Then my parents made more copies and shared them with family members. The way my parents carried on about that note through the years made me feel as if the note were the actual prize. But I guess they were just proud of the good things the judge said about my essay and about me:

"This one is, without a doubt, a cut above the rest!

1. The writer did not try to give me a history lesson.
2. She relates, "What It Means to Be an American" to herself much better than the rest.
3. Her ideas are refreshingly different. "... I'm so glad I came in the world to live in America" (odds are greater that you would be born in another country). "And being an American is just like the meaning for freedom" (None of the other papers were this concise.)

Hey Teacher!
This girl has some potential!"

I didn't really appreciate this note from the judge until I had reached adulthood because I didn't understand its meaning as a child. But to my proud parents, that little note was proof that their daughter had a gift. A remarkable gift. A gift significant enough not only to win a prize but to also be recognized by people of all races. It was a gift given to her by God. This is why God would not allow me to walk away from my gift. It was my calling. My purpose. My ministry. In fact, the journal given to me by my cousin was a sign that God wanted me to get back to writing immediately, even though the wound in my heart was still fresh.

The pink words on the cover of the journal that said, "Faith is about believing in something and knowing in your heart that it is true, even when your mind can't find the answers." were also a message from God.

He was telling me that I had to believe in Him even though I couldn't understand what He was doing in my life at the moment. I had to trust that He had allowed it for my good whether it felt good or not. He told me that my faith in Him is what had brought me this far in life, and it will be my faith in Him that sees me through the rest of my life. Just in case I had it twisted, He wanted me to know that before Erskine ever walked into my life, He was there, and He has always been there. I was His girl. And that's the only side of Tracy I needed to discover, God's girl.

About ten days after Jonita gave me the journal, I wrote my first entry inside. I was brainstorming a new book idea that I later decided to scratch.

> 3/13/13, 8:45 a.m.
> My new book will be titled *Life without Daddy*. It will be my and the girls' thoughts and feelings on life since Erskine's death. I'll open with how I started calling him Daddy in order to teach the girls to call him Daddy. Then I will go back to our dating era, discussing our letters, our dreams and goals. I'll talk about our life together, the sicknesses and other happenings along the way. Then I will bring it to a close with January 2012 through December 2012 and our first year without him.
> Writing in this journal is hard because I have to stop and cry after every sentence, but I'm willing to push through it if this is what God wants from me.

I wrote my next entry nine days later.

> 3/22/13, 8:15 a.m.
> Yesterday was three months exactly that Erskine's been gone. I realized that I've spent the first three months trying to get back what was taken from me through another man. I quickly found out that man could never be Erskine. Although he's a good man, he's still not Erskine. Just as Erskine had a unique name, he was a unique man,

God's Girl

and no one, and I mean no one, could ever take his place. He was born just for me.

The nineteenth was my birthday, and although I feared celebrating my forty-fourth birthday without my husband, amazingly I enjoyed it. My kids, their friend, my dad, and two of my good friends from church were there, and we really had a wonderful time.

The day before my birthday, Daddy went with me to purchase Jasmine a car, debt free. That was a bittersweet moment because although she and I were excited about her having her own car, the idea that her dad wasn't there to share in our joy was a bit heartbreaking. That's when it hit me that I was in for a lifetime of such heartbreaking moments. There were more cars to purchase, proms to buy for, graduations to attend, weddings to plan, and grandbabies to hold, all without Erskine's presence. I assumed every milestone for my girls from now on would be a mixture of joy, pain and tears.

Surprisingly, Ryan continued calling me every day and giving me mixed messages, which was very confusing to me. He would tell me I was his best friend, which I figured should have been the perfect reason for us to begin a serious relationship, but he kept insisting that we only remain friends. And whenever I talked to him about my desire to date other guys, he seemed to have an issue with it because he didn't want to see me go. No matter how many times I tried to ignore his phone calls, he continued to pry his way back into my world. It was evident he had grown attached to me as I had to him. I finally quit trying to pull away from him and just went with the flow, all the while holding on to a fragment of hope that his mind would eventually change.

I spent many lonely nights in my tiny bedroom under the stairs, lying in the dark, soaking my pillow in tears. I needed God to hurry and change my depressing circumstances, as I was tired of living life with a fake smile and a heavy heart. While lying there, I would have wild imaginations of Erskine miraculously returning home, or of myself going to the graveyard and digging him up. I even wondered if all of this was just a bad dream and soon I would wake up and everything would be back to normal.

As I look back upon that time in my life, I realize that the Holy Spirit had to be sticking to me like glue because I have no idea how I was able to take care of my children and other responsibilities each day with my brain in such a handicapped state.

I must admit though, God allowed much of my strength to come by way of a DVD Erskine and I purchased about three years before his death. On the DVD was the gospel singing group *Commissioned*. It was their reunion concert, which they performed in 2001. Erskine and I both grew up listening to the music of these anointed young men, so we decided to purchase the DVD for a bit of nostalgia. After watching it a couple of times, we ended up stashing it away among several other old discs and forgot all about it. However, after moving so much stuff around in preparation for the remodeling, I came across that DVD and decided to watch it again.

Back when I first watched Commission's concert with Erskine, it brought back old memories of my youth. But this time as I watched it, it brought healing. I watched that concert nearly every day, as every song was soothing to me. It seemed Fred Hammond, Marvin Sapp, and the rest of those guys all knew just what I was going through, and they decided not to stop singing until I had received a breakthrough.

Ryan eventually became like a substitute husband for me. I enjoyed talking to him, cooking for him, and spending time with him. He was also a substitute dad to my girls, and his demeanor and patience with them really turned me on. This man had more of my heart than he realized. He was like a rescuer for me in a sense. And during the times when I felt like I was going out of my mind, his words had a way of calming me.

After a few months, Ryan finally upgraded our friendship to a relationship, and he and my dad went out on a breakfast date to discuss us. He told me that he realized I would be a great choice for him as a wife because he knew my father, his pastor, had taught me how to be such. He also said he remembered the wonderful relationship I had with my deceased husband, which is the kind of relationship he wanted us to have. I was on cloud nine and very excited about telling my friends that I had a new love in my life.

In June, I went on a train trip to New Orleans, Louisiana with our church's singles' ministry. It was my first time going on a trip without my husband or children. It felt good but weird. Actually being identified as a single felt even weirder.

While there in Louisiana, I remembered that Benfordnetti Morgan, one of my best friends from childhood, lived there. When I contacted her, she was excited to come visit me at the hotel where we were staying. After spending time in the lobby catching up and visiting the rooms of other church members, we ended our time together sitting outside the hotel on a bench facing a busy street. As cars zoomed by and people walked to and fro, we were absorbed in our conversation about the new developments in both our lives, as there were an awful lot of things that had changed for each of us. As she already knew of Erskine's passing, I eagerly filled her in on my new relationship with Ryan, and she seemed very excited for me. And likewise, I was just as excited about the good things happening in her life there in Louisiana.

That meeting with my old friend was quite an experience. One I'll always cherish. Where we were once very young girls, playing together at church and spending the night at one another's houses, we were now forty-something-year-old friends, sitting on a bench outside of a fancy hotel, somewhere on a busy street in New Orleans, discussing our past and present lives. It was a bit surreal for me, as it had the feel of an emotional Lifetime movie scene.

In July, I hit the road again, driving my family to Destin, Florida, for a women's trip sponsored by our church. Though I was trailing Mama Trish the entire way, I was still proud of myself for releasing the fear of driving in unfamiliar territory. However, milestones like this did not excite Ryan, so he didn't know how to be happy for me because he didn't understand my struggle. To him, I just didn't know how to drive, and my fear was ridiculous.

Though he didn't realize it, Ryan often said and did things that belittled me, but for the chance to fill that empty void in my life with another man, I felt I needed to learn to put up with the belittling. For instance, he often discussed the size of woman he was attracted to, which happened *not* to be my size. So, in an effort to keep him, I felt obligated to try changing to please him.

Then there was the questionable relationship with his ex-wife where they did favors for one another and sometimes hung out together with their grown children as one big happy family. I wasn't invited on such dates, nor did I desire to be. And I believed them both when they'd tell me that I had nothing to worry about concerning their relationship, as they were just great friends. But my heart would break a little each time they had one of their meetings. Not able to bear the thought of them having a chance encounter with one of my friends or family members while they were together, I finally spoke out against it. But it didn't seem to change much.

These and other things Ryan did or said made me feel somewhat insecure about him and our relationship. But as I stated earlier, I did what I thought I had to do to keep a man in my life. Ignoring the caution lights that were steadily warning me that this was not the man for me, I continued trying to make him happy. Happy enough to marry me.

I guess my efforts worked because soon enough, Ryan and I were discussing plans for our future together. I was very excited about that, so much so that I gave very little thought to the string of broken relationships and bad decisions that trailed behind this man. Eagerly looking forward to finding my new purpose in him, I questioned Ryan often about his vision for his life because I desired to jump in and help him obtain it, as a good wife should. But sadly, I started to notice that this fifty-something-year-old man really didn't have a clear vision for his life, and the few goals he did have were very mediocre. That should have been a sign to me that if he didn't have a vision, he would not be successful at leading our family. Nevertheless, because I loved him, I made his mediocre goals my goals, and I was determined to help him reach them at all cost.

When the renovations were complete on our house, the girls and I began house hunting. I no longer wanted to remain in the city where we lived because it was now part of my painful past. So I searched for homes in cities that were several miles away. I excitedly told Ryan about each house we viewed, hoping he would help us pick one and thereby feel a part of the process since he would be living with us once we were married.

With the aid of a Realtor, I was hunting for houses every week. And every house that appealed to me either didn't have enough space or was over $300,000. When I finally found one that I really liked, it was around $280,000, but I figured after a hefty down payment, I could handle the notes. God allowed an interference, which hindered me from purchasing that house, and therefore I had to start looking all over again.

Earlier in my hunt, my Realtor would send me pictures and information on houses that had the amount of bedrooms and bathrooms I desired. One day, she sent me information on a nice home that was in the city where we were presently living, and I called her immediately and asked her not to send me any more homes in that particular zip code because I was not interested in remaining in the same area. I was so dead set on not staying in that city until I didn't even take the time to look at the photos or read the description of the home she had sent.

Well, since I was back at square one after not getting the house I wanted, I decided to go back and look at some of the listings my Realtor had e-mailed me previously, including the one that was in the city where I lived. That listing was for a large home in one of the upscale communities in our area. It was nearly all brick and had five bedrooms, which included an extra-large master suite, four and a half bathrooms, living room, dining room, family room, laundry room, two-car garage, a sunroom, a deck, and an extra-large fenced-in backyard, and it even included a doghouse. And amazingly, it was a move-in-ready foreclosure that I would easily be able to pay cash for, eliminating a house note. All of that sounded wonderful to me, but I just couldn't get past the idea of it being in the same city as my old house because I really wanted to move far away from my memories. But I knew this was too good of a deal to pass up, so I reluctantly went to view that house.

On the outside, the house was lovely, though it could still use a little TLC. And as I walked around the outside, I was very impressed, but I was still pouting. Then I decided to make a deal with God, saying, "I'm going to call my dad to come look at this house, and if he doesn't answer his phone or is too busy to come right now, then I will assume this is not the house for us and that I should continue looking in other cities."

As I stood in the front yard of that house, I called my dad on my cell phone, and surprisingly he answered the phone right away. That was unusual. Then, when I asked if he was able to come and look at the house, he told me to come pick him up immediately. I guess God had spoken loud and clear. He wanted me to stay in that city because He didn't want me uprooting my children in an attempt to run away from my pain.

After only seeing the outside, Daddy loved the house, and he encouraged me to contact my Realtor right away to make an appointment to see the inside. Well, long story short, a day or so later, Jessica, my dad, and I went to view the inside of the house, and we all fell in love with it, as it was well kept, very spacious, and as I stated before, move-in ready.

Two days before Christmas, I bought the house, debt free. And two days after Christmas, my girls and I moved in. After that, I put my old house on the market, hoping it would sell fast. But after six or seven months when it hadn't sold, I decided to rent it out as a way to help me pay its mortgage and to have someone help me keep it up because having to maintain two houses was a bit much for me.

Meanwhile, Ryan was still assuring me that we were going to get married, but he said he was working on straighten out his financial issues first. He even hired a financial advisor to help him. Because I trusted him, I saw no problem in using my own finances to help him out until he could get his finances straight and he was ready to say, "I do." He and I figured since we would be marrying soon, there wasn't any harm in me giving him a hand every now and then. I now realize that was a terrible mistake.

As our relationship neared a year and a half, I felt it was time for us to get serious about taking the next step, so I started giving Ryan ultimatums concerning engagement and marriage. I had always heard that when a man knows what he wants in a woman, it doesn't take him long to make the right one his wife. Well, Ryan had assured me repeatedly that I was the right one for him, but for some strange reason, it was taking him forever to solidify our relationship. In fact, it seemed my questions about it were frustrating him, and he began to pull away from the girls and me. He called less, stopped coming around as often, and started excluding me in his affairs. It was very painful watching our relationship fall apart without knowing why. And I didn't know whether to fight for it or let it go.

This was rather stressful for me, as it stayed on my mind constantly. And I did everything I could to hide it from the outside world, including my family who already had their doubts about Ryan. Soon, the stress of our relationship along with the increase of responsibilities that were upon me began to affect my health.

Around Mother's Day of 2014, I ended up with shingles, which was a severely painful rash that broke out all over my upper right chest, shoulder, and back. It was also on the right side of my head and behind my ear. My doctor explained to me that the shingles virus derives from the chickenpox virus, which continues living inside of those who've had chickenpox in the past. However, he said the main cause of a shingles outbreak is stress. He then asked me what was causing my stress. I was too embarrassed to tell him about my failing relationship with my boyfriend, so I blamed it all on being a new widow and having to raise six kids on my own.

I was in so much pain from the shingles that my girls had to cater to my needs. I couldn't wear clothing items that touched me in the areas where the rash was located, nor could I receive hugs because the slightest touch in that area would give me extreme pain. And because I couldn't wear certain clothing, I was homebound for a few weeks. Surprisingly, God used this situation to open my eyes a bit wider concerning Ryan.

Ryan rarely came by to check on me during this time because he said he didn't want to catch what I had. And whenever he called me, he'd go straight into conversing about his day, never pausing to ask me how I was feeling or what I was doing. It hurt to face the truth that this man didn't really feel the same way about me as I felt about him.

Because of his heartlessness as well as having grown tired of playing cat and mouse with him (I was the cat, he was the mouse), I tried breaking up with Ryan a couple of times. But he would always come back begging forgiveness and promising to do better. He'd then do better for a few days, but eventually he'd resume acting as if he had never promised to marry me.

It was around this time that I contacted a few of my married friends asking if they knew any single men they wanted to introduce me to because I was ready to be free of Ryan. Sadly, I thought I needed to find a replacement before I could let him go. But since neither of my friends seemed to know anyone, I assumed I was stuck playing Ryan's stupid games.

Then I decided to get a job. I started working at a local department store to help me pay some new bills I'd made and to take my mind off Ryan. I also hoped to catch another fish while I was there, but it's funny how God never allowed any fish to swim my way.

One day, after confronting Ryan about his aloofness, he shocked me when he seemed very willing to give up on what I thought we were building together. He admitted that he didn't love me the way I loved him and that he didn't think he could be the kind of man I needed him to be. He said I deserved someone better than him. When I asked why he was suddenly ready to give up on us, he found it hard to give me an answer. So he left me in the dark about it for a few days. However, he later admitted that he was afraid of commitment. He said he really wasn't ready to let go of his independence. His words knocked the wind out of me. I was devastated. I wanted to slap him, kick him, punch him, and even curse him out. But I didn't. I just cried because I felt cheated and embarrassed. But more than anything, I felt used. I had given my heart, my time, my money, and even my body to a man whom I don't believe ever seriously planned to marry me.

Not wanting to lose me as a friend, Ryan came over for dinner one evening and asked if we could have a uncommitted relationship whereby

God's Girl

we'd still hang out like best friends, going to the movies, to dinner, to the park, and other places for fun because he missed the times we used to spend together. Basically, he wanted to go back to being *just friends*. Because I also missed our time together, especially his phone calls, as he was like a drug for me, I decided to play along, though it didn't feel right.

I knew I wasn't looking for a friend to hang out with; I wanted a husband. Ryan may have wanted to hold on to the single life, but I didn't. I was not that kind of girl. I was wife material, and I needed a man that was husband material. I knew in my heart that I had made a mistake in agreeing to remain friends with the man who had broken my heart, but I didn't know how to let him go. I felt stuck.

Another verse in Kelly Price's song, "Healing for My Soul," spoke volumes to my twice broken heart as her lyrics described perfectly the way I felt after I had wasted a year and a half making the biggest mistake of my life. "Lord, I've made some terrible mistakes, gave my body and my soul away. Now I come to you because I need to be whole. Heal my soul Lord."

I was so hurt and confused that I began questioning God all over again, as to why He had allowed Erskine to die. And because I was battling the fear of no other man wanting me with so many kids, I begged God to change Ryan's heart and send him back to me as a husband, but He wouldn't.

Every Wednesday night before Bible study and every Sunday morning before 11:00 a.m. service, I could be found in my dad's office talking his head off about my pain. Yet he never turned me away; he only encouraged and strengthened me each week. And through our weekly impromptu meetings, I felt myself growing stronger and stronger.

But everywhere I went, which was mainly work, church, and the local Walmart, I was still hoping to catch the eye of another man. Many times when I went grocery shopping, I often looked around wondering, *Is he in here, Lord?* Then one day while in the Walmart near my home, as I looked around for *him*, I heard God say to me clearly, "He's not in here. He's not even on this side of town." Hearing God tell me that *he wasn't in there* led me to believe that *he was somewhere*. So I stopped looking and just patiently waited on God to send him. I didn't know how long it would take, but my peace came from knowing that he was on the way.

I slowly started to grow content with being a widow and a single mom. My life consisted of working at the department store, running up and down the highway taking Jasmine back and forth to college, working in the media ministry whenever I could fit it in my schedule, and caring for my girls. And when I wasn't doing any of those things, I was at home reading a book, as I bought a new book every week because I didn't care much for watching television. I decided snuggling up with a good book was better than entering another heartbreaking relationship. And I told myself that I would just wait until 2020, when my twins were due to graduate high school, before I started dating again. Below is one of the journal entries I wrote during that time.

> 9/ 18/14
>
> It's been awhile. A year and four months to be exact. A lot has happened in my life, almost too much to tell. I will try to make it brief, and it may not be in order, but here it is.
>
> I moved out of the home Erskine and I shared, but I still own it, and I am still paying the notes on it through the help of a tenant. Yes, I am a landlord.
>
> The girls and I found and bought (debt free) a home in a nearby upscale community. It was a foreclosure that was well kept. It was move-in ready and just needed a new roof and garage doors. I bought it two days before Christmas, December 2013, and we moved in two days after Christmas. I bought it with settlements from Erskine's Mesothelioma lawsuit. The lawsuit has made it where all the girls will have a trust fund for their college education. Thank you, Lord! Jessica and Jasmine are both in college now. Jessica goes to Lawson State Community

God's Girl

College, and Jasmine goes to Troy University. This is Jessica's second year and Jasmine's first.

I have three girls driving now, Jessica, Jasmine, and Janay. Janay needs more practice to get her license, but she has her permit. I have two girls in college, two in high school, and two in middle school. The twins have one more year in the middle school, and then they will be in high school. Wow time flies!

Jessica and Jasmine both have cars now. Jasmine didn't take hers off to school, so I drive it a lot. Janay was easy on me when it came to celebrating her sweet sixteenth birthday. She didn't want a big celebration like Erskine and I gave Jessica and Jasmine. Instead, we went to take pictures at a portrait studio across town and then went out to eat with family. Thanks, Janay!

I still lend a hand at Mt. Canaan. I help Sister Joyce edit the television show. I only do it for her and dad, as I don't really care for doing that type of work anymore. Since Erskine died, I don't care for spending much time in the media room, as that is where we spent much of our time together. I kind of feel that way about church also. It just doesn't feel the same.

Ryan and I are just friends now. We tried to make it a serious relationship, but it just didn't work out. He's better at being a friend than a boyfriend or husband. I'm just waiting on God to send me my next husband, but waiting can be so hard.

Well, I think that's about it. Oh, I can add that I am now seriously working on my newest book. God told me recently that there was a blessing on the other side of my obedience, which I assume is the completion of this book. Therefore, I am working hard to complete this task in order that I can get on the other side of this and begin to live again. A brand-new life!

Concerning that blessing on the other side of my obedience, which I mentioned in my journal entry, it was at the close of my dad's sermon on a Sunday afternoon in September 2014 when Daddy asked David Davis, who was also one of Mt. Canaan's ministers, to pray. He wanted David to pray in line with what he had just ministered. But just before praying, David said to the congregation, "Look at your neighbor and say, 'Neighbor, life begins on the other side of your obedience.'" As soon as he spoke those words, something leaped inside of me, and tears immediately flooded my eyes, giving me a sign that God was speaking to me.

I accepted David's words as a mandate from God, encouraging me to get serious about finishing this book. And from that day forward, at every given chance, I worked hard at completing it. Even through my painful memories, I wrote out of obedience, as it was once again my heart's desire to do God's will because I was ready to be healed and to start living again.

I was so sure that this book was the obedience that God was referring to that I did not consider any other way in which I was being disobedient to Him, until that weird *just friends* situation with Ryan didn't work out. I discovered that it was hard to be just friends with someone you were once planning a life with, someone who used you, lied to you, and broke your heart. And I realized that by playing his game, I was allowing him to continue playing with my heart. If Ryan wasn't the one for me, then whoever God had for me would not be able to find me while I was playing Ryan's game. I had to come to grips with the truth that if I wanted God to send me a real man who loved, needed, and wanted me, I had to let Ryan go. Completely. And as long as I continued playing Ryan's games, I was being disobedient to God.

As normal, I went to talk to my dad before Bible study one Wednesday in October. My friend Aleshia Posey also happened to be in the office, and the two of them gave me much wisdom and strength that night, so much so that the next day I felt confident enough to write a final letter to Ryan. In the letter, I expressed to him that I needed to cut the cord with him completely. And as a result, I needed to reclaim some property of mine that was in his possession, as soon as possible.

October 9, 2014

Ryan, I've made a decision. For my emotional and mental stability, I have to cut this cord with you totally. As I shared with you on the other night, since we don't desire the same thing out of this relationship anymore (you only want a friendship, I still want a marriage), then I can't go on with it "As Is." You see, although you don't realize it, I've been allowing you to play with my heart, and I need to stop it because it's unhealthy for me.

Whenever we spend any time together or spend an hour or more talking on the phone, my heart and mind start to imagine we are a couple. Then when I fall back to reality, I'm left hurting, and it sends me into a deep depression.

I guess my biggest hurt in this is why God would allow me to love you so much harder than you loved me. As I've mentioned before, I invested so much into you because I loved you so much. That was it. I wasn't trying to buy you. I just wanted to make life easier for you because I didn't like seeing someone I loved so much have to suffer such hardship. Now, I realize that although my motives were pure, that was still a big mistake. Just as sex should be reserved for marriage, a woman being a man's helpmeet should also be reserved for marriage. Therefore, I was moving prematurely. I'm not blaming you; I'm blaming me.

Anyway, I'm really tired of hurting, and I'm tired of battling this depression. I am so ready to move forward with my life and discover all that God has waiting for me on the other side of this.

As a result of my decision, I don't want to drag this property issue out any longer. Rather than waiting until next year to return it, I need you to give me my property by November 30, 2014.

I hope you can forgive me for being so abrupt, but I had to do this for me, and if for no other reason, to remain emotionally stable for my girls.

Tracy

I don't know if you've figured it out yet, but the prophecy I shared with you that I received back in 2010 from Prophet Todd Hall was a foretelling of the death of my husband and this *situationship* with Ryan.

Remember when the prophet said, "And you know what? I'm laughing and this gone sound like I'm a false prophet because the Lord is taking me back somewhere I don't want to go. He said to tell you regardless, I don't know you, whether you are married or not, but God said, 'The one who should have married you missed a millioneiress.'"

Prophecies are normally foretelling of events to come. So when Prophet Hall thought he was seeing into my past when he said, "the Lord is taking me back somewhere I don't want to go," God was actually showing him my future. This is why he didn't know whether I was married or not, because in his vision, he didn't see Erskine, as he was already deceased.

And seeing as I had never had anyone before Erskine with whom I had discussed marriage, I knew the prophet had to be speaking of Ryan when he said, "The one who should have married you."

As I think about it, I am truly amazed at how God sent me encouragement for this period of my life, four years in advance. He knew that one day there would be a man who would reject my love and break my heart. And because He loved His girl so much, He reached out to me beforehand, piercing through the fabrics of time, sending me a word of encouragement for a future circumstance.

God wanted me to know that in releasing Ryan, I wasn't going to lose a thing. In fact, I was the prize that Ryan lost. Also, completely releasing Ryan would prove to be one of the ways I needed to be obedient to God because not long after severing that relationship, God opened up the windows of heaven and poured out my blessing!

God's Girl

Before moving on, I must share with you what I learned in all of this. Rather than become my husband, Ryan became a lesson for me. Actually, he became many lessons for me and not only for me but also for many of you who are reading this book. I hate that I had to learn these lessons the hard way, by making a mess of my life. But I thank God for supernaturally turning my mess into a message for you.

The lessons I learned in dealing with Ryan are …

1. Just because he goes to church doesn't mean he is the one for you.
2. Just because he is single doesn't mean he is the one for you.
3. Just because he is handsome, sweet, kind, saved, sanctified, Holy Spirit-filled, and fire baptized doesn't mean he is the one for you.
4. Never give a man, to whom you are not married, husband benefits (sex, money, too much time, etc.).
5. Don't go changing yourself trying to please a man. If you want to change, make sure you are doing it more for yourself than you are for them because if they can't accept you for who you are, they are not the one for you.
6. Don't allow a man to waste your time. If he won't agree to solidify a progressive relationship with you in a sufficient amount of time, just move on and believe that God has someone better waiting just for you. And lastly …
7. A new man is not always the answer for a broken heart.

23

The Climb

> But as it is written, Eye hath not seen, nor ear heard, neither have entered into the heart of man, the things which God hath prepared for them that love him.
> —1 Corinthians 2:9 (KJV)

Honestly, I was very lonely after severing my relationship with Ryan, and I contemplated a lot about what I was going to do with my life. I considered leaving Mt. Canaan and going to one of the many churches in Atlanta on Sundays to experience a new atmosphere and perhaps be noticed by a new man. I wasn't bold enough to try choosing one for myself anymore, as I didn't want to make another *Ryan* mistake. But I thought maybe if I gave myself a little exposure, one would find me.

My mind was all over the place due to loneliness and hurt, and I just needed God to help me get through it because I felt so alone in the world. Though I felt alone, I knew I wasn't alone because I trusted God when He said He would never leave me or forsake me (Hebrews 13:5), but at the time, I really missed male companionship. I was grateful for the material things God had given me, but I didn't understand what good they were if I didn't have anyone to enjoy them with. In a few years, my girls would be gone off to build their own lives, and when that day came, I didn't want to be left alone with a bunch of *things*.

Early one morning I heard God's reply to my frustrations, He said, "During this season in your life, you must fly solo. But don't worry, I'll be with you." So every morning after that, whenever I would awake and

God's Girl

my feet hit the floor, my first words to Him were, "It's just me and You, God, just me and You."

One weekend in late October, Aleshia invited me along with our other friend KaShunda Dunn on a road trip to Atlanta, Georgia, to help her celebrate her upcoming birthday. Because we had no major plans for our trip other than shopping, eating, and enjoying our luxurious hotel, we happily incorporated KaShunda's plan for herself to climb Stone Mountain for exercise. So upon our arrival in Atlanta, Aleshia and I stopped by a local Walmart to purchase some athletic shoes and a walking outfit, as the idea of climbing Stone Mountain was last minute, so we had not packed anything of the sort.

We planned to arise very early the next morning, get dressed, and head to Stone Mountain. But before the sun or my friends could get up, I was already wide awake lying in bed in deep thought.

I thought about everything from the death of my husband, my turmoil with Ryan, my new single state, and even the sarcoid scars in my lungs. Because of those scars, I knew this climb would be difficult for me, as even walking on level ground proved difficult for me sometimes because of my limited air intake. But I wanted to take this climb so badly for a number of reasons. First, I knew I could use the exercise. Secondly, I saw it as part of my new YOLO mind-set, which is the reason I instantly added it to my bucket list. And lastly, the Holy Spirit encouraged me to bravely accept this challenge, as He revealed to me that morning, through a song by Miley Cyrus called "The Climb", that this climb would actually be a metaphor for my life.

"I can almost see it, that dream I'm dreaming, but there's a voice inside my head saying you'll never reach it. Every step I'm taking, every move I make feels lost with no direction, my faith is shaking, but I gotta keep trying, gotta keep my head held high. There's always gonna be another mountain I'm always gonna wanna make it move. Always gonna be an uphill battle, sometimes I'm gonna have to lose. Ain't about how fast I get there, ain't about what's waiting on the other side, it's the climb."

Through Miley's song, the Holy Spirit revealed to me that this mountain that I was about to climb represented my life and all of the turbulence I was experiencing in it. Though I had been too afraid to go through life alone, thinking that I needed a man to hold my hand and go with me, God wanted me to know I only needed Him.

I knew there was nothing wrong with me desiring to be married again, but it had to happen in God's timing and with the person that He ordained. And though it was hard to see at times, God was making me aware that with Him and Him alone, I could actually climb this mountain of heartbreak, pain, and mess that I was enduring and experience the happy and successful life He had waiting for me on the other side. But I had to have the confidence to make the first step because when I stepped, He was going to get with me and help me make it to the top.

The beginning of our climb was just fine for me. In fact, I thought to myself, *This is no problem at all. I can do this!* But the higher we climbed, I began experiencing shortness of breath, and my friends had to keep stopping to check on me. As we climbed even higher, I actually considered quitting. I figured I would just sit by a tree and allow my friends to make it to the top and pick me up on their way back down. But thank God, they didn't allow me to quit. With compassion, they encouraged me and waited on me to catch my breath each time, making sure that no matter what, we stayed together.

The higher we climbed, the tighter my chest became. And my breathing was so shallow until I just knew I was going to die. But with the help of my friends and even a stranger, I'm proud to say that I successfully reached the top of Stone Mountain. I was so moved by my accomplishment that all I could do was cry.

As we rested while sitting on a large rock overlooking the beautiful view below, I heard God say to me, "Aren't you glad you kept going?" I said, "Yes, thank you, Lord," and He reminded me, "This mountain is your life. Keep climbing. Don't quit. You can make it. I know it's hard now, but just remember, through this process, I'm molding you into the woman I have purposed for you to become."

Though we did many other fun things during our trip, that Stone

Mountain climb seemed to top them all. In fact, that was yet another surreal moment in my life, as I never thought in a million years I'd literally be standing on top of a mountain that I had climbed.

I went back home very excited about adding the story of my climb to this book. And since God had said that my blessing was on the other side of my obedience, I got very busy trying to finish this book because I assumed my new husband was one of the blessings God had waiting for me when I was done.

Life began to get in the way of my desire to complete this book in the time frame that I had set for myself because I was still working at the department store as well as trying to take my daughter Jasmine back and forth to college, which was two and a half hours each way, every other weekend. That was torture.

Because I worked in the stock room at the department store, I got up at 4:30 a.m. each morning in order to get to work by 6:00 a.m. I was due to clock out at 2:00 p.m., but that only happened if my coworkers and I were done putting out the merchandise. If we weren't done, then we couldn't leave until the job was complete. That was hard on me as a mother because my duties of taking care of my family had to take a backseat to this corporate world.

It hurt me to have to leave my kids at home preparing for school by themselves. For many years, I had faithfully seen them off to school every morning, and now that seemed to be a thing of the past. While at work, I worried about them making it to the bus on time. And because I wasn't allowed to talk on the phone while at work, I couldn't check on them, so I worried whether or not they had missed the bus or if anything bad was happening in my absence.

Not only was it difficult having to leave my children, but the job itself wasn't very easy. Lifting heavy items and walking on concrete for several hours was murder on my back. One morning when I woke up in excruciating pain, I knew I had made a mistake in taking this job so I tried to quit. But I made another mistake of allowing my manager to talk me into staying and putting me on a cash register.

I discovered each day just how much I hated working that job. But I couldn't make myself quit. You would think that the backbreaking work I was doing just to bring home one dollar above minimum wage would have given me the courage to walk away. But no, I stayed. That was until a girl twenty years younger than me, and who was in a higher position, totally disrespected me. To her, age was just a number. She had a little bit of power, and she was going to use it. And it didn't matter that she was using it incorrectly, as she had decided to put me on blast in front of the customers for something I had not grasped yet as a new cashier.

I had been thrown on the cash registers without proper training, and it was only my third day in this new position. A customer came to me with a return, and I couldn't remember how to do that type of transaction, so I asked the young girl to help me because I was instructed by management to ask her any questions I had. But because she grew tired of my questions, she abruptly took the customer's items, did the return herself, and spoke negatively about me to the customer while handling the transaction. That was my breaking point.

After speaking with management, I was moved to another area of the store, but I only worked there about two more days before I finally quit. I gained my confidence to quit when I remembered the words my dad spoke to me at Erskine's funeral. He said, "Supernaturally you're not gonna have to go back to work cause God's got your back. It's too much work at home to finish. It would not be God to put you out to work when you've been at home all the time raising these girls. God's going to finish what he started. God's gonna finish what he started in you." Those words made me realize that I was outside of God's will working that job anyway.

I remembered the volunteer work I had been doing for Mt. Canaan, helping Sister Joyce edit the television show whenever I could fit it into my schedule. I knew she really needed me more than I had been available to her, as with her other responsibilities at the church, she was stretched thin. But because I stubbornly didn't want to have anything to do with the media room after Erskine's death, I made my time in there very scarce. I'd run in, look over her work, make any necessary changes, and leave.

God's Girl

But now God was showing me that's where He wanted me, back in His business.

I decided to call my dad and asked him if I could come back to the church to work part-time editing the television show. He was so excited that he agreed immediately. Sister Joyce was also excited, as well as relieved, because she could now leave the editing to me and go about doing her many other tasks.

I was happy to be working at the church again, and surprisingly, working in the media room was not as bad as I thought it would be. Working there turned out to be a blessing because it didn't take any time away from my children, I was doing something I loved, I was surrounded by people I loved and those who loved me, and I was now back in the will of God.

On the evening of November 30, I had to take care of some unfinished business with Ryan. My daughter Jessica and I went to meet him at a local gas station to reclaim some property of mine that he had in his possession. It bothered me when I noticed he didn't seem to have a bit of remorse concerning the situation. But I remained calm.

When I returned home, I called my dad to let him know that Ryan had returned my property. Daddy's response shocked me. Rather than say, "Okay, great," he asked, "Are you okay?" I wondered why he had asked me that. I didn't think I had sounded upset. I thought I was doing a good job at holding myself together. But being a parent, Daddy knew. And when he asked me that question, I broke.

I explained to Daddy how unremorseful Ryan had been and how it hurt to see that he had no desire to fight for our relationship. He simply walked away, which proved to me he never really wanted me in the first place. Later that evening, I sent Ryan a text telling him how his nonchalant attitude had hurt me. He sent back a very brief and heartless reply, "I'm sorry. I didn't mean to hurt you." And just like that, our relationship faded to black.

God used that heartless text from Ryan to open my eyes, as I realized I had wasted my time, love, and affection on a man that had no time, love, and affection to give me in return. And soon, all those feelings I thought I had for him started melting away. In no time at all, God supernaturally broke the heart ties that were binding me to this man, revealing to me that it had never been about love at all. Only lust and the fear of being alone.

I cried often during this season as I tried hard to remain focused on the things God wanted of me rather than waste my time trying to figure out how to get another man. God in turn always had a word of comfort for me. I remember Him telling me, "Just trust Me. I have amazing things in store for you. I have great works for you to do. I have wonderful places for you to go and renowned people for you to meet. Daughter, be encouraged. I am in the process of enlarging your territory."

It was then that I remembered the prayer of Jabez, which I used to pray faithfully back in 2004, after I had released my first book. Around that time, my mom had given me a small book by Dr. Bruce Wilkinson called *The Prayer of Jabez: Breaking Through to the Blessed Life*. In that little book, I learned about the prayer that a man in the Bible named Jabez had prayed to God in 1 Chronicles 4:10. "And Jabez called on the God of Israel saying, 'Oh, that You would bless me indeed, and enlarge my territory, that Your hand would be with me, and that You would keep me from evil, that I may not cause pain!' So God granted him what he requested" (NKJV).

When I discovered that there were many miraculous blessings packed in that one simple prayer, I began praying it every day for an entire year because I desired those same blessings for my life. Now, it was ten years later, and God was reminding me of a prayer I had prayed in my past. Sometimes we forget the things we ask of God, but He never forgets. He had been waiting to bless me, but He couldn't while I was outside of His will, dating a man He didn't ordain for me and working a job He didn't authorize me to work. Now that the wrong man and the wrong job had been removed from my life, He was about to send the rain. The good rain.

One of the books I enjoyed during my reading time was Sarah Jakes's

Lost and Found: Finding Hope in the Detours of Life. Sarah, the daughter of Pastor T. D. Jakes, found herself pregnant at thirteen and in a destructive marriage a few years later. After living a young life filled with mistakes and regrets, she finally ran back into the arms of God, and her life changed drastically for the good.

I was so blessed by Sarah's story that I began following her on social media. And it was through that venue that I discovered how awesomely God had blessed this young lady after the release of her book, as He sent a new man into her life, Pastor Toure Roberts.

Sarah's story gave me hope because we had a great deal in common. Though we were years apart in age, we were both preacher's kids, we both had circumstances in our lives that detoured us from God, and we were both suffering heartbreak from a man. Also, we were both single parents, and we both had recommitted our lives back to God and His work after making the mistake of trying to live life on our own. Something inside of me just knew that if God had sent Sarah a husband, He had one for me too.

My dad was so excited that I was working with him in the ministry again that he began dreaming up all kinds of projects for us to work on together. He said he wanted to create special video segments for the television show, he wanted to develop a Christian talk show, and he even wanted me to accompany him on his trips to visit and pray for the sick and shut in. I was willing to do all of that because I was just happy to be back in the fold.

Because I had read Sarah's book and was following her online, I talked often to my dad about her amazing story. I shared with him how God had sent her a husband who was a pastor in California, which resulted in her having to leave her father's ministry in Texas and join her husband in Los Angeles. This sounded like a nice little fairy-tale story to him until I broke it down further. I said, "Daddy, you know what that means, right?" He replied, "What?" I responded, "Well, you told me that you've been praying that God sends me a husband, but have you considered if He sends me someone who does not attend our church, I will have to leave you and follow him?" Daddy's eyes got big as baseballs. "No," he said, "I didn't think about that! Well, I'm going to pray that God sends you someone who will be willing to join our church." Actually, it didn't matter to me whether the man joined our church or not. I just ready for God to send him.

One day in early December, my dad and I visited a couple of hospitals. We went and prayed for a sick member who was in one and then went to visit our cousin Jackie Sankey Harville who was in critical condition in another due to the sarcoidosis she had dealt with for years. When we arrived at the hospital to visit our cousin, we were hit with the news that she had passed. We stayed at the hospital for a while, spending time with the family and then we left for lunch.

I remember so vividly the conversation I had with Daddy as we left the hospital. The thought of my cousin's early death had reminded me of the early death of my husband. And that one thought sparked another thought and then another. Before long, as we exited the hospital parking lot, I was pouring my heart out to Daddy concerning the type of man I desired from God.

I told Daddy that I wanted a man who wanted and needed me just as much as I wanted and needed him. I wanted a man who would recognize my worth and who would be proud to have me as his wife. And I wanted a man who wouldn't mind how many children I had but would love, cherish, and protect them all as his own. Less than two weeks after this conversation, I discovered God had been listening to my requests and taking notes.

Because we were in the season of Impact, Mt. Canaan's praise convention, after leaving the hospital, Daddy and I went out to lunch with Pastor Kim Pothier. Pastor Kim, or Real Talk Kim, who many of you may know from the television show *Preachers of Atlanta*, was on program to be our guest minister during the services that night. As we ate, I found myself sharing my story with her through tears, and she spoke words of comfort to me, saying that God had allowed Ryan's rejection to be my protection. In other words, God was protecting me when He removed Ryan from my life. I knew she was right.

God's Girl

A week before Impact, during the Thanksgiving holidays, I started the process of bringing Jasmine home from college little by little. When I picked her up for Thanksgiving, we crammed the SUV with as many of her things as possible and planned to get the rest of it during the Christmas break.

After spending a semester away in college, Jasmine and I agreed that she should come home and attend Lawson State Community College with her sister Jessica. Our decision had nothing to do with her grades, because surprisingly her grades were good, considering she had been taking seven classes that semester. I was not at all upset when she told me she had passed all but one of her classes, as I considered it an accomplishment for her to pass the six.

But our decision to bring her home was for other reasons. Mainly because I was tired of driving her back and forth to college every other weekend just because she was homesick. Her school was two and a half hours one way. And because she was not confident driving such long distances yet, I had to do all the driving. This was a lot on me while working at the department store because after getting up at 4:30 a.m. and getting off work around 3:00 p.m., I would be extremely tired while driving. My breaking point came when I fell asleep one day while going to pick her up. When I woke up and realized I had fallen asleep while driving, I panicked. I thank God He didn't allow me to have an accident. After stopping at a restaurant for coffee to help me stay awake, I made the decision that day that she was coming home.

Jasmine wanted to come home anyway because, as it turns out, I was not the only one suffering from depression after losing Erskine. Jasmine, Jessica, and some of the other girls were also suffering from depression after the death of their dad. But being home together, with the freedom of talking out our feelings and sharing our memories, was healing for the remaining girls and me. But being away from home slowed down Jasmine's healing because she was not only dealing with the loss of her dad but also homesickness, and she ended up suffering mentally. So I brought her home in order that she could heal with the rest of us.

Having all of my kids back under one roof again was a good feeling. I guess it took bringing my daughter home from college to help me finally see that it was never my job to replace what I had lost in Erskine. That was God's job. My only job was to love and take care of what remained, our girls.

One day while leaving the church, Brian Courtney Wilson's song "Worth Fighting For" came on the radio. The song hadn't played a good thirty seconds before there were tears streaming down my face. Although I'd heard his song a few times prior to that moment, I had never paid close attention to the lyrics. But this day, I heard God speaking as this man sang my testimony!

> You met me deep in my despair to show me You would never leave me there. You claimed because I was made for so much more, I am Your child and I'm worth fighting for.
> Though heavy with the weight of my mistakes, You carried me and refused to let me sink under the pressure. You meant for me to soar. I am Your child and I'm worth fighting for.

This song touched my heart because after losing my husband, I didn't know how to pray anymore. I remembered how my girls and I did all of that praying and scripture quoting for his healing, and it didn't work. After that, I was so confused about prayer that whenever others asked me to pray for them, I found it hard to do. I figured what was the point in praying when God was still going to do what He wanted to do.

I finally understood the vision I saw of myself at the end of 2011 when my own face flashed before me. God was encouraging me to intercede for myself because of the great trials that were headed my way. Those trials not only included the sickness and death of my husband but also the hurtful rejection I would experience from Ryan and my wayward mind-set. And during that period of grief, heartbreak, and confusion, while I was busy trying to discover me and fix me, I ended up losing me and nearly destroying me, because I no longer knew my worth.

But God was there all along, sweetly loving on me, keeping His eye on me, never giving up on me, and fighting for me because He knew that I was worth so much more than what I was trying to sell myself. Even when my heart grew cold toward Him, God loved me too much to allow me to leave Him. He gently guided me back to the calling that was on my life while steadily mending my broken heart, all because He knew my worth.

24

From Mourning to Dancing

> Thou hast turned for me my mourning into dancing: thou
> hast put off my sackcloth, and girded me with gladness.
> —Psalm 30:11 (KJV)

In many ways, my actions during my season of mourning reminded me of the prodigal son whom Jesus speaks of in Luke 15:11–32. The son took his inheritance, left his father's house, and while making many bad decisions, tried to handle life on his own. Soon he was completely broke and forced to work a miserable job feeding pigs. That's when his eyes were opened to the error of his way, and he went back home.

In my case, my mom and dad had apprehensions about me dating Ryan, and Daddy warned me several times concerning him. But because I assumed my parents were just being overprotective—after all, I was forty-four years old—I quit taking their advice for a season and tried living life on my own.

Before long, the blessings were no longer flowing freely, my money was drying up, and I was barely making ends meet. I had worn myself out trying to do things my way, running from my parents' advice and ignoring the call God had on my life. I soon reached a point where I was out of strength, out of plans, and almost out of money.

The difference between the prodigal son and me is that I didn't need to end up in the pigpen to see the error of my ways. I only needed to see my pigpen from a distance. And seeing the destruction that was awaiting me up ahead, I suddenly made a U-turn in my life, which placed me in proper alignment for God's blessings to begin flowing in my direction again. Had I not made that U-turn when I did, I would have missed the colossal blessing that God had waiting for me.

But before I tell you about my great blessing, I'd like to share with you just some of the lessons I learned regarding it:

1. Many times God waits until we have given up trying to do things on our own before He enters and works it out for our good.
2. God loves those moments when it looks like there's no possible way for us to achieve our dream; that's when He steps in with the supernatural.
3. God's thoughts are truly not our thoughts, nor are His ways our ways (Isaiah 55:8–9).
4. Life may not be a fairy tale, but God does sprinkle a few fairy-tale moments in the mix.
5. There are amazing blessings waiting for us on the other side of our obedience.
6. Rejection is not always bad, as it can put us in a position to receive God's best for us.
7. God loves me, and I am His girl!

On Tuesday morning, December 16, 2014, I was out with Ann, my attorney, finalizing the trust accounts for my girls. As we sat in the waiting area of the bank, Ann and I engaged in a bit of small talk. In my hurt and frustration, I told her that after being in such a disappointing situation with Ryan, I'd decided to lay low for a while. I said I was no longer interested in dating and that I would probably wait until the last of my girls graduated high school in 2020 before I even considered talking to a man again. Ann seemed to agree that waiting was my best option.

After leaving the bank, my plan was to go work at the church, but since I was still pretty close to home, I decided to stop by the house for a few minutes before going. When I walked in the front door, my cell phone rang. It was my old friend Ronda Henderson.

Ronda and I used to attend church together years ago before she married her present husband. She was also one of the friends I had consulted during my issues with Ryan when I was looking for a new man to replace him. It was now three months later, and Ronda was calling to see if I was still interested in meeting someone new. I thought it was funny that she would call to ask me this after I'd just had this conversation with my lawyer only a couple of hours earlier. I told her no. Not right now. I said I was just going to focus on raising my girls and wait a few years before dating again.

Ronda didn't take no for an answer. She asked me was I sure, because there was a guy she had spoken to about me who was interested in meeting me, and she wanted to know if it was okay to give him my number. At that moment, I was in total shock as I thought, *A guy? Wants to talk to me? With all these children?* Then I asked her, "Girl, did you tell him how many kids I had?" and she replied, "No, I haven't told him anything about you other than that you were a sweet girl." Then I burst my own bubble when I thought, *He'll change his mind when he finds out how many kids I have.*

I just knew that man was not going to want me, so I tried to spare myself another broken heart by telling Ronda I didn't want to go through with it. But still not taking no for an answer, Ronda encouraged me saying, "Just talk to him." So, before giving her a definite answer, I asked her a million questions about him, but she was only able to answer just a few.

She said she had gone to high school with him, but she had graduated a year or two before him. And she remembered him being a nice person in school. Because they were social media friends, she noticed that he would always post scriptures and inspirational messages. And she noticed that he'd also post comments about his desire for a wife. One day, after reading one of his posts, Ronda messaged him and asked if he was interested in meeting a friend of hers. He said he was, but Ronda forgot to tell me. A week or so later, the guy reached out to Ronda again, saying, "I'm still waiting," and that was why she was calling me, to get my permission to give him my number. *Lord, what on earth should I do?* I wondered. *If this is Your way of blessing me with my heart's desire, I sure don't want to miss out on my blessing by being stubborn.*

I knew I could trust Ronda because we had known each other for many years. She knew that I was Pastor O'Neal's daughter, and she knew the type of girl I'd always been. She even knew the caliber of man I had lost. So I felt she wouldn't be introducing me to just anybody. He must

God's Girl

have been a very decent and respectable man for her to want to introduce him to me, so I figured I would go for it, but I needed to know one other thing, what he look liked.

I told Ronda to give me the guy's name so that I could go and look him up on social media. She said his name was David Lee, and she told me to call her back once I'd found him.

I couldn't tell much about David from his profile picture because it was a selfie that had been taken way too close to his face. And not wanting to frustrate Ronda or miss my blessing, I gave her permission to give this stranger my number, and I told her to tell him not to call me until after six, as I figured by then I'd be home and settled in for the evening. Then when we hung up, I thought about my dad.

Now that I was welcoming Daddy's advice again, I was interested in what he had to say concerning this new prospect. When I called and shared the news with him, he, being the protective dad that he is, decided he wanted to talk with Ronda too. So he called her up, and she gave him all of the same information about David that she had given me. But, because of what I had gone through with Ryan, Daddy was still hesitant, and I totally understood. Not only was he trying to protect me from heartbreak, but he was being protective of my assets as well.

―――⁂―――

I went on to work that day, but all I could think about while there was my conversation with Ronda. And as the hours ticked away, I became very nervous about my upcoming phone rendezvous with this stranger. *Will he like me? Will I like him? Will he run away when I tell him about my girls? Should I really be putting myself through this?*

After work, I went by Walmart to pick up some items for dinner. I was in there a little longer than I anticipated, as it was the Christmas season, which made for a much-crowded store. After loading the groceries in my SUV, I decided to check my phone before pulling off. I noticed I had a missed call. I didn't remember hearing my phone ring, so I figured it must have been the bad reception inside of Walmart. I looked at the number and didn't recognize it. Then I noticed I had a message, so I called my voicemail and was stunned to hear the deep voice of a strange man. It was David Lee.

I guess when Ronda told this man to call me after 6:00 p.m., he waited until 6:01 p.m. then called. But I wasn't ready to talk to him yet because I still had things to do like fixing dinner, getting into my pajamas, and talking to my children. I decided I'd return his call after I'd done all of those things. However, by the time I reached my driveway, he was ringing my phone again, so I answered his call.

After engaging in small talk, I told him to let me call him back after I had cooked dinner for my girls. He replied in a smart-aleck tone, "They should be cooking dinner for you." Though I knew that he meant no harm, that sly remark made me wonder if I really wanted to call him back, as I thought, *He doesn't even know me, and he's already getting on my nerves.* But after making him wait until I'd done everything I needed to do, I went into my room, shut the door, climbed into bed, and called Mr. Lee.

In the beginning of our conversation, I remember this man sounding a bit robotic, as if he was reading a resume. "My name is David Lee. I'm forty-eight years old. I'll be forty-nine in January. I have four children, two boys and two girls." As he continued with his resume, he mentioned that he was six two and about 215 pounds. He was a disabled army veteran, a former employee of FedEx, and presently an assistant head basketball coach at one of Birmingham's top high schools.

I noticed the longer we talked, the more relaxed he became, and he began to allow me free access into his world as he encouraged me to ask him whatever questions I desired. The first question I remember asking was about my girls, as I wanted to get that out in the open first. I asked him if my having six young daughters would be a problem for him. I just knew he would try to back out, but rather than backing out, he confidently told me that he had no problem with the amount of children I had. In fact, he began to tell me of his VA benefits that, in the event we were to marry, my kids could use them for their college tuition. What? Was this man really talking marriage to a woman he'd just met by phone? I had been so concerned about him backing out, but now *I* was the one considering backing out. However, I tried to ignore his marriage comment and just continued to ask him more questions.

I asked him if my height would be a problem for him because I was only five one and a half. Very quickly, he responded, "I like short women." This made me giggle like a little schoolgirl.

As we delved deeper into our conversation, I discovered that I had never met a man as sure and straightforward as David Lee was. In fact, during our conversation, which lasted about three hours, this man bared his soul. He was a man who loved God more than life. He had been single for over fourteen years and had raised his four children on his own for the majority of those years.

Because of the terrible hurt he suffered in his previous marriage, David had fears of reaching out to love again. And he said that when he did gain the courage to do so, he experienced rejection from women who didn't like the idea of being with a man who was raising so many children on his own. This increased his fear of ever finding true love. I think it's funny how that was the same fear I had, as I worried that no man would want me because of my number of children.

After sending his last child off to college in 2011, David became serious about finding love. He wanted someone with whom he could spend a lifetime loving, traveling, and growing old. Having someone to grow old with was important to me as well, because I felt robbed of that when I lost Erskine.

David expressed the great amount of love he had in his heart that he had been just waiting to bestow upon a future wife. He said he had enjoyed being married the first time, but due to unfortunate circumstances, the marriage crumbled. However, he truly wanted the opportunity to be a husband again. And he said that if God was to send him another wife, he promised to try his best to be a great husband to her and give her the world.

Though David's sentiments were very sweet, what truly turned me on about him was how he said he had finished raising his kids, especially his daughters, on his own. He explained how he prepared himself to teach his girls about their monthly cycles by going to the library and first educating himself on the subject. He said he also styled their hair for a while by reading up on how to apply chemical relaxers. And though he never perfected it, he did enough to get by until God sent people in his life to help him.

David expressed how he had worked two and three jobs trying to make ends meet for his family. As a result, he kept his kids involved in sports and other activities to keep them occupied and out of trouble. As you can imagine, all of this impressed me because I felt that if this man had raised his kids on his own, he would be the perfect candidate to help me raise mine. Actually, he sounded too good to be true. I couldn't believe I had encountered such an amazing man.

While giving David information about myself, I was extra careful not to tell him where I lived or what I owned. And surprisingly, he never asked. But that night, I learned that he and I had many things in common. One being that he hated debt as he'd spent the last fourteen years trying to dig himself out from under a mound of debt derived from his broken marriage. I also learned that he and I attended the same type of churches, nondenominational teaching ministries. And we both worked in our church's media ministry; he was a camera operator, and I was an editor. Also, his pastor of over twenty years, Dr. Michael Moore of Faith Chapel Christian Center, was one of my dad's good friends. And if you can remember, Dr. Moore is the pastor who was reading the scriptures on the healing CD that my friend LaTanya brought over for Erskine the night before he died.

David began sharing with me how much he loved and respected his pastor. He appreciated him for being an additional father figure who taught him how to be a godly man. This is another reason he was so excited about finding a wife, as he was ready to put all of the great teaching he'd gained over the years from Dr. Moore to good use. His story reminded me of my own because I had obtained my wifely skills growing up in Mt. Canaan. The wisdom I absorbed from my parents' teaching through the years is what enabled me to be a good wife to Erskine and a good mother to my children.

David mentioned being an unofficial minister as he ministered alongside his head coach, Kelly Cheatham, to the young boys that they coached in basketball. Coach Cheatham was also a member of Dr. Moore's church, and he, David, and the other coaches with whom they worked felt it was their duty to teach their students not only how to excel in basketball but how to excel in life.

After texting pictures of ourselves to one another that night, David raved repeatedly about my smile and how it had captivated him. And during our three-hour conversation, after receiving a taste of my spirit and godly personality, he felt very positive that he had found the right woman. But I wasn't so sure just yet. I mean, this was all happening too fast for me.

David shared with me how he had a desire to be married before he turned fifty. Now mind you, he had previously told me that he was about to turn forty-nine in January, which was only weeks away. His words startled me when I realized he only had about a year before he would be turning fifty. That was too fast if he was considering marrying me. I didn't know this man yet. We needed time to get to know one another. We were strangers. And besides, I had planned to wait six years, when my twins graduated high school, before getting too close to another man.

Regardless of how I felt, David boldly declared that I was his wife, even quoting Proverbs 18:22, "He who finds a wife finds a good thing, and obtains favor from the Lord." And when I asked him how he could be so sure so fast, he responded, "It doesn't take long for a man my age to know when he has found the right woman. I knew exactly what I was looking for, and I found it in you." Then I asked him, "What if I said I wanted to wait three years before marrying you?" He replied, "I'm willing to wait." Then I said, "What if I said five years?" and he answered, "It'll be hard, but I'll wait." I didn't have the heart to pile on any more years.

I must admit, the longer I talked to David that night, the more I was impressed because I realized this man had purpose, he had vision, and he had a relationship with God. That's the kind of man my spirit longed for. I also realized David was a husband in search of a wife, and I was a wife desiring a husband. As a result, God supernaturally allowed our paths to cross. And though he still sounded too good to be true, I kept in mind all of the supernatural ways God had moved for my family and me in the past, and I figured this was probably another one of those instances, so I was not about to act crazy and walk away from my blessing.

After recognizing how serious David was, I felt obligated to tell him about the other four people that were apart of my package, as Mama Doll and Erskine's three nieces were still an important part of my life. I explained to him that Mama Doll and I were like a modern-day version of Naomi and Ruth because after losing her husband and both of her children to death, I was her only remaining child. Therefore, she would always be one of my moms, my third mom to be exact, coming after my biological mom and my stepmom.

I told him how when my sister-in-law, Nikki, was on her deathbed, Erskine and I made her a promise to look after her three daughters. And I was not going to relinquish my end of the promise just because Erskine was gone. I needed David to understand that if he truly wanted me, then he had to be willing to accept more than just my six girls and me; he would have to accept these four other females from my previous marriage as well.

David said he had no problem with me still being attached to Mama Doll. In fact, he said he would consider her his mom too. That really touched my heart. Then he told me of family members that he was still close to from his first marriage, saying that he would need me to understand his situation as well. Of course, that was very understandable to me.

By the end of our conversation, David said it felt like he had known me for nine hundred years. And to be honest, I felt the same way about him. Something about him just felt so familiar to me, and I was surprised at how comfortable I felt talking to him. Actually, the longer we talked, the closer we grew. Supernaturally, our spirits connected. I'm sure our connection came about because we were both in much need of healing, and the time we spent talking on the phone seemed to deliver a healthy dose of that.

When we finally said goodbye, I lay on my bed in a complete daze. This was simply an amazing night. *God, is this You?* I wondered. I really needed to know if this man was definitely in God's will for my life because I didn't want to set myself up for another heartbreak. And since I wasn't quite sure, I decided I would take things very slow, telling myself that I was not going to jump into this relationship with two feet as I did with Ryan. I was just going to take my sweet time.

The next day, David said he pondered on his decision to get involved with me because of my six children. He actually had begun to get a little nervous. While talking to his youngest daughter, Jade, who was away in college, he confided in her. She set his mind at ease when she told him, "Daddy, maybe those girls need you. Maybe that's why God sent you into their life. You were a great dad to us. And you did a good job raising us. All of my friends said they wished you were their dad, so I know you will be a great dad to those girls." Her words remarkably sealed the deal for David.

Though I had decided to take my time in this relationship, it was not easy to do because David was not trying to take his time at all. He was moving very fast, as he was not about to lose the *good thing* God had allowed him to find. He texted me every morning, called me to chat during his lunch break, and held long conversations with me each night. As you can imagine, all of this attention from him made it difficult for me to take it slow because I was falling for him so fast. Our matchmaker, Ronda, called me every other day to see how things were going. She was thrilled to know how well we were getting along, and she was very proud to have had a hand in bringing us together.

My issue with driving outside of my comfort zone is actually worse at night, as I have a problem seeing in the dark. I will drive at night if I have to, but I try not to do it too often. I had to explain this to David when he asked me out on our first date.

Two days after our first phone conversation, he tried to arrange a meeting between us because he wanted so badly to see me in person. But since I was trying to take things slow, I'd always tell him I had something to do. Well after about four days of good phone conversations, David was adamant about a face-to-face meeting. However, since I wasn't ready for him to know where I lived or to meet my girls, I decided to step out of my comfort zone, which involved night driving, and meet him some place not too far away rather than have him pick me up.

We met at a quaint little area in Birmingham called Uptown. Uptown was a fairly new dining district that encompassed various kinds of restaurants. Since David and I both had never been there before, we didn't know which restaurant to choose, so we ended up choosing one called Southern Kitchen and Bar, which was one of the first restaurants we saw as we exited the parking lot.

Laying eyes on this stranger in real life was almost breathtaking, as I had never been involved with a man so tall besides my high school sweetheart Chris. And while looking up at him, my first thought was, *Wow, big ole you really wants little ole me?*

Walking from the parking lot to the restaurant, David did a simple gesture that to this day touches my heart and makes me struggle to hold back tears. Without thinking twice, he reached for my hand. This was my first sign from God that he was the one. I know this doesn't sound like much to get excited over, but for this widow and single mother who had reluctantly made peace with doing life all on her own, this *was* a big deal.

With his legs being much longer than mine were, he was a step ahead of me as we walked. So, as we prepared to cross the street, he instinctively reached back for my hand as if he were reaching for a child's hand. But it didn't bother me. In fact, it made me feel safe, as if he were a guardian angel sent to watch over me. And that simple gesture to hold my hand felt more than an effort to help me across the street, as through it, I could feel him saying, "Let me help you. Let me love you. Let me take care of you."

After scanning the menu, I decided on a salad topped with grilled shrimp. And David, who was struggling with the menu because he had left his reading glasses at home, decided he'd have what I was having.

I gained my first real impression of David while waiting for our food to arrive. I realized he was such a zany and fun-loving guy. He kept me laughing the whole time. I welcomed this because I not only loved to laugh, but at this time in my life, I needed to laugh. I also noticed something else about him; he had that same familiar spirit that I felt over the phone. I say that because we were still so amazingly comfortable with one another. You would have thought we'd known one another all of our lives.

After dinner, he asked me if I wanted to go to the movies because we were enjoying one another so much and were not ready for the night to end. I agreed, but I reminded him that I didn't drive very well at night and that I would need him to stick close to me as I followed him to the movie theater. I actually expected him to make fun of me, but he didn't. He just very sweetly agreed.

God's Girl

Inside the theater, we went our separate ways to use the restroom, and when I came out, David was standing nearby waiting on me. As I approached him, he stood with his arms open wide, saying, "So this is me. What do you think? Do you like me? Do you want to be with me?" I guess he was not in the mood to play games. He had already made his decision about me, and he wanted to know if I felt the same way about him. I was trying so hard to take my time in this relationship, but he was making it very difficult to do so.

I was fearful of giving David an answer because I felt a *yes* would be premature and a *no* would run him away. But as he continued to stand there, awaiting my answer, I decided not to make him wait any longer; I gave him the answer he wanted, by faith. And as I agreed to be exclusively his, I prayed that God would allow my feelings to catch up with his feelings very soon because I knew how it felt to be in a relationship with a person who didn't feel the same way about me as I felt about them.

After the movie, we sat in the parking lot and talked awhile before parting ways, and the more we talked, the more at peace I became in my decision to say *yes* to him. When we left the theater, he had me follow him so that he could show me the way to the interstate entrance that I would need to take to get home, as he would be going home in a different direction. While on the phone with him, he guided me until he saw me safely out of his sight. This was just as touching to me as his holding my hand, and it increased my feelings of him being my guardian angel.

The next morning, which was Sunday, I broke my silence as I sent some of my family members and a few friends a text message that read, "New Developments in My Life," and it included a head-to-toe photo of David. Everyone was ecstatic for me.

Three days later, on Christmas Eve, as I was out doing some last-minute shopping, David called. He was trying to arrange for us to meet again. I told him all of the things that were on my agenda, including having dinner at my mom's house that evening. I told him he could come and have dinner with us if he wanted, and he accepted the invitation. This would be the first time he and my family met. This would also be the first time he learned where I lived.

When David entered my neighborhood, judging by the caliber of homes he saw in my community, he said he wondered if I might be a snob. He nervously assumed I would turn out to be like many others who looked down on him because of what he didn't have, as his vehicle wasn't the best and he lived with his parents. He figured that because of those things I would consider myself better than him. But he had me all wrong. I understood that he had lost a lot in the collapse of his marriage and even during his fourteen-year struggle to raise his four children by himself while trying to come out of debt. So why would I look down on him? If anything, I applauded him.

But while David was busy thinking his thoughts about me, I had my own thoughts concerning him. I wondered if he would think twice about being in a relationship with me after laying eyes on all of my children, because hearing about them was one thing, but seeing them all together was totally different.

When the doorbell rang, the girls and I were in my bedroom, which, due to its size, often doubled as a family room. They were scattered about wrapping last-minute gifts for their friends. After answering the door, I invited David to join us in my bedroom, but he refused, saying he didn't go into people's bedrooms. I was finally able to convince him to come anyway.

As he followed me to the room, I continued to walk in, but he stopped at the doorway. And when I turned around, I saw him panning the room in silent slow motion, looking at all of my girls scattered about. Then slowly he started backing away. This actually frightened me because I seriously thought he was about to leave; however, the girls thought it was hilarious. I begged him to come back in, which he did while saying he was just kidding. His sense of humor caused him to click with my girls instantly.

David rode with the girls and me to Mama and Papa Dewey's house for Christmas Eve dinner. He seemed very comfortable around my family, which impressed me. And he was great with my girls and my nieces who were there with Mama Doll. Some of the girls enjoyed talking his head off, and he seemed to enjoy listening. I imagine working in a school around children every day is why he was so comfortable with them.

When dinner was ready, Mama asked David to say the blessing, and during his prayer, he said something that stunned us all. After only knowing me for eight days, and my family for about an hour, in his prayer, David confidently thanked God for his new family. It seems this man's faith was going full speed ahead.

After leaving my mom's house, I asked David if it was okay with him if we went by my dad's house. Since he had already met so much of my family, I thought it was only befitting that he meet the other side. However, when we arrived, he only had the opportunity to meet my dad and my friend Aleshia who is also Mama Trish's armor bearer. Mama Trish was already in bed.

After about forty-five minutes of conversation, I could tell Daddy liked David. And Aleshia not only liked him, but she was literally bubbling over with excitement for me because she remembered what I had gone through with Ryan. She was also in awe at how quickly God had moved on my behalf after my obedience to release Ryan completely.

I was in awe as well, because I remembered how we had lost Erskine around Christmastime in 2012, and now God had sent David to us at Christmastime two years later. I think He did that on purpose, to replace our bad Christmas memories with good ones.

David came into my world treating me like a queen and my daughters like princesses. I could tell that he was extremely grateful to have us in his life. It impressed me how he never tried to separate me from my children as I've seen men do to other single mothers, but he actually seemed happy about the idea of gaining this large family. He said after being on his own a few years since his last child went to college, he rather missed having children around.

He also told me how he really missed being married and having his family all together. He said he knows he made some mistakes in his first marriage and in the raising of his kids but he felt that now God was about to give him a second chance to get it right. And he continuously expressed to me how much he wanted to share a life with the girls and me.

I was excited to share with my coworkers at church about the new man

God had literally dropped from the sky into my life, and they all were so happy for me. And each week, like giddy schoolgirls, Sister Carolyn Robertson and Sister Brenda Williams eagerly questioned me about the latest developments in my evolving relationship with David. I actually looked forward to sharing with them those juicy details. But as to be expected, everyone in my life wasn't so happy for me.

I remember introducing David by way of Facebook. I posted a picture of us together and wrote an emotional paragraph where I called him King David and my soul mate. Though I received hundreds of likes for that post, behind the scenes there were just as many dislikes. I understood that many people felt I was moving too fast after losing Erskine, and I couldn't be mad at them for how they felt, as they were entitled to their feelings. But subsequently, I couldn't allow their feelings to control me. I felt as long as I had the blessings of God, my parents, and my children, I was good.

When David and I first met over the phone, he said he would be willing to wait until I was ready before pressuring me into marriage. But after spending time together and getting to know one another, he realized he couldn't wait three or five years; he wanted his wife as soon as possible. So one night in January 2015, he asked me to marry him, even though he didn't have a ring yet. He even got down on both knees saying, "Please." I could feel this man's sincerity, and I had a desire to be married just as much as he did, but I was so torn.

I was torn because once again I was worrying about other people's opinions, as I wondered what they would say about me marrying so soon. And after telling people that I was going to wait until my twins graduated high school in 2020 before I'd date again, I didn't know how I would face them with this surprising update. But then it hit me. I had literally begged God for this man. And now that He had sent him, I was about to allow other people's opinions to keep me from receiving my blessing. The devil is a lie!

I realized I wasn't a young girl anymore as I was actually pushing fifty myself. And if I were to really wait until 2020 before I started dating again, I would definitely be fifty and probably tired, set in my ways, and not wanting my life disturbed by a strange man.

I took the opportunity to talk to my daughters one night after dinner. I told them how David really wanted to marry me soon and that I wanted to marry him too but it was important to me to have their blessing. My twins, Karen and Kamille, said they had no problem with it. They were actually excited about it. And Janay and Joycelyn said they just wanted me to be happy, but they didn't want their dad's memory erased. I assured them that there was no possible way their dad would be forgotten, especially since I often saw pieces of him in each of his girls.

Jessica had the same sentiment as the twins. She said she was perfectly fine with me marrying David. Ever since she caught me one night lying in bed crying, she wanted nothing more than for God to make me happy again. However, Jasmine was the one who gave me a problem, as she was adamant about not having another man come into our lives trying to take her dad's place.

Though I didn't want to, I had to get a bit firm with my daughter that night. I told her that I was only asking for her blessing out of respect but that I couldn't allow her feelings to control me. I also had to force her to face the painful reality that her dad was never coming back. She left the table crying and went upstairs to her room. And using all of the emotions that were erupting inside of her, she wrote the most heartfelt letter to her dad, which she then e-mailed to me and gave me permission to insert into this book:

> Are you sure you're not coming back Daddy? You were more than a father to me. And more than a hero too. You were someone that could not be described, as your precious character could not be explained. You were in no way a god, but oh boy you were one of God's most spectacular creations.
>
> Daddy, as cliché as it sounds ... I miss you. And I need you like the air that I need to breathe. You made me feel safe, and you made me feel happy. The thought of having someone take your place in my life really tears me up on the inside. Call me stubborn, but it's seriously

a struggle to accept someone new when I was so used to having you around. Hearing the words, "Your dad is never coming back" is what breaks me the worst. I've come to the realization that my problem is, to this day, I haven't accepted the fact that you're never coming back. And whenever it is brought to my attention, my heart sinks, my stomach tightens, my knees get weak, my face gets warm as I feel the tears rush up and ready to fall. And my throat ... it begins to ache with the lump that forms there. It's mind-boggling because all of this is still a shock to me and it feels like a bad dream that I still haven't awaken from yet! It literally feels as though someone is breaking the bad news to me all over again, and I often wonder, *When will this be over? Will I ever be able to think of you and not fall apart?* This isn't how things were supposed to be. You and Mama were supposed to be together forever, you know. You were supposed to see me graduate high school, right? You were supposed to be here to watch me go off to college, you were supposed to intimidate my boyfriends and remind them to open the car door for me. Daddy, you were supposed to someday look at me and say, "You look so beautiful," just before you walk me down the aisle on my wedding day.

Things just don't seem right anymore without you. Everything's out of whack, and I mean everything. I wasn't finished loving you yet. I just wasn't. I was just beginning to appreciate you more and more. You were only here for a moment, and then you were gone, just like that. I will always remember what you used to tell me, "We have bad days in our life so that we are able to appreciate the good ones." And although that is true in many cases, Daddy, I'm still looking for the next good day for me to appreciate because after losing you, it feels like I've been stuck in this really bad day for a long time. I constantly search my sky for the sun, but it seems like it's ever so cloudy. But because of what you told me, I know that one day soon, a better day is coming, and this won't hurt as much anymore.

I want to thank you for having been the marvelous father and example that you were to my sisters and me. And the outstanding husband that you were to my mother. It's so hard to wrap this up because it feels like I'm having to let you go all over again. I never want to say goodbye, but I'll end with saying that I surely was beyond blessed to call you Daddy. I know that God is so happy to have you home with Him because I was always so happy to have you at home here with me.

Writing that letter was how God allowed Jasmine to release her secret hopes of her dad ever returning. This was something she needed to release in order to make room in her heart for David. And also, Jasmine and her sisters needed to understand that David was not trying to take their dad's place. He knew he could never do that. He just recognized that they were missing a father figure, and he wanted to be one for them.

As I thought about it, there were things that I needed to release as well in order to make room in my heart for David. First of all, I needed to release my expectations because I didn't want to make David feel as if he had to compete with Erskine. Erskine was the husband God had appointed for the first part of my life. Now that the first part was over, God was appointing David as the husband of the second part.

Erskine and David were two very different men. They didn't look the same, nor would they act the same. Therefore, I couldn't treat David the same as I did Erskine, nor should I expect the same performance from him that I was familiar with receiving from Erskine. I had to let go of any preconceived ideas of how my second husband should or shouldn't perform based on my first one. In essence, I had to let David be David.

I also had to let go of that nagging question I'd been asking God ever since Erskine passed, "Why? Why did You let him die?" I had to understand that God might never reveal to me why He allowed Erskine to leave us. But just because his life ended didn't mean mine had to end.

I couldn't sit around stuck in my feelings waiting on God to answer my question before I moved on with life. I had to move on by faith and trust that in due time God would reveal an answer or give me the peace to stop worrying about it. I had to accept that the purpose of the first part of my life had been fulfilled. I was predestined before birth to be Erskine's wife, his caregiver, his business and ministry partner, and the mother of his seven children. For the twenty-one years that we were married, I was assigned to take care of him and our children, as they were my ministry. But now that he was gone, my assignment was complete and it was time to move on to the next phase of my life.

There was another thing I needed to let go of in order to accept the love David was offering me, and that was the hurt that Ryan had caused me. Sometimes it was hard to let my guard down with David because of the pain I had experienced from Ryan. I kept expecting David to change on me and at some point disappoint me as Ryan had. But just as I had to remember that Erskine and David were two different men, so it was for David and Ryan. It was unfair for me to judge David based on Ryan's past actions. And besides, all I needed to do was trust God. If He sent this man to me, then He would make sure he always loved, honored, and respected me.

After releasing her dad through that letter, Jasmine said she felt free, and she soon made an about-face saying she was happy to have David join our family. She even said that she was especially happy to know that her future kids would have someone to call "Granddaddy". Pretty soon, she and her sisters fell in love with David, and they dubbed him "Coach Lee." They soon understood that he only wanted to give them the love, care and affection that their dad could no longer give them.

It wasn't long before we all could see that David had been sent by God to look after us. My parents even recognized this. And Mama Doll felt the same way. She even went as far to say she believed Erskine had asked God to send David to us.

Then one day, without any knowledge of our thoughts or feelings concerning the matter, David shared with me a conversation he had with

God. As we were riding along, he said, "You know what I asked God?" And I said, "What?" and he responded, "I asked Him to let your late husband know that I was going to be taking care of ya'll for him." I was shocked. I mean I was literally dumbfounded at those words because they proved to me that the supernatural hand of God was still working in my life.

God began to reveal to me more and more that He had definitely sent David to the girls and me. For instance, do you recall when I said that as my dad and I were leaving the hospital after the death of my cousin in early December 2014, I was sharing with him the type of man I wanted from God? I told Daddy I wanted a man who wanted and needed me just as much as I wanted and needed him. I wanted a man who would recognize my worth and who would be proud to have me as his wife. And I wanted a man who wouldn't mind how many children I had but would love, cherish, and protect them all as his own. Well David Lee was God's answer to that prayer. And there's more.

Do you remember when I said God spoke to me one day while in Walmart near my home, as I was grocery shopping and looking around for a man? Remember He told me that I could stop looking because the man He had for me wasn't even on that side of town? Well, turns out that was David as well, because he lived on the east side of town. I lived on the west side.

Also, do you remember the dream my cousin Linda Stallworth had of me right after Erskine died, where she saw me getting married to a wealthy man that adored my girls and me? Again, that was David. And God even revealed to me that the wealth she saw was more than financial wealth as I had first suspected; it was spiritual wealth, as David had gained a wealth of spiritual wisdom and knowledge from abiding under the teachings of his anointed pastor, Dr. Michael Moore, for over twenty years.

Recently, my oldest three girls were discussing a similar dream they each had when they were very young. The dream actually became a reoccurring dream for Jasmine. I remember her coming to me a couple of times when she was a little girl telling me she had dreamed that I was married to someone other than her dad. It made her worry that her dad and I might be getting a divorce. Each time I would assure her that Erskine and I loved each other very much and that we would never divorce.

Jessica and Janay said they both had the same type of dream. And though each dream entailed a different scene, the overall meaning was the same; the man they saw me with was not their dad. After comparing notes, each of the girls remembered certain features of the man they saw in their dreams. Jessica and Jasmine remember a man with a light skin complexion, and Janay says she remembers the man in her dream being tall. Surprisingly, these were features of David.

Lastly, do you remember the vision God gave me not long after Erskine's death of the tall, bald man that walked past me as I stood in my kitchen doorway? Remember how I assumed it was Ryan because I thought the meaning of the dream was the opposite. Well, I've told you that David was tall, but what I haven't revealed to those of you who don't already know, he's bald.

As I think about the girls' dreams along with my cousin's dream and the vision God gave me, I can understand why David and I felt so familiar with one another from the beginning. Our spirits had already connected in that vision and those dreams.

With the assurance that David was indeed the man God had promised me, I had no reason to be caught up in what others were saying or thinking. I only needed to focus on what God had said, and He said that He was about to make all things new and restore the lost years for me and my family (Revelation 21:5; Joel 2:25). So with great confidence, I happily said yes to David.

One night, David came over to my house with a video that he was eager for me to watch. It was a Father's Day tribute to him that his church's media ministry had composed and aired in-house a few years prior. In the video, David was spotlighted for his touching story of being a single father of four, with three kids in college and one in high school at the time. They highlighted his struggle of having to be both father and mother to his children and the challenges he faced in raising his girls alone.

David and his youngest three kids were interviewed in the video, but

Caleb, his oldest, was not featured as he was away in college. His daughter Diamond talked about the pros and cons of being raised with only a father. And his daughter Jade, the baby of the family, talked about her dad's struggle in learning to comb her and her sister's hair and buy their clothes. Joshua, the third child, mentioned how his dad had taught him how to be a man and how to respect his sisters and other females. And David spoke highly of Dr. Michael Moore, whom he referred to as Pastor Mike, saying he not only taught him how to be a godly man, but he gave him the wisdom and encouragement to make it through the struggles he faced being a single dad.

Watching that video opened my eyes even more to the caliber of man God had sent into my life, as He didn't send me a random John Doe, but He chose for me one of His best. A man after His own heart. A man who loved God as much as I did. And a man who had a testimony just as amazing as mine.

On New Year's Eve 2014, David invited me to service at his church, and together we ushered in 2015. It felt amazing to spend this holiday with a true significant other by my side versus having spent it depressingly alone in 2012 and with a man whom I was shamefully chasing in 2013.

I always enjoyed spending time with David as I found myself doing things and going places that I'd never even considered. He introduced me to a whole new world of entertainment, mainly sports, which was very exciting. With him, I attended more sporting events than I had attended in my life. But I didn't mind, as I had already been itching to do something different. During the time that I was in the mind-set of going against God and doing things my own way, I considered doing some nightclubbing because that was all I could think of and it was something that I had never experienced before. But God hindered that ridiculous plan and sent David along with better plans.

Since we were thinking about marrying in the coming months, David and I thought it befitting that our families come together as soon as possible. So, utilizing his January 25 birthday, we planned a birthday party / meet-and-greet whereby my parents, his parents and our children, could fellowship. The gathering was a success, as our families clicked in the exact same manner David and I had. We talked, laughed, and comfortably enjoyed one another regardless of being strangers.

And my girls thoroughly enjoyed meeting David's children because they were very sweet and down to earth just like David. And not only that, but several of them were highly amusing like their dad. It blessed me how the four of them happily welcomed my and David's impending marriage just as most of my girls had. And because Diamond was less than two months away from giving birth to a baby boy, my girls looked forward to gaining a nephew, who would turn them into instant aunts. That was a beautiful night, and we sealed it with our first family portrait, a cell phone snapshot of David, our 10 children, and me.

In February, David and I began six weeks of marriage counseling at his church with Minister Alondio Hill, and we set a wedding date for May 30, 2015.

During this time, in an effort to win even more the hearts of my girls, David surprised them with two new additions to our family, twin, black-and-white pit-bull puppies, which they happily named Cocoa and Oreo.

On March 3, David's first grandchild, Khari, entered our world. And God used that little baby to pull our two families together even closer. But a grandson wasn't the only blessing David received that month. Since our final counseling session was coming up the week before my March 19 birthday, I told David I was willing to marry him sooner than May 30. So, on my forty-sixth birthday, David and I went to the courthouse and eloped.

We knew that the longer we waited to marry, the further in sin we'd fall because the temptation to sleep together had presented itself a few times. Sometimes we passed the test, and sometimes we failed. But we didn't want to continue failing. So for that reason alone, we knew it was better to marry than to burn (1 Corinthians 7:9).

We kept our eloping plan a secret, not from our parents and children, only the rest of our family and friends. And as we had no rings yet, my mom, in her excitement, ran out and bought inexpensive rings for us. Jasmine went with us to the courthouse that morning to be our photographer, and afterward, the girls and my mom and pop went out to eat with us to celebrate my birthday and our marriage. That was an amazing day!

The week after we married, David and I were blessed with the awesome opportunity to see President Barack Obama speak live at Lawson State Community College. Mama and Papa Dewey were given tickets to this event by their friends Dr. and Mrs. Perry Ward. Dr. Ward was the school's president. But because my parents were not able to attend the event, they invited David and me to go in their stead.

Standing in an exceptionally long line that encompassed the school's campus, David and I were numbers 728 and 729 in line to see the president. We waited so long that we chatted with old friends and even made new friends. Had I known I would be standing in line for that long, I would have made a better choice in shoes because my feet were aching something awful. Eventually, one of my new friends and I disregarded our dainty little dresses and sat on the curb to rest our feet.

Almost an hour later, we finally reached the building where the event was taking place, but just before we could approach the doors, a female White House employee came walking through the crowd, randomly putting stickers on people's tickets. After putting stickers on our tickets, she instructed us to go into a different door from the rest of the crowd. When everyone with a sticker had gathered in a certain area, White House officials announced to us that we had been chosen to sit behind the president during his speech. Wow! We were going to be on television with President Obama! Our extra-long wait and aching feet had paid off!

David and I soon realized we had awesome seats, which were directly over the shoulder of the president, when our friends and family began blowing up our phones with text messages and social media notifications saying they could see us as the president delivered his speech live on television. That was such an incredible way for us to begin our new life together, with our faces being embedded in Lawson State's history as having hosted America's first African-American President.

―――∽∿∾⨀⦿⨀∾∿∽―――

Through our union, God blessed David with several of his heart's desires all at one time, the first being his desire to marry before he turned fifty, as he was forty-nine when we tied the knot. Then, after losing so many possessions with the crumbling of his first marriage, David constantly asked God for restoration, which is what God gave him when He gave him me.

Like me, David took tithing very seriously, and as a result, he took each opportunity to tithe as an opportunity also to make his request known to God. He said he learned from Pastor Mike to name his seed whenever he tithed. So every Sunday he wrote on the backside of his tithe envelopes exactly what he was expecting to reap as a result of his giving. He wrote such things as: Debt Free! New Home! New Wife! Debt-Free Wedding! Blessed & Obedient Children! New SUV! New Truck! No Lack! More Than Enough! Blessed to Be a Blessing! Then on March 19, 2015, God not only gave him the wife he asked for, but He gave him several of those prayer requests in one big heap! This also relates to his spiritual wealth that I referred to earlier because though David was not rich in the natural, he had the ability to pray his needs and desires into existence.

David laughs often about his prayer request for *blessed and obedient children*. He said he was actually referring to his own four children when he wrote that request, but seeing as God has a sense of humor, He gave him six more blessed and obedient children!

―――∽∿∾⨀⦿⨀∾∿∽―――

We continued to plan a big wedding for May 30, which we only had two months to pull together. Our grand affair would encompass all ten of our kids, our new grandbaby, both of our sisters, several of David's closest friends, fifty of my friends and family members as hostesses, and several other participants.

While shopping for my ring, David took me to three different jewelry stores and asked me to show him the rings that I liked. Then, on another day, he went shopping without me and he purchased a ring from among the ones I had chosen. Because the store didn't have my size available, they said they would have to order it, and the delivery date would be very close to our wedding date, with the potential to come even later. We prayed hard that God would speed up the delivery process.

During our wedding planning, David teasingly asked me if he could wear sneakers to the wedding with his tuxedo. I shocked him with my answer, as I gladly said yes and told him that I thought it would be a wonderful idea if the entire wedding party wore sneakers. So, with our wedding colors of lime and tangerine, we decided on orange Converse for the girls in the tangerine dresses, green Converse for the girls in the lime dresses, and white Converse for me. Then we chose black Vans for the groomsmen and black-and-white Vans for David.

My mom was a lifesaver during the wedding planning because after ordering our ten bridesmaid dresses online, most of them came back too small, and a couple of them were too large. And because there was no time to send them back and wait for new ones, Mama, who owns her own sewing business, altered them all, including my wedding dress.

As our date drew closer, our days were filled with such things as securing a caterer, a decorator, a florist, a reception hall, and so much more. We didn't have to worry about a church, as we would be getting married at my dad's church. And we didn't have to worry about a preacher because my dad was not only going to walk me down the aisle, but he was going to do exactly as he had done in my first wedding, which was turn around and marry us. And my brother William had agreed to come over from Atlanta and assist Daddy in performing the ceremony.

A few weeks before the wedding, David's older brother, Flozell, who lived in California and had not seen his family in about fifteen years, decided he was coming home. The amazing thing about this is that Flozell had no idea David was about to get married when he made this decision. Overwhelmed with how God had orchestrated his brother's long-awaited return to coincide with his long-awaited wedding, David gave his brother a position in the wedding as one of our ushers.

God answered our prayers concerning my ring, as it arrived about a week before the wedding. It was incredibly stunning and well worth the wait. But oddly, I couldn't remember choosing that ring. I didn't even remember seeing it in the store. But David insists that I chose it. I think God chose it for me.

The ring displayed a 1.70-carat pear-shaped diamond, set in 14k white gold. However, to me, the pear-shaped diamond looked like the shape of a teardrop. One day, while admiring it on my hand, God revealed to me that it was symbolic of all the tears I had shed during my grief and loneliness, which He bottled up (Psalm 56:8) and turned into a diamond for me. That beautiful sentiment made me shed more tears.

On our wedding eve, after the rehearsal dinner, David went to his parents' house to spend the night, as he wanted to stay within the tradition of the groom not seeing the bride until the moment she walked down the aisle. Though it was just for one night, we missed each other something awful. He called me before going to bed, just as he used to do during our short-lived dating era. It brought back such wonderful memories.

Tracy O'Neal Daniel & David Janssen Lee
Request the honor of your presence
At the celebration of their union
May 30, 2015
Three o'clock in the afternoon
Mount Canaan Full Gospel Church

Though David and I had already been married for a little over two months, this day somehow felt magical, as if we were about to do it for the first time.

After the hoopla of my bridesmaids and flower girls getting dressed in one area of the church, me getting dressed in another, the men gathering

God's Girl

in yet another, and Jeff King, our photographer, and his assistant, running back and forth from place to place, trying to get pictures of us all, it was finally time for the celebration to begin.

The largest concern I had was for our wedding to start on time, as I didn't want to repeat history, because, if you can recall, I mentioned in an earlier chapter that my first wedding was over an hour late. But thank God, history didn't repeat itself. Our wedding, which was due to start at 3:00 p.m., started at about 3:05 p.m.

As Janice Cobb, my wedding directress, guided the ceremony along, her assistants, LaKeisha Pruitt and Jamillah Williams, were busy moving me in place for my impending entrance. They guided me up the stairs from the dressing room and into my dad's office. While waiting there, I took a look at myself in his mirror to admire the beautiful job my daughter Jasmine had done on my makeup. Suddenly, my mind fell on the awesomeness of God.

I was in awe because I had planned 2015 to be the year that I released my book, as I assumed that the blessing God had for me on the other side of finishing it would be the husband that I greatly desired. But God decided to bless me sooner than I expected, allowing 2015 to be the year I remarried. This left me wondering, *What more does God have waiting for me on the other side of my obedience?* Though I was sure whatever it was would be amazing, I felt in my heart that if He never did another thing for me, He had already done enough.

As the church doors were opened, I stood there in my lovely ivory wedding gown and headpiece while locking arms with my dad before slowly marching down the aisle to the beat of Kenny Latimore's soulful ballad "For You," which David specially requested. As I marched, I noticed that I felt much different than I did during my first wedding, as I was more confident, very relaxed, and genuinely happy.

My happiness was based on a lesson I learned while dealing with the loss of my first marriage, which was *life is too short to spend it waiting for happiness to begin.*

Though my first marriage was a good one, my husband and I made the mistake of spending our time trying to reach that unrealistic happily-ever-after place in life. We assumed that life was about having the spouse, the good job, the money, the house, the vehicles, debt freedom, and good health. And we worked hard to obtain these things, figuring that once we obtained them, we could then say we had made it in life, to that ultimate happy place. Sadly, we never truly focused on learning how to be happy regardless. Please don't get me wrong. We were very happy with each other, but I can't say that we were happy with life.

After my husband's death, when I experienced an excessive amount of money, debt-free cars, and a debt-free home, I learned that none of these things brought about true happiness. I also realized that there would never be a point in life when I would have everything I desired. For example, it would have been nice if my husband was alive and able to enjoy the money and the new house with the girls and me, but life just doesn't work that way.

With this revelation, I decided I would stop waiting for things in my life to line up perfectly in order to deem myself happy. I only needed to adopt the mind-set of being happy in whatever situation I found myself (Philippians 4:11).

Author Mandy Hale sums up my thoughts best in this great quote of hers that I came across on social media, "Happiness is letting go of what you think your life is supposed to look like and celebrating it for everything that it is." Because we didn't have this mind-set, Erskine and I spent twenty-one years chasing a happy place that never existed, and before we knew it, he was gone, and our marriage was over. However, true happiness came for me when I let go of that fairy-tale mentality and made up my mind to be happy with life—as is.

While marching down that aisle, I was happy just to be happy. In fact, I was so happy that I tried to greet every smiling face in the audience with an acknowledging raise of my brows and a great big smile of my own. David was happy too. I could see him in the distance as he stood on stage with our ten children and the other members of our wedding party. He was so overcome with emotion that he found himself wiping away grateful tears.

As I stated in the beginning of chapter 1, I never thought I'd be in such a place in life, married for the second time. However, I did have a desire for a second wedding a few years back, but that was only to commemorate my and Erskine's twentieth wedding anniversary. I had it all planned out mentally with my daughters as my bridesmaids. But insufficient finances halted that idea, making this present wedding truly ironic for me.

Though I desired my first marriage to be my only marriage, I thank God He didn't allow it to end in the most common way—divorce. In hindsight, I realized He had amazingly graced me with one of my deepest desires, which was to break the generational curse of divorce that ran so prevalent in my family. Having done this, I didn't waste time worrying whether my next marriage would survive the curse of divorce or whether it would be just as good as the first marriage because God had taken away all those worries when He promised in His Word that my latter would be greater (Job 8:7).

Rather than repeat the traditional wedding vows, David and I decided to express our own personal vows to one another. But he didn't write his vows on paper because he said they were written in his heart. They were ...

"First and foremost, my number-one vow: I always vow to love God more than I ever love you because as long as I love Him first, I will always love you. And I vow to be the best dad I can be to all of these children. I'm not just marrying you; I'm marrying them all. I vow to be a man of God before them and always be high priest in the house to lead, guide, and encourage. Most of all, I vow to just treat you like the queen you are because you mean everything to me. You know, everybody talks about diamonds, but I've got you. You're the greatest diamond I've found."

My vows were also written in my heart, but I still needed the assistance of paper, which my brother William held for me in his pocket until the opportune time. This is what I said to David ...

"David, I feel so blessed to be the girl who gets to marry you because you are truly a one in a million kind of guy. I am honored to be the one who gets to laugh with you and cry with you. To care for you and share with you. To run with you and walk with you. Be angry with you and make up with you. To build with you and live with you. To dream with you and grow old with you. To hold you and, most importantly, to love you.

"When I first presented you to the world by way of Facebook, I introduced you as King David. It was, and still is, so easy for me to call you a king because you have always made me feel like a queen. You even make my girls feel like princesses. You've taken such great care of us already, as if we have been yours from the beginning.

"David, we are more than happy to become a family with you and your kids. Having you all in our lives makes us feel happy and whole. I must say I am truly enjoying the beginning of this lifetime adventure with you. And I'm sure it will only get better from here because God has promised us in His Word that our latter shall be greater, and I believe Him.

"David, today I not only promise to be your wife, but I promise to be your helpmeet, your lover, your partner, your best friend, your confidant, your consoler, your cheerleader, your sidekick, your ride-or-die chick, your good thing, and your favor.

"I promise to lie by your side as you watch your sports channels. I promise, that in good times and bad times, I will cheer for your school's basketball team. I promise to console you when the Dallas Cowboys lose and celebrate with you when they win. And I promise to always, always Roll with the Alabama Tide ... forever and ever. Amen!"

When all was said and done, my dad had us face the audience, and he presented us to the congregation as husband and wife. Then he told David to salute his bride. David seemed to be very bashful, holding his head down and laughing as if he were afraid to kiss me in public. However, the audience soon discovered it was all a joke when he grabbed me around my waist, pulled me in close, and planted the longest and most passionate kiss on my lips. Daddy yelled in jest, "That's enough! That's enough!"

The music I chose for our dramatic exit was Dorinda Clark Cole's prophetic song "Take It Back," as that song served as a testimony for both David and me:

God's Girl

Everything that the devil stole, God's giving it back to me.
Everything that the devil stole, God's giving it back to me.
Can't have my joy, Can't have my peace,
Can't have my faith, I want everything.
Everything that the devil stole, God's giving it back to me.

Having lost my only son, my first husband, my joy, my peace, and, at one point, even my faith, God gave it all back to me plus interest! When I couldn't figure out how He was going to fix my situation and I botched it up trying to fix it on my own, He came through for me with flying colors. When I tried to hold on to a pauper because I feared there would be no one else to love and accept me and my children, God gladly proved me wrong when He gave me a king.

God not only replaced the husband I lost, but He replaced the son I lost by giving me two handsome sons for the price of one. Then He gave me two beautiful daughters to add to the beautiful six He had already given me. And, as if that wasn't enough, He gave me an awesome grandson that I am enjoying sharing with David. He also gave me an unspeakable joy and an increase of faith in Him. And all of these wonderful blessings and more were waiting for me on the other side of my pain.

As Dorinda's song begin to play, I stood there thinking about how good God had been to me and before I knew it I was giving David my bouquet of flowers, then I lifted my dress and began to praise God in a dance. I just *had* to praise Him because He had brought me through one of the worst trials of my life and now I was experiencing a most incredible supernatural triumph! And after going through a terrible divorce, losing all of his possessions, digging his way out of debt, raising his children on his own, and waiting fourteen years to find his *good thing* and *favor*, David decided he wanted to cut a step too!

After a wonderful reception, the next morning David and I flew to Orlando, Florida where we enjoyed a free trip to Disney World, compliments of my uncle and aunt, Gene and Patricia Dorleus. And we spent our evenings relaxing in a luxurious condominium compliments of Daddy and Mama Trish.

After months of watching David interact with my family, I realized God had given me more than just a king in him, but this man was actually my modern-day Boaz. In the Bible, when Ruth lost her husband, Boaz not only married her and gave her a child, but he assumed the responsibility of caring for her mother-in-law, Naomi, as well. Well, in my case, David not only married me and promised to help me raise my daughters, but he has submitted himself as a son to *my Naomi*. He's also an uncle to my nieces, helping me to be there for them as well. He had no idea God would give him such responsibilities when he asked for a wife; nevertheless, he didn't run away when he discovered the obligations that came along with his answered prayer. He willingly accepted his duties, and as a result, God has blessed him with way more than he ever lost.

I've heard it said that a man who owns up to his responsibilities is a good man, and a man who owns up to the responsibilities left behind by another man is an exceptional man. Erskine Daniel Jr. was a very good man. And David Lee is no doubt an exceptional man. One day, Sister Carolyn Robertson asked me, "Tracy, do you realize God has given you two *good* men in your lifetime?" I told her, "Yes ma'am, I sure do." Not only was I was aware of that, but the thought of it was quite humbling because it forever reminds me of how I almost messed up my life trying to do things my way, but God blessed me regardless. In the words of my brother William, "If I had known God was going to work it all out for me the way He did, I wouldn't have acted the way I did."

I was also in awe at how God gave me a man spiritually wise enough to ask Him for anything and believe that he would receive it, thus the spiritual wealth I told you he possessed. His faith to name his seed concerning a debt-free wedding was also answered by God, as He allowed us to pay off every one of our wedding expenses within six months. I've had the opportunity to watch God perform many other miracles for David all because of his faith. Having a husband with such a relationship with God led me to express my thoughts about him one day on social media.

Every morning, he joins hands with me, and he prays for our entire family. He faithfully calls out the names of our ten children from the oldest to the youngest and prays a hedge of protection around each of them. He also lifts up our parents, our pastors, other family members, friends, and even our dogs. He has brought such a sense of security to my girls and me. It feels as if he is a guardian angel assigned by God to watch over us. The way he loves our children and me just blows me away.

To him I am a treasure, and I feel it in the way he always wants to hold my hand (even while lying in bed), the way he looks at me, the way he is so patient with me, the way he seeks to please me, the way he loves my girls, and the way he serves our God.

After being married for twenty-one years, then losing the love of my life to cancer, I constantly prayed for God to give me the opportunity to love again, as I secretly feared no man would want me ... a woman with six young daughters. Now today, I am truly humbled by the awesome way God blessed me with this man of God. He did it when I least expected it. When I stopped searching for him myself. When I set my mind on being His girl, taking care of His business, and being a good mom to the children He had given me. That's when it happened. Suddenly! Thank you, Lord, for the treasure I've found in David Janssen Lee!

Late one night, about five months after our wedding, I received a text message from David's sister, Sandra Calloway Fields, saying, "Thanks for making my brother happy, I really appreciate it. He was sad for so long, and now that he has you and the girls, I see a spark in his eyes that I have not seen since we were young. This may be corny to you, but I love David with all my heart, and I have prayed for this day. Now I am very happy, very happy. I just wanted to share that with you, sis."

Sandra's message blessed my soul, because it was more confirmation that my and David's relationship was destined by God. Not only was David an answer to my and my family's prayers, but I was an answer to his and his family's prayers. He and his children needed us just as much as my girls and I needed them.

My daughter Jessica's faith in God was even renewed when God sent David and his family into our lives. In fact, she wrote an essay about it for one of her college classes, and she has given me permission to share it with you:

The Time I Thought God Wasn't Real
by
Jessica Daniel

Growing up, I thought that life would be like a fairy tale or at least go great for me. I had both my parents who loved my sisters and me, and many aunts and uncles who loved us as well. I even had a close relationship with God. But life turned from great to a disaster, and I never thought anything like this would ever happen to my family and me.

In February 2012, my dad was diagnosed with lung cancer. Mesothelioma. He had already fought cancer and won back in 2000, and now, this had to happen. And he had just recently lost his sister, his only sibling, in 2011.

Throughout the whole year of 2012, my family and I were believing God for a miracle that my father would beat cancer once again. Every day my mom, my sisters, and I would pray and say scriptures over him and declare healing.

December 21, 2012, my father lost his fight against cancer. He was on hospice in our den when he died. For me, that whole day was full of nothing but inward and outward cries. I cried until I couldn't cry anymore. The thought of not having a father had destroyed my dream that every girl dreams. I started to think about things like:

God's Girl

Who's going to teach me how a guy is supposed to treat me? He won't get to see me off to prom. He won't get to see me graduate. Who's going to walk me down the aisle on my wedding day? Who's going to tell my children old family stories? And who's going to pick me up and wipe my tears away when a guy breaks my heart? Who, God? Who? This is the time when I began to think that God wasn't real because I felt that He had let me down on everything in my life.

More of my family members on my father's side began to die, and as a result, my family and I spent less time with our extended family on that side because it hurt too much.

I couldn't stand seeing or even hearing my mom cry because it broke my heart every time. All I could think about was: If God is real, why did He have to take away almost everyone that we loved and cared about? It didn't make any sense to me. So I stopped praying, and I stopped listening to gospel music.

Two years after my father died, my mom met a new man named David. My mom had been believing and praying to God that she would meet a man who was willing to step in and take over where my father left off. Funny thing about this situation is that Mr. David had been believing and praying to God for a wife.

After spending more and more time around my mom and our family, Mr. David and my mom were engaged in 2015. Mr. David had his four children to come over to meet my five sisters and me, and they treated us as if we had been brothers and sisters forever. After all of these amazing things happened (and are still happening), I've come to realize that God is so real.

For several months after the wedding, David and I tried being faithful to both of our churches. Twice a month we attended his church, and twice a month we attended mine. But after a while, we were no longer comfortable with this arrangement, and we didn't think God was either. So, in a meeting with my dad, I shared with him my desire to follow my husband, and he sadly released me. When Daddy released me, I felt so free, like a weight had been lifted from my shoulders. But at the same time, I felt a little awkward, as if I were doing something wrong.

Back when I married Erskine and followed him to Nebraska, things were different because I had actually left the state; therefore, I had no other choice but to join another church. But now, living in the same state yet attending a church that wasn't my dad's church felt so strange. However, I welcomed the change because I was excited about a new beginning. And actually, the change was much needed because my girls and I had not felt very comfortable at Mt. Canaan since Erskine died. So I figured, just as God had allowed us to change houses, He was allowing us to change churches.

We attended Faith Chapel Christian Center for at least three months before I officially joined in October 2015. But my membership was short-lived because God soon began moving on David's heart, giving him a desire to be a part of my dad's ministry. So after talking to Pastor Mike and receiving his blessing, David brought us back home to Mt. Canaan in April 2016 when he joined and I rejoined the church. And though the girls were attending Faith Chapel with us, they had not had a chance to change their membership, so they were still official members of Mt. Canaan.

Daddy was terribly distraught when the girls and I left Mt. Canaan, but he tried his best not to kick against our decision because he knew it was God's will that I follow my husband. However, through her gift of prophecy, Mama Trish kept him encouraged by telling him that she was sure we would be back soon. Not only was her prophecy correct, but I imagine our return was also God's answer to the prayer Daddy prayed weeks before I met David. The prayer that he promised me he would pray for God to send me a husband who was willing to join Mt. Canaan, because he didn't want me to leave him.

David not only brought us back to Mt. Canaan, but I credit him for bringing us back to God. Though I had given my heart back to Him before meeting David, I was not as committed to Him as I had been before Erskine died. But God used David, who was highly committed and now the head of our family, to encourage the girls and me to continue walking in the direction of holiness.

As I draw near to the close of this book, it is May 2017, and David and I have been married for two years. I will not lie to you and say that we have enjoyed total bliss and no problems because that is far from the truth. However, I will say that we have had more bliss than problems because of the utmost appreciation we have for one another. My pain of losing my first husband to death and David's sad memories of his unhappy fourteen-year single state have given us a bond that is not easily broken because we both have a desire never to lose the other.

Also, as in all families, blended or whole, there are issues concerning our children that are not always perfect, but through God, we deal with them as they come. Nevertheless, I am beyond blessed by the relationship God has allowed me to have with David's grown children as they reciprocate my love for them with a love and respect for me that I have no doubt is from God. I am also quite blessed by the relationship between David and my girls because it is evident that he loves them just as much as they love him. It does my heart good to realize I do not have to raise my girls alone, especially when I see how much of an interest David shows in all of their endeavors, from academics to extracurricular activities. And he is always present when possible, expressing his pride in them, as if he were their biological dad. Even when it comes to boys desiring to date the girls, David steps in like a guard dog, ready to protect their integrity and their hearts. And when there are disagreements between him and the girls, the girls never stay upset with David for long, as they respect him as their dad and authority figure because they remember how it feels to be without such.

Recently, while celebrating our two-year anniversary in Orlando, Florida, God gave me a mind-blowing revelation. During the entire week that we were there, David did nothing but spoil me. There was nothing I wanted or wanted to do that he didn't make sure happened for me. We spent time visiting several theme parks, shopping, eating whatever we desired, and relaxing. And to be honest, not having to cook or even think about what we were going to eat each day felt like heaven to me. Our time there in Orlando felt like a dream that I didn't want to be awakened from, as being a mom with so many children, I was accustomed to catering to the needs and desires of everyone else while forgetting my own. But for the first time in my adult life, here was someone looking out for my needs and desires, and it felt awesome!

Toward the end of our trip, while dreading the thought of returning home to the real world, God reminded me of Erskine's dying wish. Often during his last days, Erskine expressed how he wanted God to allow him to live just so he could spend the rest of his life making me happy. He said God had given him a new love and appreciation for me as a result of my caring for him during his illness and therefore he desired to prove it to me. However, though He still allowed him to die, God didn't forget Erskine's prayer, as He allowed David to walk in and pick up where Erskine left off. That amazes me every time I think about it. God is such an awesome God.

The supernatural way God brought David and me together along with the supernatural events we have watched unfold for us have been great confirmation for David and me that we are truly walking in God's will for our lives. Therefore, we are very excited about our future, knowing that if God orchestrated all of this, then He definitely has more surprises awaiting us up the road.

25

God's Girl

> Being confident of this, that he who began a good work in you will carry it on to completion until the day of Christ Jesus.
>
> —Philippians 1:6 (NIV)

It gives me such joy to realize I have emerged from my darkest trial and my four-year journey of writing this book with a greater confidence than I've ever had before. My entire family and church family can attest to the fact that I am no longer the same woman I was five years ago, as I not only look different, but I am different. After having struggled through my toughest trial and this book journey, it is now very hard for me to be the same or view life the same as I did before because both experiences enlightened my view of my life tremendously. For instance, growing up as a child of divorce, I assumed I had been cheated out of a perfect life and a perfect family, and I set my heart on obtaining such in my future. My experience with divorced parents, a broken family, and then a blended family gave me a desire to do everything just right in my life and marriage so that I wouldn't have to repeat history. Nevertheless, I still ended up with a broken and later a blended family. While spending my life trying to avoid the D word, divorce, there was no way I could have avoided the other D word, death.

Also, I have come to accept that no matter how unconventional, broken, or stressful my family situation was when I was a child, today I wouldn't trade my experiences for anything in this world, as they have all become pieces *of* me and lessons *for* me. The things I went through with being a child of divorce and growing up in a blended family of seven children gave me the knowledge and wisdom I'm using today in raising my own blended family of ten children. This is another example of Romans 8:28 working in my life, "And we know that all things work together for good to those who love God, to those who are the called according to *His* purpose" (NKJV). God used all of my experiences, the good, the bad, the happy, and the sad, to all work together for the good of my future.

This writing experience also made me aware of how God literally reached back into my childhood and fulfilled the desire I once harbored of my blended family resembling that of the television sitcom *The Brady Bunch*. But He is allowing me to relive a far better experience with my new family, whom I've dubbed *The LeeDaniel Bunch*. It's funny how God never forgets our desires, even if we do.

This journey has made me aware of the truth in Philippians 1:6, which I added in the opening of this chapter. You see, after losing my husband, I assumed my life would change for the worse because I couldn't fathom life without the person I spent twenty-one years dreaming with and setting future goals with. But Paul's words, "He who began a good work in you will carry it on to completion until the day of Christ Jesus," reminded me of the words my dad said to me at Erskine's funeral, which were "God's gonna finish what He started in you." To me, his words revealed that God had already begun a work in me long before Erskine and I were married and long before I exited my mother's womb. In fact, He said in Jeremiah 1:5 (NIV), "Before I formed you in the womb I knew you; before you were born I set you apart." So His plan for me existed long before I existed, and He is not going to allow anything to stop Him from seeing it to completion.

In his foreword to this book, my dad mentioned that he didn't realize he was planting an incorruptible seed in me as an infant when he took me to Sunday school with him on Sunday mornings. Well, that seed not only took root, but as I grew, it was constantly watered by every church service I attended, every scripture I read, every praise and worship song

I sang, every sermon I heard, every piece of counsel I received from my parents and mentors, and every prayer that was ever prayed for me. Then, as I reached adulthood, that seed, which had grown into a large plant, was tested through the many storms of life that came my way. And though I struggled to make sense of everything I was going through, I now realize those storms were all related to the work God was doing in me because, with each storm, He allowed the plant inside of me to steadily grow into a resilient, deep-rooted palm tree. The kind of tree that bends but won't break. But then entered the ultimate storm, the death of my husband, which I was sure would be the end of me as well. However, it wasn't my ending as I thought; it was only a new beginning because that palm tree inside of me sprang back up when I least expected it, catapulting me further into the good work God had placed inside of me.

Another discovery I made on this journey concerns my newfound happiness. Before my life-altering trial, I was too busy being strict on others and myself to be genuinely happy. You see, it was hard to be truly happy and free while trying to live a perfect life. Though I knew God was a forgiving God, I thought He really wanted us to be the perfect saints with the perfect life, and I assumed that if we did this, He would reward us to live happily ever after. I wanted this perfect life so much that I had a hard time understanding others who were not trying to live their lives in the same manner. That is, until my perfect world came crashing down. Then I discovered that all of my perfect desires had been a waste of time. For God to welcome me back into His loving arms and continue to bless me unconditionally after I'd turned my back on Him and fell into sexual sin opened my eyes even more to how much He truly loved me and how He never expected me to be perfect. In my waywardness, I learned that it's not possible to walk the straight and narrow without falling from time to time. But the key is getting back up, dusting ourselves off, and continuing the journey to holiness. I spent years trying to live perfectly in order to obtain my happily-ever-after life, only to discover the hard way that there is no such life. So today, I've decided to stop wasting my time waiting on such, and I'm learning to be happy with the not-so-perfect life that God has given me. Now, I'm happier than I've ever been in my life.

Every since I was old enough to remember, I have always felt God's presence with me. This is why I was able to request more of Him at such a young age, even though I didn't understand what I was asking for. He, in turn, honored my request by giving me a part of Him that I wasn't familiar with, which was His salvation and the Holy Spirit. I realize now that He put that craving for more of Him inside of me to help me endure the trials that would come about in my life, as there is no way I could have made it through without a close relationship with Him.

God recently revealed to me that just as my faith was being tested during the birth of my third daughter, whom I assumed would be a son, my faith was also being tested to an even greater extent during Erskine's illness.

During my pregnancy with Janay, I had to know beyond a shadow of doubt that God was capable of giving me another son whether He did it or not. But not only that, I had to resolve in my spirit that if He decided not to replace the son I lost, I would not lose my faith in Him. Thank God, I passed that test.

However, in the case of Erskine's healing, I had to know beyond a shadow of doubt that God was capable of healing him if He so desired. But, more importantly, I had to resolve that if He decided not to heal him, I wouldn't withdraw my faith in Him just because He didn't give me what I expected. Well, let's just say I failed that test, but God didn't flunk me out. As my dad always says, "Though I may shake on the rock, the rock will never shake under me." Daddy has repeated these words for many years, and after making it through that dark trial, I now realize just how true those words have been in my life. Those words actually tie in with a revelation I received on Thanksgiving morning of 2016 when God revealed to me the meaning of the very first prophecy He gave me concerning the dark trials that were about to invade my life.

If you can recall, I shared with you in chapter 16 how during the summer of 1995 our church hosted a youth conference in which Dr. Angel Smith from Detroit, Michigan, was the guest minister. After entering her prayer line, the words she spoke as Erskine and I approached her were, "God says He can trust you." I assumed her words meant God could trust us in the area of giving tithes and offering and living a life pleasing to Him. But I had no idea the trust she mentioned included so much more.

On Thanksgiving morning in 2016, as different members stood to give their testimonies, which is our church's annual Thanksgiving tradition, my cousin Esker Ware stood up to testify. As he spoke, one of the things he said that stood out to me was, "Everything you went through, God trusted you with it because He knew you would come out giving Him the praise." Immediately, my spirit leaped, and God brought Dr. Angel Smith's words back to my remembrance as I thought, *So that's why God said He could trust us.* God knew He could trust our family to handle our trials in faith, and He trusted us to continue standing, to continue serving Him, and to continue to be an example to others long after the dust had settled. And He trusted that we would never renege on our praise.

My cousin's words helped me to realize that every trial I've gone through, God *trusted* me with it. And though I briefly lost my trust in Him when I lost my husband, He never lost His trust in me because He knew long before the trial came my way just how I would react concerning it. However, He also knew that I'd eventually come back to Him, giving Him the glory, the honor, and the praise. While standing on the rock, which is God's Word, I have shaken many times out of fear, worry, anger, and doubt. But as that rock stood firmly under me through the years, it never shook.

I've often viewed the supernatural triumphs I've experienced in life as God's way of proving to me that He was always there, that He loved me, and that I was His girl. However, I'd like to share with you one subtle way He proved this to me one night, which meant more to me than any of the other dramatic ways He's ever revealed Himself to me. This inspirational moment happened back in August 2014 when the relationship between Ryan and me was deteriorating.

Due to severe depression, I went out to the front porch at around eight thirty one evening to get a breath of fresh air before going to bed. Actually,

I was afraid to go to bed because I knew all I'd do was lie there in mental anguish and cry myself to sleep.

While sitting in the chair on the front porch and viewing my beautiful surroundings, I began to thank God inwardly, then outwardly. I was so grateful for how He had blessed me with such a lovely home and for how He had kept me through all of my self-inflicted turmoil. I also repented to Him for having been so caught up in trying to build a new life with Ryan that I had not taken the time to tell Him just how much I loved and appreciated Him for everything He had done for me.

After sharing with God the issues of my heart, I looked toward the sky and said to Him, "I love you, I really do," as a stream of tears rolled down my face. Immediately after saying those words, a gentle breeze came out of nowhere and began whistling through the trees and blowing across my face. Then, in the distance, I saw the sky light up in three back-to-back flashes, and it wasn't even raining, nor was there a threat of rain. Instantly, I knew this was God stroking my face and saying to me, "I love *you*."

I realized this sweet message was meant just for me when afterward there were no more flashes in the sky, the gentle breeze had ceased, and the only sounds that could be heard were the nighttime lullabies of the crickets and tree frogs in the distance. With my heart full from this supernatural display of affection, I went back into the house, climbed into bed, and enjoyed a very satisfying night of peaceful rest with the assurance that God loved me and that He was concerned about everything that concerned me.

As I mentioned in an earlier chapter, while growing up, I had no real idea of what I wanted to be in life other than a wife and mother. Of course, I had random thoughts in college like a news anchor, a teacher, or even a filmmaker, but as far as something solid that I held close to my heart, nothing comes to mind but a wife and mother.

Today I find it amazing how God fulfilled the desire of my heart twice, by giving me two husbands and two sets of children to whom I have performed my wifely and motherly duties with my whole heart because they were answers to my prayers. Now I feel that God is in the process of fulfilling His personal desires for my life as I feel Him calling me to another level of ministry. A ministry that He has not completely revealed to me but one that He is shedding light on with each step I take and one that I am most certain will be shared with David, whom God has anointed for ministry as well. But whatever it is that God desires of me, my answer to Him is simply, "Yes, Lord. I'll go." I mean, how could I say no to Him? He has done too much for me.

While gathering materials for this book, I stumbled across a note of prophecy that my friend Vanessa Walker wrote me back in December 2001. God allowed me to find her note in order to remind me that He had been giving me small glimpses of my future for many years. Vanessa said...

> Tracy,
>
> We've never discussed what you feel God has called you to or what your vision for your life has been, but I had another impression (that's what I call what God has shown me) of you. Right now, you think of your gifts and your ministry in connection with what you do for Mt. Canaan but God is preparing you for a ministry the dimension of Joyce Meyer or Marilyn Hickey. God's putting a word in your mouth even as you travel through these many trials. When I looked at your picture in our programs the other night, for a split second, the picture looked like I was looking at a picture that showed how you looked "in the early days" (as if I was in the future looking at an old picture of you as you looked in your "early days"). I'm glad to have gotten to know you in your early days.

Later, in November 2014, while writing this book, I experienced a brief vision, which led me stop what I was doing and eagerly post some words on social media that said, "I'm so excited because God just gave me a glimpse into my future!"

In the vision, which I purposely did not divulge on social media, I saw myself standing amongst a number of renowned people. I can't remember who they were; I only remember that they were very well known. Then, nearly a year after that vision, in October 2015, I received a message from

Erskine's cousin Brian Evans. Brian was the cousin that I mentioned in an earlier chapter who, on Christmas Eve of 1996, said God had told him to bring a certain amount of money to our house or I would be upset. It had been three months since I last saw Brian, but for some reason, God had dropped me in his spirit. In his message, he said …

> Hey Tracy,
> I thought about you this morning. Know that I'm praying for you and the family. Be encouraged. I sense that God is about to release you into a place of prominence. Be wise as a serpent and harmless as a dove as you approach your destiny. I don't know what this means, but hopefully you do. Just being obedient. I love you much.

I was brought to tears by Brian's message because it confirmed the vision God had given me and the prophecy Vanessa had given me. And in thinking about all of this, I realize that God is definitely up to something. He is working on something big for my life, and I can say this with assurance because, as I mentioned earlier, He told me Himself that He was in the process of enlarging my territory.

To be honest, not knowing what God is doing or how He is going to do it doesn't bother me because I trust Him. And not only that, but I'm thoroughly enjoying life at present because it has always been and will always be about His glory and not mine. But whatever He decides to do with me and through me, and wherever He decides to take me, I'm a willing vessel. I have no need to wonder or worry about my future because, though I may not know exactly *what* it holds, I know exactly *who* holds it, and that's all I need to know.

David often teases me about my long name. At some point, before the day is over, he will call me by my whole name and then add random names to it. For example, to get my attention, he may yell, "Tracy Elaine O'Neal Daniel Lee Murphy Calloway Rodriguez Smith & Jones!" I always find this hilarious.

As you can tell by my book cover, it's true—my name is long. This is because I proudly carry the surnames of the three men who've all played very important roles in my life. While writing this book, God revealed to me that with each of my name additions and the trials and triumphs I've experienced during each, I was steadily evolving into an extraordinary woman of God. I grew up as Daddy's girl (O'Neal), then I became Erskine's girl (Daniel), and now I'm David's girl (Lee). But I've always been and will forever be God's girl as I continue to live my life for His glory.

There was a powerful anonymous quote that I read online recently, "The price you pay to be who you are is exactly what it cost." Well, considering all the things I've endured in life, I would say that it cost me a whole lot to be Tracy O'Neal Daniel Lee, God's girl, as I paid for this title with my life.

But to be honest, I haven't always considered myself special enough to be called God's girl, but evidently He has. And He feels the same way about you. By taking some time to reflect on all He has done for you, you will not only realize just how special you are to Him, but you will also realize that you too are His girl or His son. And if you haven't already, I pray that you will make a conscious decision to begin living your life for His glory.

I appreciate you for joining me on my journey. This has been such a life-changing experience for me. I pray that it has been for you as well. I hope that some kind of way my words connected with you. Maybe you grew up, as I did, in a broken family. Maybe your life didn't turn out exactly the way you assumed it would. Maybe you've considered giving up on God because your fairy tale didn't manifest. Maybe you or someone close to you has suffered a terrible illness. Maybe you've lost a loved one to death. Or maybe you've made some terrible mistakes in your life. Whatever your situation, I pray that this book has been a source of great healing for your soul.

Thanks again for journeying with me. I hope you enjoyed the ride.

Erskine in the media room (circa 2007)

Erskine fixing church A/C (circa 2010)

Our family in 2011

Me with William, Triola, and Fran after my 2009 graduation from Lawson State Community College

Karen with our children's book (2011)

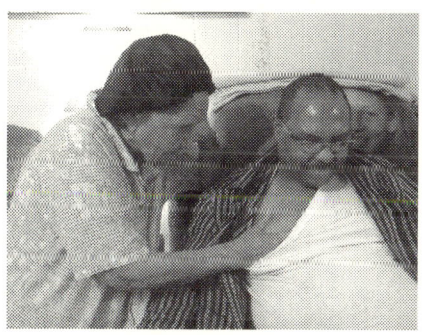

Grandma Fannie praying for Erskine (2012)

*The photo we thought we were taking
for our book cover in 2012*

Erskine and his girls (2012) 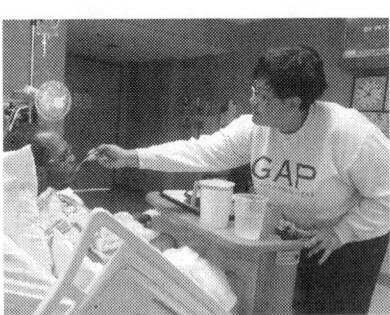   *Aunt Gale feeding Erskine (2012)*

*Erskine and me, outside of the hospital,
getting a breath of fresh air (2012)*

With my brother Philemon (2013)

The "new me" with Jasmine in November 2013

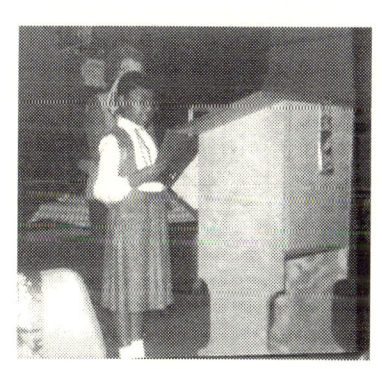

Me, reading my winning essay (circa 1980)

Daddy, Mrs. Walker, me, second and third-place winners and others (circa 1980)

Me and Aleshia sitting on top of Stone Mountain in October 2014

David with his children in 2006. (Left to right) Joshua, Jade, Caleb, Diamond

Me and David sitting behind President Obama at Lawson State Community College (March 2015)

*Daddy walking me down
the aisle (May 2015)*

Me and David giving God praise (May 2015)

*Me and David with Ronda Henderson,
our matchmaker (May 2015)*

Me and David with our parents (May 2015). (Left to right) Willie and Patricia O'Neal, Marilyn Daniel, Dewey and Teresa Murray, Martha and John Calloway.

Me and David with our grandson, Khari (May 2015)

I love this picture of us! (May 2015)

The LeeDaniel Bunch, May 2015.
(Left to right) Karen, Joycelyn, Janay, Jasmine, Jessica, David, Joshua, Caleb, Diamond
(On the floor) Kamille, Tracy, and Jade

The O'Neal Bunch (circa 2007)
(Left to right) Triola, Dedrick, Tracy, Chop, Fran, Patrick, William, and JaCarlos
(Sitting) Mama Trish and Daddy

The LeeDaniel Bunch: extended version (2017)
We've added two daughter-in-laws: Dawn, wife of
Caleb Lee, and Raven, wife of Joshua Lee
And a soon-to-be son in-law, Herbert Moye, fiancé of Jessica Daniel

Acknowledgments

God, I give You all the glory, honor and praise for commissioning me to write this book. Though it was sometimes a painful task, You never allowed me to give up. You simply helped me to work through my painful memories in order that I might help someone else. Thank you, Lord!

King David, my sweet husband, I thank you for allowing me to finish this large project. You could have easily complained about me being too busy, but you never did. You only tried your best to help me by praying for me, encouraging me, and giving me all the quiet time I needed. Thank you, Bae! You are such an awesome husband! I love you very much, and I hope I have made you proud!

Jessica, Jasmine, Janay, Joycelyn, Karen, and Kamille, I want to thank you all for being in this project with me from the beginning, encouraging and motivating me. I'm sorry you had to endure my ever-changing emotions, my hundreds of questions, and my isolated behavior. However, this was not only *my* project; this was *our* project because I could not have completed it without the help of your brains. But in the end, we discovered that by discussing our past, God allowed each of us to receive our healing. I love you all!

Caleb, Diamond, Joshua, and Jade, I am so happy to have you all in my life! Thank you so much for your love and respect for me and for lovingly sharing your father with my girls and me. I love each of you very much, and I thoroughly enjoy the time we spend together, one on one and as a family. I am so excited about spending forever with you!

Khari, my amazing grandson, it is by no mistake that you are here. God had a plan for you long before you entered your mother, Diamond's, womb, and part of it was for you to be the common thread that holds the LeeDaniel Bunch together. I call you *amazing* for a reason, because you are so smart, and you never cease to amaze us in what you say and do. Having the opportunity to watch you grow up gives me so much joy because I never had that opportunity with my little boy. I am very proud to be one of your grandmothers Khari, and I love you very much!

Teresa Murray and Willie B. O'Neal, my Mama and Daddy. Thank you for giving me life, for raising me in the Lord, for keeping me in your prayers, and for being my friends. I've wanted nothing more in life than to make you and God proud. Thank you for being so loving and understanding of me when I closed my ears to your counsel and tried to live life on my own terms. As you can see, your persistence and prayers paid off, because I made it through those dark days, and now I have the victory, and I'm still giving God the praise! I love you!

Patricia O'Neal and Dewey Murray, my Mama Trish and Papa Dewey. Thank you for being so instrumental in my life and for loving me as your own. And thank you so much for the words of wisdom and encouragement that you have given me over the years. I know you were praying for me as well during my dark days, thank you! You both have been exceptional stepparents and friends. I love you!

Marilyn Daniel, my third mom, thank you for giving birth to the man with whom I shared my life for twenty-one years. He credited you for teaching him to respect females and to serve God, and I must say, he did both amazingly well. Thank you for staying close to me as a mother and a friend, even after your son's death. You are and will always be my Naomi. I will always be your Ruth, and David will always be our Boaz.

John and Martha Calloway, my new in-laws, thank you for loving and accepting my girls as your granddaughters and me as your daughter. Thank you also for doing such a good job of raising the man with whom I plan to spend the rest of my life. I appreciate the good moral values and good work ethic you instilled in him, as it has helped him to excel in life and to be a good leader for our family. I love you both so much.

Elaine Newell and Eddie Mae Henderson, my grandmothers, thank you for your love and your prayers for me and for the important role that you played in helping to raise me. I have very fond memories of the time I spent with both of you as a child. I love you both very much!

William B. O'Neal (Bridgette), Willie Ellis (Keshia), Franchesca O'Neal Johnson (Courtney), Philemon Williams, Dedrick O'Neal

(Kenya), JaCarlos O'Neal (Tynea), and Patrick Fisher (Alecia), my siblings and their spouses. I thank God for giving me each of you as my lifetime friends. I thank Him for the bond we share and for each of you having my back just as I have yours. Thank you for your love and your prayers also. I love you all so much!

Flozell Lee, Sandra Calloway Fields (Peter), Earnest Calloway (Kristy), my new siblings and their spouses. Thank you for your loving acceptance of my girls and me into your family. I thank God for placing you in my life and I thoroughly enjoy the time we spend together. I love you all so much!

Pastor and First Lady George and Daty Keys, my godparents, thank you for being surrogate parents for Erskine and me while we were in Nebraska. I appreciate how you've never forgotten me and how the girls and I remain in your thoughts and prayers.

Dr. Michael Moore, thank you for the godly wisdom and knowledge you imparted into David Lee at Faith Chapel Christian Center over the span of more than twenty years. He credits you for teaching him how to be a godly man, husband, and father, and it shows, as he has been an outstanding husband to me and a loving and dedicated father to our children.

Ronda Henderson, my awesome friend, no amount of words would be enough to thank you for bringing David and me together. You could have chosen to introduce him to any of your friends, but God allowed you to remember me. Thank you for pressing the issue and not taking no for an answer. As a result, you helped me discover my Boaz. I love you, sis!

My youth pastors Nathaniel and Valencia Newsome, and my youth leaders, mentors, and good friends (there are too many of you to name). Your love, wisdom, guidance and friendship helped to shape me into the woman I am today. I'm grateful for all of you!

And special thanks to ...

David and Jacquita Davis, for being our first support system at the start of our storm in 2012 and for being my additional siblings and an additional uncle and aunt to my girls.

Zambia Harris and Andrea McArthur, for putting your lives on hold for half a year and dedicating yourselves to caring for my girls while I cared for their dad. May God forever rain blessings upon your lives!

Corey Lawson, for dropping whatever you were doing to come by our house and help me dress Erskine that day. And for making sure Jasmine had the book that she needed for her class when I called on you at the last minute.

Cledis Ward, for being like a brother to Erskine and looking out for his health when the two of you were partners at the county board of education.

Mary Strong, Rodreccas Brown, Robert Mauldin, Joyce Johnson, for making sure my girls had a way to and from church during their dad's illness.

Robert Dismukes, Rozita Smith, and Larry Greene, for taking a few hours out of your busy schedule to sit with Erskine during his many hospital stays, freeing me to handle other pressing business.

Shelia Porter, for helping me to care for Erskine during his last days and for being a source of strength for me.

LaTanya Lee, Shannon Edwards, KiKi Edwards, and Erika King, for using your gifts and talents to bless my family in our time of need. May God bless and anoint you with amazing success in all of your endeavors.

Chrys McDaniel, for spending Christmas 2012 at my house helping me put together Erskine's obituary. Whenever I've needed you, you've always been there. I love you, sis!

Paulette Fisher, Aaron Saxton, and Angela Brazzill, for allowing me to cry on your shoulders when I couldn't see my way. You helped nurse me back to life!

Jaunita Hogan and family, for being my family's personal photographers and for everything you've done for us through the years, especially for helping the girls and me move into our new house.

My cousin Esker Ware, for stepping in after Erskine's death and doing several odd jobs around my house. From cutting the grass, changing light bulbs, and hanging mirrors, the girls and I greatly appreciated all the help you gave us. Thank you Sharon for lending us your man of God. I love you both.

Aunt Patricia and Uncle Gene Dorleus, for driving up from Orlando, Florida, to video my and David's wedding and reception. And for the wonderful wedding gift of a honeymoon in Disney World.

To all others who've ever prayed for my family and me, offered encouraging words, cooked us a meal, sent some kind of token of love our way, gave us clothes for our children, and all other acts of kindness, thank you from the bottom of my heart! I love you!

In Loving Memory
of

Erskine Nile Daniel Jr.
June 16, 1969–December 21, 2012
"I shall not die, but live, and declare the works of the Lord."
—Psalm 118:17 (NKJV)

*In Loving Memory
of*

Triola Michelle Ellis Crawford
July 10, 1967–October 19, 2012
"I have fought the good fight, I have finished
the race, I have kept the faith."
—2 Timothy 4:7 (NKJV)

About the Author

Tracy O'Neal Daniel Lee is a preacher's daughter, a devoted wife to her husband, David, a loving mother of ten beautiful children, and a proud grandmother of an amazing grandson. She is also a faithful member of Mount Canaan Full Gospel Church in Birmingham, Alabama, where her father and stepmother, Drs. Willie B. and Patricia O'Neal, have pastored for forty years. Having graduated in 2009 from Lawson State Community College in the field of radio and television broadcasting, Tracy is the television broadcast editor for her church. This is her fourth published book.

Connect with Tracy online

Facebook: Tracy Lee
Snapchat: @tracydavidlee
Instagram: @busy_livin_my_life
E-mail: tracyodlee@gmail.com

www.tracyodlee.com

www.godsgirlbook.com

Printed in the United States
By Bookmasters